Travel Adventures

Honolulu, Waikiki & Oahu

Sharon Hamblin

HUNTER

Hunter Publishing, Inc.
30 Mayfield Avenue
Edison, NJ 08817
☎ 800-255-0343 / Fax 732-417-1744
Web site: www.hunterpublishing.com
E-mail: comments@hunterpublishing.com

IN CANADA
Ulysses Travel Publications
4176 Saint-Denis
Montreal, Québec H2W 2M5 Canada
☎ 514-843-9882, Ext. 2232 / Fax 514-843-9448

IN THE UK & EUROPE
Windsor Books International
5, Castle End Park, Castle End Road, Ruscombe
Berkshire, RG10 9XQ England
☎ 01189-346-347 / Fax 01189-346-368

ISBN 978-1-58843-665-8

4 3 2 1

Contents

Aloha!

This book will help you navigate the fascinating island of O`ahu with ease and show you some of my favorite spots to eat, shop and spend the night.

Travel Adventures Honolulu, Waikiki & O`ahu was a lot of fun (and work!) to write and I owe mahalos to many people who helped make this endeavor possible.

First of all, I'd like to thank publisher Michael Hunter and the staff at Hunter Publishing for offering me the job and fine-tuning the manuscript. Thank you, Michael, for giving me this chance and for my previous book – *Adventure Guide to Maui* – which has opened so many doors for me!

My family in California has also helped make many of my dreams come true. Thank you Dad, Romane, Marc and Judy, Keith and Jana, Bibi and Eric, and all of my little inspirations – Amanda, Jared, Donovan and Olivia. Mahalo to my younger brother Dale who promoted my Maui book with his own marketing style and always encouraged me while I was writing this one.

Thank you very much to my biggest fan, Paul Ogden. You're the best! Thanks to Betty Young, who always has a smile on her face, for her endearing loyalty.

More mahalos to Vinnie Colón, who gives me tons of support and advice on life, writing and on following your dreams. Also, thanks to Jessie Fitzgerald, who I hope someday gets the chance to live in Hawaii.

As with my last book, I dedicate this tome to my late mother, Karen Hamblin, who provided me with unconditional love and tons of support. I love you so much and wish you were here to share my happiness.

Writing a book is a huge undertaking and I can't believe I'm doing it again. There are another hundred people I need to thank, including all of those in O`ahu, such as the Hawaii Visitors & Convention Bureau and all of the other public relations officials across the island. I couldn't have done this without the editing help of Mary Davis – I hope you make it to Hawaii someday!

And thank you to Buttercup, my miniature schnauzer, who shows me daily how to let go and see the beauty in chasing a leaf across a field.

I've tried to be as accurate and up-to-date as possible with this book but O`ahu is an ever-changing oasis. If you have any suggestions or comments, please do e-mail me at sharonhamblin@sbcglobal.net.

I hope you enjoy the book and O`ahu – a spectacular island with so much to offer!

Sharon Hamblin

Preface

You may have been to the island before, but this time be prepared for a whole new Waikiki and O`ahu!

The island, especially the famous and fabulous Waikiki stretch, is experiencing a huge revitalization. First of all, the Waikiki Beach Walk has been created, providing a facelift to the iconic beach and the surrounding area. Years of planning and over $535 million in renovations have created a brand new Waikiki with a stylish shopping district full of "Aloha Spirit" with its new shops, restaurants and ongoing free activities.

O`ahu, the main island in the Hawaiian chain, is only 44 miles long and 30 miles wide, but it's full of adventure at every angle. There is so much to explore and experience that you could spend every moment of your vacation on the move. Or, leave that to the adventurous types, and spend your days taking some sunshine and enjoying an afternoon Mai Tai before an elegant dinner cruise on the Pacific Ocean.

This diverse island brings you a little bit of what each of the neighbor islands has to offer. You have the nightlife of Maui, the beaches of Kauai, the exotic quality of the Big Island of Hawaii, the "old Hawaii" atmosphere of Moloka`i, and the luxury of Lana`i.

During my travels, I found this poem, which made me cry. The copy I have is a version created by Nancy Lake, who found the complete poem at a library in the Big Island. The author is unknown.

I Shall Never Leave the Islands

I may go tomorrow and never return.
But still, I shall never leave.
My heart is in the beating surf.
My breath is in the touch of the trade winds.
Forever the fragrance of plumeria shall be with me.
I cannot close my eyes
without finding there these fluid, emerald mountains.
And in my ears the sounds of the islands:
lilting doves, waves crashing against coral reefs,
palm fronds whispering softly
and always, Hawaiian music.
I shall never leave the islands.

Enjoy your trip to O`ahu and I hope this book helps you enjoy all that this fabulous island has to offer.

Aloha!

Hawaiian Islands
KAUA`I
NIIHAU
O'AHU
Honolulu
MOLOKA'I
LANAI
MAUI
KAHOOLAWE
HAWAI'I
Pacific Ocean
N
HUNTER PUBLISHING
50 MILES
100 KILOMETERS

Introduction

Using This Guide

This guide divides the island into seven sections, with whole chapters devoted to the Waikiki and Pearl Harbor areas, along with chapters focusing on the different shores of this diverse island.

Each chapter describes the area, offers you shopping suggestions, details adventures of the area and then provides you with a list of dining and accommodation options.

IN THIS CHAPTER

O`ahu at a Glance

Nickname: "The Gathering Place," but is also promoted as "The Heart of Hawai`i."

Area: 597 square miles (1,545 square km).

Population: 902,704.

Highest Point: Mt. Ka`ala (4,003 feet/1,220 meters).

Language: English, but it helps to know some Hawaiian words, like *aloha* (hello) and *mahalo* (thank you).

Biggest City: Honolulu.

Distance from Los Angeles: 2,551 miles.

Coastline: 112 miles.

Flower: `Ilima.

Color: Yellow.

Since 1850, when the Hawaiian royal court moved to Honolulu permanently, the city has been the seat of government for the monarchy, republic, territory, and state.

O`ahu is Hawaii's most heavily populated island and is considered to be "Tourist Central" for visitors. It has some of the country's most intriguing attractions, such as Pearl Harbor, `Iolani Palace, Diamond Head, Waikiki Beach and the Punchbowl Cemetery.

***`Iolani Palace** in downtown Honolulu, is the only royal palace in the United States.*

10 THINGS NOT TO MISS ON O`AHU

- Pearl Harbor
- Waikiki Beach
- Diamond Head Hike
- North Shore
- `Iolani Palace
- Shangri La
- Lanikai Beach
- The Pali Highway
- Punchbowl Cemetery
- Aloha Tower

Information: For information about O`ahu and the other Hawaiian islands, visit the Hawaii Visitors and Conventions Bureau, 2270 Kalakaua Avenue, Ste. 801, ☎ 808-923-1811 or 800-464-2924 (toll free), www.gohawaii.com. The bureau offers information about tours and has maps and brochures for many activities. The Visitors Bureau is open from 8 am to 4:30 pm Monday through Friday and closed on holidays.

IMPORTANT PHONE NUMBERS

- **Emergency**: ☎ 911.
- **Police** (non-emergency): ☎ 808-529-3111.
- **Time**: ☎ 808-983-3211.
- **Weather**: ☎ 808-973-4380.
- **Hospitals**: Queen's Medical Center, ☎ 808-538-9011; Straub Clinic & Hospital, ☎ 808-522-4000.
- **Honolulu International Airport**: General Information ☎ 808-836-6411; Visitor Information ☎ 808-836-6413.
- **US Customs**: ☎ 808-237-4600.
- **Lost and Found**: ☎ 808-836-6547.

Climate

RAINFALL ON O`AHU

Honolulu Coastal – 22 inches (56 cm)/year
Kailua – 73 inches (193 cm)/year
Mountains – up to 200 + inches (508+ cm)/year

The weather on O`ahu is pleasantly temperate, with temperatures ranging from a low of 62°F to highs of 89°F in the summer. The windward side of O`ahu has more rain than other areas with December being the wettest month with an average of 7.9 inches of rain and June being the driest with an average of 3.6 inches of rain. Honolulu and Waikiki are a bit drier with a December average of 3.2 inches of rain and a June low of .4 inches of rain. On the North Shore, the average rainfall in December is 4.1 inches while the average in June is .4 inches.

For O`ahu weather forecasts, call ☎ 808-973-4381. For surf report information, ☎ 808-596-7873.

Culture

The Hawaiian Language

In the Hawaiian language, an *`okina* (`) or glottal stop is frequently seen between two vowels. A glottal stop indicates a total break in sound, so whenever you see one, pause for a second as if you were saying "uh-oh." "Hawaii" doesn't get one because without one it means the state of Hawaii and with a stop it means the Big Island of Hawai`i.

Hawaii is the only state to have two official languages – English and Hawaiian.

The Hawaiian alphabet (the shortest in the world) contains only 12 letters – the five vowels (a, e, i, o, u) and seven consonants (h, k, l, m, n, p and w). You'll soon figure this out when every name of every street, beach, park, town and Hawaiian person seem to be all "K"s and "W"s.

The sounds of the letters are the same as in English except in the case of the "v" which is often pronounced as a "w." For example, many people pronounce the state as "Ha-vi-e." The language isn't as simple as it seems – the Hawaiian language has 33 words to describe a cloud and 179 terms for sweet potatoes.

When trying to navigate through the Hawaiian language, it may be easier if you break the words into syllables. Hawaiian syllables never contain more than one consonant (h, k, l, m, n, p, w) and each syllable must end with a vowel (a, e, i, o, u). If you follow these rules, you'll realize that each word in the Hawaiian language ends with a vowel.

One of the most popular and intriguing words in the Hawaiian language is the name of the unofficial state fish – the Humuhumunukunukuapua`a! If you break it down, it is a bit easier and can actually be fun (kids love it!). Try Hu-mu-hu-mu-nu-ku-nu-ku-a-pa-a-`a.

Want a Head Start? **www.thehawaiichannel.com** has a section called "Hawaiian Word of the Day" which is brought to visitors by Kamehameha Schools. You can view the website or, when you're on O`ahu, check out Channel KITV 4 News every morning from Monday to Friday. Also, a website, **www.hawaiianlanguage.com**, is dedicated to preserving the Hawaiian language.

Common Hawaiian Words

ahi (AH-HEE) – yellowfin tuna
`aina (EYE-NA) – land, earth
aikane (EYE-KAH-NAY) – friend, companion
akamai (AH-KAH-MY) – smart or clever
ali`i (AH-LEE-EE) – a chief or member of nobility
aloha (AH-LO-HA) – hello, goodbye, love
aloha `oe (AH-LO-HA OH-A) – farewell to you
aloha nui loa (AH-LO-HA NU-E LO-AH) – very much love
auwe (OW-WAY) – Oh! or Ouch!
`awa (AH-VAH) – Kava root, chewed in native Polynesia in a relaxing social ritual
ea (EH-AH) – sovereignty, rule, life force
halau (HA-LAOW) – hula school
hale (HAH-LEY) – house or home
hana (HAH-NA) – work
hanai (HA-NAI) – adopted or foster children
haole (HA-OH-LAY) – foreigner
Haoli Makahiki Hou (HA-OH-LEE MA-KA-HE-KEY HO) – Happy New Year
heiau (HAY-EE-OW) – ancient temple, place of worship
holoholo (HO-LO-HO-LO) – a trip or excursion
hono (HO-NO) – bay
huhu (HOO-HOO) – angry
hui - (HOO-EE) – club, association
huna (HOO-NA) – secret
imu (EE-MOO) – underground oven
kahuna (KA-WHO-NA) – priest or expert
kai (KAH-EE) – sea water
kama`aina (KAH-MAH-EYE-NA) – a person born in or familiar with a place
kanaka maole (KA-NA-KA MA-OH-LAY) – the true Hawaiian people
kane (KAH-NAY) – man
kapu (KAH-POO) – taboo or sacred, keep out, forbidden
kau kau (COW-COW) – food

keiki (KAY-KEE) – child
kokua (KOH-KU-AH) – help, assistance
kuleana (KOO-LEE-AH-NA) – immediate garden or taro patch near a home
kupuna (KOO-POO-NAH) – elders, grandparents
ku`uipo (KOO-OO-E-I-PO) – sweetheart
lani (LAH-NEE) – heaven
lei (LEH-EE) – flower wreath
lolo (LOW-LOW) – crazy
lua (LOO-AH) – bathroom
luau (LOO-OW) – Hawaiian feast or celebration
mahalo (MAH-HA-LO) – thank you
mahalo nui loa (MAH-HA-LO NU-EE LO-HA) – thank you very much
makai (MA-KAI) – toward the sea
mele (MAY-LAY) – song or chant
menehune (MEH-NEE-HOO-NEE) – legendary race of tiny people who worked at night building fish ponds, roads and temples
mauka (MAO-KA) – inland, toward the mountains
Mele Kalikimaka (MAY-LAY KA-LEE-KEE-MA-KA) – Merry Christmas
moana (MOH-AH-NUH) – ocean
mu`u mu`u (MOO-OO-MOO-OO) – traditional Hawaiian gown for women
`ohana (O-HAH-NA) – family, relatives
`oi (OY) – best
`ono (OH-NO) – delicious
opala (O-PA-LA) – garbage
pali (PAH-LEE) – cliff, steep hill
paniolo - (PAH-NEE-OH-LO) – Hawaiian cowboy
pau (POW) – finished
pilikia (PEE-LEE-KEE-AH) – trouble of any kind
poi (POH-EE) – mashed taro
po'okela (PO-OH-KELL-AH) – regarded as the best by the community
pono (POH-NO) – righteous
pua (POO-UH) – flower
puka (POO-KAH) – hole, door or entryway
pupu (POO-POO) – appetizer or hors d'oeuvres
tutu (TOO-TOO) – granny
wahine (WA-HEE-NAY) – woman
wai (WAH-EE) – fresh water
wai wai (WHY-WHY) – property or assets

wikiwiki (WEE-KEE-WEE-KEE) – hurry
E komo mai (E-KO-MO-MY) – welcome

Da Pidgin Guide

Pidgin is slang used on the islands by locals. It is not recommended that you use it casually – some people might think that you're making fun of them. If you want to learn more about pidgin, ask a local to explain some terms. In order to understand pidgin a little better, you may want to browse through these definitions:

an' den – and then

broke da mouth – If you eat something and it was really good then it is "broke da mouth"

brah – All guys call each other this, a greeting for locals ("whassup brah?")

da – the

da kine – When you can't think of the word you mean to say, you just say "da kine," i.e. "Where did I put da kine?" You could be looking for any thing – your car, your lunch, your kid....

fo real – This can be a question or a statement. "Fo real?" could be a question meaning "Really?" Or it could mean agreement to a statement as if someone says, "That ahi dinner hit the spot." The reply, "Fo real," implies agreement.

garans – guaranteed

garans ballbarans – Also means guaranteed and if you're fortunate enough to have the name "Sharon" as I do, you will probably be called Sharon Ballbarans for the rest of your life.

grind – eat ("I'm so hungry, I'm gonna grind so hard")

grinds – food ("Let's go get some grinds in Hale`iwa")

haole – Caucasian

haole feet – tenderfoot (what you say when you see a pale tourist running across the beach because the sand is so hot)

hele on – moving on

holoholo – to go out ("Let's go holoholo tonight")

howzit? – common greeting meaning "How is everything?"

junk – lousy, horrible ("Last night was so junk")

laydahs – later ("See ya laydahs")

mo bettah – more better (a popular catchphrase on Moloka`i where you'll see the "Moloka`i mo bettah" slogan all over the place)

okole – butt, bottom

ono – delicious ("This poke is so ono")

pakalolo – marijuana

pau – finished, done

pau hana – finished with work (also the name for the beer/drink that you have after work, i.e., "Did you have a pau hana yet?")

puka – hole ("My shirt has a tiny puka")

shaka – hand signal waving thumb and pinky

shishi – pee (used to ask children – "Do you have to go shishi?"

sistah – sister

slippahs – flip flops

stink eye – a dirty look ("That girl over there is giving you stink eye")

talk story – casual talk or gossip ("I'm going to go over to Vinnie's to talk story")

tanks - thanks

tink – think ("I tink I saw a shark in the water")

If you want a completely different view of the Bible, check out **Da Jesus Book** *for a translation like no other. The book is available at Hawaii bookstores or through www.pidginbible.org. For a humorous view of pidgin, check out* **Peppo's Pidgin To Da Max,** *which is available at most book and novelty stores in Hawaii.*

The Hawaiian People

In general the Hawaiian people are a unique group – full of aloha, spirituality and they have a special bond with their heritage. O`ahu is home to many people who were born on the island and lived there all their lives. Family is very important to the Hawaiian people and don't be surprised to see a group of Hawaiian having a barbeque on the beach or celebrating a special occasion (a baby's first birthday is a HUGE deal in the Hawaiian culture and enormous luaus are held).

The Hawaiian people also practice what is called "aloha spirit." This is a way of life in Hawaii and encompasses a rare combination of generosity, camaraderie and genuine friendliness. Don't be shy about asking for directions or about the history of the island. You'll be surprised at the heart-warming responses you may get.

"Aloha Friday" is celebrated every Friday and follows a decades-long tradition of wearing informal island attire to work. On this day, you'll see men in Aloha shirts and women dressed in *muumuus*. Some lucky employees are allowed to leave work an hour early on "Aloha Friday." Now, that's Aloha!

Also, in Hawaii (well, maybe not in busy Waikiki) we tend to use our car horns as a way to say hello to someone.

Elders in Hawaii are affectionately called "auntie" and "uncle," but don't call someone this without their invitation.

A ukelele lesson
(HVCB/R. Dahlquist)

It is customary in Hawaii to leave your shoes at the front door and enter a home barefoot. I would assume that this tradition stems from a desire to keep the house clean as people trample in and out with sand all over their bodies.

Canoeing is the official state sport of Hawaii and there are several canoe clubs throughout O`ahu. Paddlers take this sport seriously and you can often see them practicing on the beaches, especially along Waikiki. As you stroll down beaches, you'll see the long, skinny outrigger vessels parked on the sand waiting for the next race. Races are rigorous, team-oriented events and often entail paddling across the rough oceans between islands. For more information about this competitive sport, check out www.y2kanu.com.

No More Tiny Bubbles: Legendary Hawaiian crooner Don Ho, known for his raspberry-tinted sunglasses and signature song, *Tiny Bubbles*, died in April of 2007. Ho entertained Hollywood's biggest stars and performed thousands of tours for four decades. His Waikiki show was a mix of songs, jokes, double entendres, Hawaiian history and audience participation. Donald Tai Loy Ho, who was of Hawaiian, Chinese, Portuguese, Dutch and German descent, was born August 13, 1930 in Honolulu and grew up in the then-rural countryside of Kaneohe.

Flora & Fauna

Flora of Hawaii

Pink angel's trumpet

Most visitors are dazzled by the colorful array of flora seen abundantly throughout the islands. Some of the most prevalent plants include the angel's trumpets (which resemble upside-down trumpets), heart-shaped waxy-feeling antheriums, spiky orange and blue birds of paradise, fragrant white and yellow ginger flowers, bold yellow, red and orange heliconia, hibiscus, aromatic plumeria and ever-present orchids.

Fruit trees also grow freely throughout the islands. During avocado season, where I live there are so many of the fruits that you can't even give them away. During your travels you may see banana, avocado, breadfruit, macadamia, mango and papaya trees. Mango season occurs in July and August and many local chefs take advantage of these delicious fruits when creating their specials. Mango margaritas are also ultra-tasty! Exotic lychees are rarely available outside of July but these much-treasured treats, which look like grapes with a seed on the inside and a spiky hard outer coat, are a must-try if you're lucky enough to find them in season.

There are many plants, trees and flowers that can only be found in Hawaii, including the Koa tree which is found in higher elevations (3,000-5,000 feet). Its hard wood is rare and something of a treasure. Koa is a member of the acacia family and can grow to be very large. Traditionally it was used to make outrigger canoes, but today many shops in O`ahu sell items like bowls, furniture, cribbage boards and desk accessories made out of Koa.

Flower Greetings: One of the most recognizable images of Hawaii is the lei, a wreath made out of flowers given or received for a number of reasons – a welcome gift, a farewell present, birthday greetings and any other kind of celebration. The most popular flower leis are made out of plumerias, orchids or the fragrant puakinikini. The proper way to wear a lei is to have it loosely draped over your shoulders, hanging down in both the front and back.

Fauna of Hawaii

There are only two mammals endemic to the Hawaiian Islands – the small hoary bat and the Hawaiian monk seal. Others have been brought over, either on purpose or accidentally, and now Hawaii has many different animals, including some endangered species.

The State Bird of Hawaii is the nene (pronounced "nay-nay"), which shares a common ancestry with the Canadian goose and can only be found on the Hawaiian Islands. It is believed that in 1778 when Captain Cooke arrived in the island, the nene population was around 25,000. In 1952 there were thought to be about 30 birds and in 1967 this beautiful animal was listed as the eighth-most endangered waterfowl in the world. But, after nearly becoming extinct, nene are now thriving on the islands. Due to efforts to reestablish them, there are some 1,300 of the birds on the Big Island, Maui, Moloka`i and Kaua`i, with about half living on the Garden Island of Kaua`i.

Pests in Paradise

Everybody loves Hawaii – including bugs and other pesky animals. The tropical climate is attractive to many of these pests and provides a pleasant breeding ground. Even the nicest hotels and restaurants have the occasional cockroach or ant problem and it doesn't necessarily mean they are dirty. Here's a list of Hawaii's most annoying pests and some suggestions on what to do if you see one, or worse, get bitten by one.

Cockroaches

There are 19 different kinds of cockroachs in Hawaii and they may differ from the ones you see at home, They are very big and some of them fly (we call these "747s"). Cockroaches do not have very sophisticated palates – they will eat everything from paper and leather to hair and toenails. The best way to prevent cockroaches is to keep all food covered and to take out the garbage frequently.

Mosquitoes

Many visitors are surprised to discover that there are mosquitoes in Hawaii. Apparently they like the warm weather, too. Only the females bite and it's true – mosquitoes find some people more attractive (well, at least they find their skin secretions more attractive) than others, which is why if two people go on the same hike, one will return covered in red, swollen, itchy spots and the other will be untouched. The best way to prevent bites is by using repellent (those containing Deet are the most effective but do a skin test first as many people are sensitive). Or wear long pants and long-sleeved shirts. Many people swear by Avon's Skin-So-Soft bath oil as a mosquito repellent although there's no scientific proof that it works. And there's nothing more irritating then hearing a mosquito buzzing around your head when you're trying to sleep. I keep a fan blowing on me at night, which seems to keep them away.

Did You Know? Mosquitoes are tourists, too. They reportedly arrived in 1872 aboard the Wellington, a merchant ship, headed to Lahaina, Maui. Like many locals, they decided to stay.

Centipedes

Centipede
(www.britannica.com)

The centipede is probably the most hated and feared insect in Hawaii. Almost everyone who lives here has a story about seeing one, getting bitten by one or killing one. Chances are you won't see one on your vacation, but don't be surprised if you do run into one of these creepy crawlers. This long (up to nine inches), multi-legged, scaly creature is more flat in shape than round and can live up to six years. And, contrary to the name (centipede means "100 legs"), this pest has one pair of legs per body segment and the number of body segments is always an odd number. They move very quickly with a snakelike motion and will bite in self-defense. The bite can be painful, but is rarely fatal. The wound will swell and redden and the pain may last for several hours. If the pain doesn't go away or the wound is in the face area, see a doctor. One of their few redeeming features is that they eat cockroaches.

Check Your Shoes: Centipedes often find refuge in tennis shoes left outside the front door. It only takes one bite to for you to create a lifelong habit of always looking in your shoes before putting them on. I have a friend who went for a walk with his wife and then played tennis for quite a while before feeling something funny in his shoe. It was a centipede squished up in the toe of the shoe that finally found some space to move around in. Luckily my friend wasn't bit. That time.

Centipedes like damp, dark living conditions and may enter the home if it is very dry or wet outside. Many people have been bitten while sleeping so if you are staying in a damp, jungle-like area, check your bed before you hit the sack. If you do see one, the best way to kill it is to chop it up into several pieces with a sharp knife.

Lucky Charms: *Geckos, the small, lizard-like creatures that you may see scaling the walls, are NOT pests. They are, in fact, the opposite. These friendly creatures feed on cockroaches, mosquitoes, ants, moths and spiders and can often be found near light bulbs or behind wall hangings as they look for their next meal. If you don't see them, you might hear them – they make various chirping sounds. It is considered good luck to have geckos in your home. The downside to geckos is that they leave messy droppings along windowsills and on the floor.*

Spiders

There are no tarantulas in Hawaii, although you may think you've seen one if you view a cane spider. This large, brown, long-legged spider is more helpful than heinous, though, and is probably more scared of you than you are of it. Mostly found outside, cane spiders are also frequently seen inside houses and other buildings, especially in the wetter parts of the islands. They do not spin webs and they rarely bite unless provoked. Cane spiders are beneficial as they eat cockroaches and flies. If you do see one, the best thing to do is to trap it and move it outdoors. It is considered bad luck to kill them.

JELLYFISH WARNING

O`ahu is the only island that has a serious jellyfish problem and the buggers usually only show up on south shore beaches when they mate, seven to 10 days after a full moon.

Recently, 300 box jellyfish washed up on Waikiki Beach and were seen all the way to Hanauma Bay, Pokai Bay, Makaha Surfing Beach and Waimea Bay. Although most of the stinging creatures are off the shore by mid-morning, keep your eyes open for lingerers. Lifeguards are aware of this situation and if you have any questions, feel free to ask them. The influx usually lasts a day and warning signs are posted at the affected areas. If you do get stung, the lifeguard should be able to help but, if not, a vinegar spray and a cold pack should ease the swelling. A jellyfish sting can be dangerous to those who are allergic to the toxins and anyone who suffers breathing problems, muscle spasms or constant pain should get immediate medical attention.

Ants

There are over 40 types of ants found in Hawaii, most of them harmless – just pesky. Ants usually come in seeking food, so try to cover up all open containers and thoroughly clean up all spills.

Did You Know? There are no snakes in Hawaii unless you count the ones in the Honolulu Zoo.

Fleas

Fleas are generally only a problem if you have a cat or dog but, if you're in an infested area, their bites can be irritating. The Hawaiian name for this pest is *`uku* and legend has it that the small four-string musical instrument called the *`ukulele* was named after Edward Purvis, whose nickname was *`Ukulele* (leaping louse). Purvis popularized the use of the instrument that was then named after him.

Bedbugs

Bedbugs have recently become a problem across the United States, and Hawaii is no exception. Actually, the moisture in the air probably makes it a nice place for them to call home. The National Pest Management Association said reports of bedbug infestations have climbed more than 60% in the last four years.

Experts thought the little pests were eradicated in the 40s and 50s, but they're back. At hotels, look for red specks on the mattresses and bedding and check for the quarter-inch-sized bugs in draperies and behind moldings. Bedbugs aren't deadly, just very irritating. They are night creatures and their telltale symptoms are itchy, red welts and tiny blood droppings.

If attacked, be at ease – bedbugs don't spread disease. They are tiny, browning, flattened insects that feed exclusively on the blood of animals and humans. If you fall victim to these little bloodsuckers, immediately call the manager and prepare to move to another room or another accommodation.

Your best way to prevent an attack is to check the room before you unpack. Experts think that the creatures are transported through luggage, so check your bags to make sure you're not taking home any unwanted souvenirs.

History

King Kamehameha I

The ocean has always had a vital role in the history of the Hawaiian Islands. The island chain was uninhabited until Polynesian navigators steered their double-hulled canoes more than 1,800 miles from the Marquesas to Hawaii.

Although the island of O`ahu was populated before 1000 A.D., one of the first references to the islands was recorded by Spanish sailors who visited in 1627 and described the volcanic eruption in the ship's log. O`ahu was added to the Island kingdom in 1795 when King Kamehameha I, leader of what we call the Big Island of Hawai`i, fought the O`ahu king's troops until they surrendered at the famous Battle of Nu`uanu Pali. At this time, O`ahu was controlled by Maui's chief, Kalanikupule. After many battles, he was driven up Nu`uanu Valley to Nu`uanu Pali, where an estimated 400 warriors were pushed off the cliff to their deaths. Victorious, Kamehameha became the first king of the Hawaiian Islands.

The Honolulu Harbor was discovered before 1800 and became a key Pacific port for whale, sandalwood and fur traders. From the 1820s to the 1850s, Hawaii was a huge port of call for hundreds of whaling ships based in Honolulu and Lahaina, Maui.

During this time, travel between Honolulu and the Windward Coast of O`ahu was a difficult trek. Travelers had two choices – paddle a canoe around the island or hike over the treacherous cliffs of the Ko`olau Mountains. This steep and slippery trail was difficult but the ancient Hawaiians traversed it, carrying containers of poi, bundles of taro and sweet potatoes, pigs, chickens and goats to sell in Honolulu. In 1897, the Kingdom of Hawaii built a new 20-foot-wide carriage road, which was the only option for cars until the 1950s when the two Pali tunnels were created.

Called the *puka* (hole) in the Pali by locals, the tunnels were completed in 1957.

RELIGION IN EARLY HAWAII

Early Hawaiians believed in *mana*, a supernatural energy that gave form and function to everything above, upon and below the earth. To safeguard this *mana,* the Hawaiians established a system of sacred privileges and a governing body of laws, or *kapu. Kapu* were upheld by a priestly class of Kahuna, who officiated at sacred sites and temples of worship. There was little tolerance for infractions or violations of the *kapu*.

Kamehameha I, a warrior king who had consolidated power over most of the Hawaiian Islands by 1795, understood the power of *kapu* to ensure control over all social classes, land and resources.

Near the end of Kamehameha's reign, a young war orphan named `Opukaha`ia swam to the *Triumph*, an American ship anchored at Kealakekua Bay. He befriended the captain and returned to the United States with him, attending the Foreign Mission School at Cornwall, Connecticut and becoming one of the first Christian Hawaiians.

`Opukaha`ia planned to bring Christianity to his people but the plans dissolved when he fell victim to typhus and died on February 17, 1818.

After the death of Kamehameha I, in May of 1819, his eldest son and successor Liholiho (Kamehameha II), abolished the *kapu* system and destroyed all the temples, or *heiau*, throughout the Hawaiian Islands. Religious patronage shifted to the work of Christian missionaries, who worshipped a new god they called Jehovah. With the support of Ka`ahumanu, a favorite wife of Kamehameha I, the missionaries took hold in the Hawaiian Islands.

Honolulu, with its convenient harbor, gradually became the state's political, economic, military, education and cultural center. Until the 1940s, most visitors to Hawaii arrived in Honolulu Harbor by ocean liners from the West Coast.

During that time, Waikiki was primarily a swampland producing some agricultural goods. Actually, investors were reluctant to invest their money in Waikiki as it was a quiet backwater area, surrounded by swamps, taro fields, rice patties and mosquito-infested duck ponds.

A few fishermen and well-to-do families lived in beachfront homes on Waikiki. In 1837 the Hotel Waikiki opened. If was followed in the 1880s and 1890s with the opening of the Sans Souci in 1884, Park Beach in 1888 and Waikiki Seaside in 1894. The Sans Souci was built in 1884 by Allen Herbert and named for Frederick the Great's palace of the same name. The hotel's bungalows were demolished during World War I. The Waikiki Seaside is now the site of the famous Royal Hawaiian Hotel.

In 1917, the Hau Tree Hotel opened on Lewers Street. It was the converted home of Robert Lewers and is now the famous and elegant Halekulani property. In 1928, the Hotel Niumalu was built on the present site of the Hilton Hawaiian Village, which opened in 1956. After the first 2,270-mile trans-Pacific flight from San Francisco to Hawaii was completed in 1935, tourism boomed. Soon thereafter, the state became the center of attention for another reason. Pearl Harbor became famous when the nation set about to establish strategic military bases. It became infamous when the harbor was bombed by the Japanese on December 7, 1941, killing 2,390 people and igniting World War II.

Hollywood Meets Hawaii

Many television shows and feature films have been filmed on O`ahu. The Kahala Hotel and Resort has memorialized the bar from *Magnum P.I.* with a plaque noting its significance. Most recently, Hollywood has moved to Hawaii for the tremendously popular show *Lost*. O`ahu has so many diverse locales that it has been used to double for many exotic locations on the show. For example, on *Lost*, O`ahu has doubled as Pittsburgh, Seoul, Nigeria, France, Miami, London, Bangkok, Albuquerque and, of course, Hawaii.

Getting Here

By Air

Finding a deal on a flight to Hawaii is like gambling – a flight one day might be $50 more or $50 less when you check the next day. I've found that the best way to get the best fare is research. Check all of the airlines websites (many have special web fares) and if you are flexible with your dates, check the different days to see the differences. These days you can buy your ticket, choose your seat and check in for your flight over the web without ever talking to anyone. In fact, many airlines charge a fee to book a flight over the phone.

Here's a list of the major airlines that travel to Hawaii:

Ata Airlines, ☎ 800-435-9282, www.ata.com, offers several flights to Hawaii, including Las Vegas to Honolulu, Los Angeles to Maui, Oakland to Maui, Phoenix to Maui and Oakland to the Big Island.

Hawaiian Airlines, ☎ 800-367-5320, www.hawaiianair.com, has several flights from Hawaii to the Mainland, between the islands and to Australia and the South Pacific. Flights to Honolulu depart from Los Angeles, Sacramento, San Diego, San Francisco, San Jose, Las Vegas, Phoenix, Portland and Seattle. You can also fly Hawaiian Airlines from Honolulu to Sydney, Australia, Papeete, Tahiti and Pago Pago, American Samoa.

> *Hawaiian Artist Paints a Plane: One very special Boeing 737-700 honors Hawaii's precious marine life and ocean environment by having renowned artist Wyland paint some of the island's most famous residents on the sides of the airplane. Whales and dolphins are depicted as well as a seal, turtle, triggerfish, shark and an albatross. The jetliner was named Koholalele, which translates as "flying or leaping whale." Wyland created the Wyland Foundation, www.wylandfoundation.org, a non-profit organization dedicated to promoting, protecting and preserving the world's oceans, waterways and marine life.*

United Airlines, ☎ 800-864-8331, www.united.com, flies to the islands from Chicago, Los Angeles, San Francisco, Denver, Tokyo and Osaka.

American Airlines, ☎ 800-433-7300, www.aa.com, flies to Honolulu from Los Angeles, San Francisco, Chicago and the Dallas/Fort Worth area.

Continental Airlines, ☎ 800-523-3273, www.continental.com, flies from New York, Los Angeles and Houston to Honolulu.

Delta Airlines, ☎ 800-221-1212, www.delta.com, has flights from Atlanta, Los Angeles, Minneapolis/St. Paul, Salt Lake City, San Francisco, Seattle/Tacoma, Seoul (Korea) and Taipei (China) to Honolulu.

Korean Airlines, ☎ 800-438-5000, www.koreanair.com, has one flight a day from Seoul to Honolulu.

Island Air, ☎ 808-484-2222, www.islandair.com, flies between the islands and can take you to Kaua`i, Moloka`i, Maui, Lana`i and the Big Island of Hawai`i (Hilo and Kona).

Northwest, ☎ 800-225-2525, www.nwa.com, has flights from Los Angeles, Memphis, Detroit, Minneapolis/St. Paul, Osaka (Japan) and Guangzhou (China) to Honolulu. The airline also flies directly from Los Angeles to Kaua`i, Maui and the Big Island of Hawai`i.

Australian newcomer **Jetstar**, ☎ 866-397-8170, www.jetstar.com, has flights from Sydney and Melbourne to Honolulu. Jetstar started flying within Australia in May 2004 and internationally in November of the same year. It is owned by Qantas airlines but operates independently. The airline flies from Sydney to Honolulu on Tuesdays, Thursdays and Saturday and from Melbourne to Honolulu on Mondays and Fridays.

Qantas, ☎ 800-277-4500, www.qantas.com, an Australian airline, has one daily flight from Sydney to Honolulu.

By Cruise Ship

The **Norwegian Cruise Line** (NCL) has three ships (*Pride of Hawaii, Pride of Aloha* and *Pride of America*) that roam around six Hawaiian Islands, including O`ahu. The cruise line offers its signature "Freestyle Cruising," which allows guests a more personal and flexible voyage. The cruise line also works with over 135 properties across the islands if you want to stay on one island for a longer period.

Package Vacations

The **American Automobile Association** (AAA) has partnered with **Pleasant Holidays** to provide organized tours according to your needs and preferences. The company will arrange your airfare, accommodations, activities, automobile rental and dining options. If you prefer to have your vacation pre-arranged this is a nice option and you will receive exclusive discounts at restaurants, activities and attractions. The downside is that you won't have as much flexibility as if you were on your own. If you're a member of AAA, contact your local office for more details.

Getting Around

TheBus

TheBus, ☎ 808-946-5555 or 808-848-5555 (from 5:30 am to 10 pm HST), ☎ 808-848-4444 (lost and found and bus pass information), www.thebus.org, has $2 fares which will take your around the whole island of O`ahu. Nearly a quarter-million riders a day use TheBus, with its 4,000 stops on almost six dozen lines. The bus hits many of the popular tourists spots, including Pearl Harbor, the Bishop Museum, Diamond Head and the Waikiki Aquarium. Try to bring exact change! A time schedule is usually available from the headquarters at 811 Middle Street, at libraries or at any City Hall.

TheBoat

TheBoat, ☎ 808-848-5555 (from 5:30 am to 10 pm HST), ☎ 808-682-2555 (lost and found), www.trytheboat.com. In September 2007, the City of Honolulu launched its own island ferry service called TheBoat. The service can accommodate up to 149 passengers and does not take reserva-

tions. The ferry, which does not carry vehicles, is designed as an alternative to driving for commuters from Waianae, Kapolei and Makikilo to downtown Honolulu. Two boats make a total of three trips in each direction every day and the best part is that the hour-long ride is only $2, just like TheBus. What a deal!

The Waikiki Trolley

For a fun ride through Waikiki, hop on the Waikiki Trolley (www.waikikitrolley.com), which stops at all the popular sites. There are four lines: the Honolulu City Line (Red Line), the Ocean Coast Line (Blue Line), The Local Shopping & Dining Stop (Yellow Line) and the Ala Moana Shopping Shuttle Line (Pink Line). The Waikiki Trolley schedule is available at most hotels and popular tourist destinations. It can also be viewed on the website. There are a couple of price options. An all-day ticket that includes unlimited rides on the Red, Blue and Pink Lines costs $25 for adults and $12 for children ages four to 11. Four-day tickets are also available and must be used on four consecutive days. Check the website for military and senior discounts.

Airport Shuttle Services

Most hotels can provide you with shuttle services from your hotel to the airport. Don't be surprised if your shuttle is full of passengers dressed for a day of sightseeing rather than a luggage-lugging caravan to the airport. Many tour companies will pick up airport passengers and drop them off on their way to Pearl Harbor. Smart way to fill those empty seats!

Shuttle prices are about $10 one-way or $15 round-trip to and from the Honolulu Airport to Waikiki. Most companies allow two pieces of luggage, with additional charges for odd-sized, oversized and extra luggage pieces.

Here are some of the many companies that have airport shuttles and/or tour options:

Airport Shuttle, ☎ 808-954-8605, www.airportwaikikishuttle.com, is the only state-authorized airport shuttle between the airport, cruise ships and Waikiki.

Tahiti Trans, ☎ 808-455-7300, runs from 6:45 am to 11 pm.

Hawaii Super Transit, ☎ 808-841-2928, runs from 6 am to 9 pm.

Roberts Hawaii, ☎ 808-954-8608, runs from 7 am to 6 pm. For same-day reservations or if calling after 6 pm, ☎ 808-831-1555.

Ilima Tours and Transportation, ☎ 808-836-1881. Hours vary but are generally 5 am to 10 pm.

Mahalo Shuttle, ☎ 808-922-4900, runs from 6 am to 10 pm.

Ohana Express, ☎ 808-390-9563 or 808-753-5593 (toll free), www.honoluluairportwaikikiexpressshuttle.com, has a shuttle to the airport as well as transportation to the Swap Meet, Waikele Premium Outlets, Pearl Harbor and Aloha Tower.

VIP Trans, ☎ 808-836-0317, offers 24-hour-a-day service

Waikiki Express, ☎ 808-690-3185, runs from 6 am to 10 pm.

Rental Cars

I highly recommend reserving a car before you leave for Hawaii if you're the kind of visitor who loves the freedom of having your own wheels and aren't on a tight schedule. Renting a car or van is usually the most economical choice unless you plan on staying at your resort or rental property for the whole time. Car rental prices are one of the few things that are cheaper when compared with the Mainland. Always select "unlimited miles" and, if asked, choose to fill the tank before you return the car or else they'll fill it for you at a much higher price.

Your best bet is to shop around, especially on the Internet where great rates can be found. If you have AAA, always mention your membership to see if you can get a discount.

Here are some of the most popular rental car companies on O`ahu:

Enterprise Rent a Car, ☎ 800-261-7331, 808-836-2213, www.enterprise.com, Honolulu International Airport.

Hertz Rent a Car, ☎ 800-654-3131, central toll-free reservations, www.hertz.com. Hertz has three O`ahu locations: the Honolulu Airport, ☎ 808-529-6800, Hyatt Regency Waikiki, ☎ 808-971-3535, and the JW Marriott Ihilani Resort, ☎ 808-671-2366.

Budget Rent a Car, ☎ 808-921-5808 in Waikiki, ☎ 808-836-1700 at Honolulu International Airport, ☎ 800-527-0700 central toll free reservations, www.budget.com.

Alamo Rent a Car, ☎ 808-947-6112 in Waikiki, ☎ 808-833-4585 at Honolulu International Airport, ☎ 800-327-9633 central toll-free reservations, www.alamo.com.

Avis Rent a Car, ☎ 808-971-3700 in Waikiki, ☎ 808-834-5536 at Honolulu International Airport, ☎ 800-331-1212 central toll-free reservations, www.avis.com.

Dollar, ☎ 808-944-1544 central toll-free reservations, ☎ 808-952-4264 Waikiki (at the Ilikai Hotel), ☎ 808-922-1877 Japanese reservations, www.dollar.com.

Thrifty Car Rental, ☎ 808-831-2277 at Honolulu International Airport, ☎ 808-971-2660 in Waikiki, www.thrifty.com.

National Car Rental, ☎ 808-973-7200 in Waikiki, ☎ 808-830-3800 at Honolulu International Airport, ☎ 800-227-7368 central toll-free reservations, www.nationalcar.com.

V.I.P. Car Rentals, ☎ 808-922-4605, is a locally-run company that offers daily, weekend and monthly rentals. They offer free pick-up and free mileage.

Paradise Rent-A-Car, ☎ 808-946-7777, www.Harleys-andsportbikeshawaii.com, is a locally-owned company offering exotic cars, convertibles, Jeeps, Harley-Davidsons, mopeds and bicycles for rent.

Hawaii Rent-A-Car, ☎ 888-308-7154, www.rentexoticcars.com, has Ferraris, Porsches, Hummers, Corvettes, and many more top-of-the-line vehicles for rent. Their inventory also includes Harley-Davidsons and scooters. Check out the website for more information!

The downside to having your own car is that traffic in Honolulu can be a little daunting, but proper planning and avoiding busy commuter traffic can ease that pain. Parking is also expensive (average $15 a night for a Waikiki hotel) and there's no way to get around it.

Taxis

The CAB, ☎ 808-422-2222, www.thecabhawaii.com, info@thecabhawaii.com, provides service 24 hours a day, 365 days a year. The company has acquired a fleet of ramp-equipped Ford Windstar vans to provide service to physically impaired passengers. The basic cab fare is $2.45-$2.75 a mile with an additional charge of about $4 for oversized or heavy suitcases.

Star Taxi/Honolulu Hawaii Airport Shuttle, ☎ 808-942-7827 (reservations) or 808-739-1300 (Uncle Bob's line). Uncle Bob offers taxi pickups from the airport, www.startaxihawaii.com, as well as mini-van island tours, www.honolu-luhawaiiairportshuttle.com. Check the website to see how much it will cost to get a ride from the airport to your hotel (he has a list of over 100 Waikiki accommodations). Taxi pickups are by reservation only and each taxi carries a maximum of four passengers. If you have more than four people in your party, you must reserve another taxi. Island tours are $35 per hour for one to four people.

Uncle Bob offers many guarantees with his service, including at least 20% off the price of any metered taxi ride. He also guarantees that a real person will answer your call any time, day or night, and he dares potential customers to check it out. A test call in the middle of the night might hook you up with "Nick at Night," who never tires of talking about surfing. To make your shuttle or tour ride a bit smoother, Uncle Bob requests that you have the following information available when you call: date of arrival, approximate time of arrival, name of airline, flight number, number of people in your party, approximate number of large pieces of luggage, your destination and a cell phone number, if possible.

Charley's Taxi, 680 Ala Moana Blvd, ☎ 808-531-1333 or 808-947-0077; at the Hilton Hawaiian Village, ☎ 877-531-2333, www.charleystaxi.com. Established in 1938, Charley's Taxi has an informational website that provides lists of things to do and see in O`ahu. You can even read about "Auntie Myrtle," the `ukulele-toting "Singing Cab Driver." Charley's also has limousine rentals.

Limousine Services

If you have a large group of people in your party and want to go out for a night on the town, it can sometimes be more economical to rent a limousine by the hour than hiring several taxis. Once, some friends of mine and I were going from Waikiki to Aloha Tower Marketplace for dinner and, after some investigating, we discovered that it was a much better deal to get the limousine. And the small children we had with us had a great time in the "limbo."

Alpha Limousine Service, ☎ 808-955-8898.

Carey Hawaii Chauffeured Services, ☎ 888-563-2888, www.careyhawaii.com.

Cloud 9 Limousine, ☎ 808-524-7999.

Duke's Limousine, ☎ 808-738-1878.

Elite Limousine Service, ☎ 808-735-2431.

First Royal Limousine, ☎ 808-722-6037.

Hawaii Luxury Car Rentals, ☎ 808-222-2277.

Hawaii Car Service, ☎ 808-926-4444 (has vans and town cars).

Sharp Limousine, ☎ 808-951-6144.

Showtime Limousine, ☎ 808-926-4444.

*For Something Different: Try cruising the island in a dunebuggy! **Dunebuggy Adventures**, ☎ 808-371-6578, www.dbahawaii.com, has been renting street-legal dunebuggys for more than 30 years. Or if you're looking for a scooter-like vehicle, check out **Hawaiian Style Rentals**, ☎ 808-946-6733, for a large selection of scooters, three-wheelers and bikes. They'll deliver the vehicles to your hotel for free. **Paradise Cruisers**, ☎ 808-926-2847 or 808-368-4223, www.paradisecruisershawaii.com, rents motorcycles, scooters, beach gear and the "Hawaiian Luv Bugs."*

Between the Islands

Interisland Flights

go!, ☎ 888-435-9462, www.iflygo.com, is the newest competitor in the interisland airline wars and definitely a breath of fresh air with ultra-low prices. The airline, owned by Mesa Air Group, took to the sky in June 2006 and offered special one-way fares of $39 (competitors were charging between $80 and $100 for a one-way trip). Currently go! operates about 60 flights a day from its Honolulu hub to Lihue (Kaua`i), Kahului (Maui), Kona and Hilo (the Big Island). They also branched out in 2007 with the launch of go! Express which offers 12 flights a day between Kona and Kahului, Kahului and Kapalua (Maui) and Kapalua and Honolulu.

Hawaiian Airlines, ☎ 800-367-5320, www.hawaiianair.com, has several flights daily between Honolulu and Kaua`i, Maui and the Big Island of Hawai`i as well as code-sharing service daily to Moloka`i, Lana`i and west Maui. Hawaiian Airlines has been around since 1929 and is a reliable way to get around the islands. Booking over the Internet is easy, convenient and you can print out your boarding passes through the website.

Hawaii Superferry

And some more competition has arrived! The Hawaii Superferry, ☎ 877-HI-FERRY (877-443-3779), www.hawaiisuperferry.com. Call for reservations from 6 am and 7 pm (Hawaiian Standard Time). It started traveling between islands in July 2007 and offers travelers a very different way of getting around. The brand new ferries have space for 866 passengers and 282 vehicles. The trip is a bit long (three hours between Honolulu and Maui) but you can kill the time with four big-screen TVs, video games, free Wi-Fi, a 200-square-foot area for kids, and floor-to-ceiling windows with amazing views.

The 350-foot catamaran-style ferry leaves Pier 19 in Honolulu daily at 6:30 am bound for Maui, with a return scheduled to depart at 11 am. The Superferry leaves Honolulu Sunday to Friday at 3 pm for the island of Kaua`i, with a 7 pm return. Plans are being made to have another ferry run the Maui-O`ahu run and a round-trip between Honolulu and the Big Island of Hawaii is scheduled for 2009.

For locals, bringing your car with you can be a money-saver but for tourists rental cars are still being disputed as of press time. An old state law requires a vehicle's owner to give approval before it's taken interisland. Hopefully, this will be resolved soon and would allow families to rent a car once and still travel to several islands. At press time, Superferry tickets were $52 one-way for adults from Tuesday to Thursday and $62 from Friday to Monday. Children ages two to 12 pay $11 less. Infants are charged $17. The fee for bringing a car starts at $59.

Tour Companies

There are dozens of companies on O`ahu that provide various kinds of tours. There's a tour for everyone – adventure seekers, newlyweds, seniors, children, history buffs, you name it....

Here are a few of the companies that offer island tours.

Polynesian Adventure Tours, ☎ 808-833-3000, www.polyad.com.

Polynesian Hospitality, ☎ 808-526-3565, www.kobay.com.

Roberts Hawai`i, ☎ 808-539-9400, www.robertshawaii.com.

Discover Hawaii Tours, ☎ 800-946-4432, www.discover-hawaiitours.com.

Ko Olina Resort Tour Company, ☎ 808-382-6547, www.koolina.com, operates out of the Ko Olina Resort & Marina on the Windward Coast of O`ahu.

E Noa Tours, ☎ 808-591-2561, www.enoa.com. E Noa has been around for more than 30 years and offers 15 varied tours throughout the island of O`ahu or gives you the option of designing your own tour. Tours include an all-day Grand Circle Tour of the entire island and a Pearl Harbor/Circle Island tour. All guides are certified by the State of Hawaii.

DRIVING AROUND O`AHU

As Waikiki is the epicenter of O`ahu, here are the distances from Waikiki to other popular destinations:

From Waikiki to:

Honolulu Airport	9 miles	30 minutes
Arizona Memorial	11 miles	30 minutes
Downtown Honolulu	4 miles	15 minutes
Hanauma Bay	11 miles	30 minutes
Pali Lookout	11 miles	25 minutes
Pearl Harbor	14 miles	30 minutes
Diamond Head	1 mile	10 minutes
Hanauma Bay	12 miles	30 minutes
Sea Life Park	16 miles	40 minutes
Polynesian Cultural Center	38 miles	75 minutes
Kualoa Ranch	25 miles	50 minutes

Makaha	37 miles	75 minutes
Turtle Bay Resort	37 miles	75 minutes
Waimea	35 miles	75 minutes
Waimea Valley Audubon Center	35 miles	75 minutes
Hale`iwa Town	32 miles	60 minutes
Ko Olina Resort	26 miles	45 minutes
University of Hawai`i	3 miles	10 minutes
Nu`uanu Pali Lookout	11 miles	30 minutes

What Time Is It? *Hawaii does not participate in Daylight Savings Time. We have our own time zone, Hawaiian Standard Time, which is two hours behind Pacific Standard Time during the months of November through March. We are three hours behind Pacific Standard Time during the rest of the year. This can get confusing, especially if you're traveling, and I've talked to visitors who actually think their flight home on the day of the changeover will be an hour shorter!*

Trip Planning

Before You Go

TRAVEL TIPS

Security at airports is at an all-time high so here are some tips to help you get through the procedures in a timely and trouble-free manner:

- The Transportation Security Administration (TSA) has come up with a "3-1-1" promotion to explain what can be brought onboard in your carry-on luggage – three-ounce containers or less of liquids, gels or aerosols in a one-quart clear plastic zip-lock bag. One bag is allowed per traveler.
- Pack all liquids, gels and aerosols in your checked baggage. Exceptions to the rule include baby for-

mula/breast milk/baby food while traveling with a small child, medications and liquids or gels needed for diabetics or other medical needs. Any exceptions must be declared to the security officer for screening and will take up additional time.

- Pack all undeveloped film in your carry-on bag because screening equipment for checked bags may damage film. Pull out the clear plastic bag when going through screening to avoid delays.
- Wear shoes with a low sole (less than one inch), such as sandals or flip-flops. Most people have to take their shoes off to have them scanned and it's the people who are wearing tennis shoes and other lace-up shoes that hold up the lines. Also take off jackets, metal jewelry and put keys, coins, PDAs and mobile phones in your carry-on baggage.
- If you have a laptop computer, keep it handy (not at the bottom of your carry-on), as you will be required to screen it separately.
- Most airlines require you to check in two hours prior to the flight. This is a good rule of thumb as it allows you enough time for check-in, security and will alleviate any anxiety if the lines are long.
- Check with your airline about weight restrictions on luggage. I've watched people open their luggage and transfer some of the contents into large garbage bags so they could meet the limit. Most of the airlines limit luggage to 50 lbs before they assess a fee.
- Travel early in the day – I usually try to take the first flight of the day and I almost never run into lines at the airline counter or in security. Most of the crowds travel in the early afternoon and that is when you could run into delays.
- If you have any questions about what you can and cannot bring, visit the Transportation Security Administration website at www.tsa.gov/public, or call the TSA Contact Center toll-free at ☎ 866-

289-9673. As the rules of what you can and cannot bring are hard to predict, check out the website so you don't have some of your possessions confiscated. For example, a bottle of wine is forbidden, but corkscrews are allowed. Gel candles and gel shoe inserts are not allowed but three ounces of Jell-O and gel-filled bras are okay. You can bring an unlimited amount of K-Y Jelly, but a large jar of grape jelly will cause you trouble. Rounded butter knives are allowed but scissors with blades longer than four inches are forbidden.

Helpful Website: www.smartpacking.com was created by Susan Foster, the author of **Smart Packing for Today's Traveler**. *Foster offers many tips on how to avoid involuntary bumping by airlines, checking out and understanding an airline's "Contract of Carriage," and making the most out of your carry-on luggage.*

When To Go

The weather in O`ahu is generally great but there are some seasons that are wetter and chillier than others. And remember, the Windward side of every Hawaiian Island gets more rain than the drier Leeward sides. For example, in the month of December, Honolulu varies from a high of 82°F to a low of 65°F, with an average of 3.2 inches of rain. The Windward side in December has a high of 78° and a low of 67°, with 7.9 inches of rain on average. And on the North Shore, temperatures in December range from 82° to 65°, with an average of 4.1 inches of rain.

The holidays (Christmas, New Year's Eve and spring break) are the busiest (and most expensive) times to visit any of the Hawaiian Islands. Keep in mind that if school is out, then the islands will be busy. During the summer you'll find a lot more families on the beaches compared to the slower months of January, February, October and November. If you do decide to travel during this busy time, don't do it on the weekends. Tuesday, Wednesday and Thursday are the best days to travel, crowd- and cost-wise.

What to Bring

It can be a little overbearing to bring beach towels, beach mats, snorkel gear, water toys, ice chests, etc. I recommend stopping at the Costco (if you're a member), Longs Drugs, K-mart or Sam's Club to pick up these items as well as groceries and souvenirs. There are three K-marts on O`ahu (500 N. Nimitz Highway, ☎ 808-528-2280, 4561 Salt Lake Blvd, ☎ 808-486-6118, and 500 Kamokila Blvd, ☎ 808-674-9355). Costco also has three locations in O`ahu (94-1231 Ka Uka Blvd. in Waipahu, ☎ 808-678-6103, 525 Alakawa Street in Honolulu, ☎ 808-526-6103, and 333A Keahole Street in Hawaii Kai, ☎ 808-395-5538).

Also, most vacation rentals provide these items as part of the rental (although there's no guarantee they will have your flipper size!) and most resorts are associated with a beachside company that rents equipment on a daily or weekly basis.

If you do purchase these items, don't lug them back home. Instead, leave them at the vacation rental for the next family or, if you're staying at a resort, pass them off to another family.

Getting Married

Hotel Help

Outrigger Hotels & Resorts has launched an online honeymoon registry with a service called TheBigDay.com. Couples who choose an Outrigger or Ohana property for their honeymoon are provided with a "registry wizard." It helps them create a registry that includes activities and experiences they will enjoy on their honeymoon. There is no fee for couples that sign up for the service and they will have their own wedding webpage, announcement cards and an e-mail account for organizing their wedding-related correspondence.

Wedding Planners

A sunset Hawaiian wedding
(www.dreamweddingshawaii.com)

Dream Wedding Hawaii, 47098 Halemanu Place, Kaneohe, ☎ 800-557-1310, www.dreamweddings-hawaii.com. Steve Young, who calls himself "The Wedding Guy," has been doing full-service weddings for about 10 years. His philosophy is to keep everything fun and as simple as possible.

Haiku Gardens Weddings, ☎ 808-247-0605, www.haikugardens.com/weddings.html, weddings@haikugardens.com. This company caters to couples who want to have their wedding at Haiku Garden on the North Shore. Options include full-service wedding planning or couples can pick and choose from an "à la carte" menu.

Accommodations

Before you select a place to stay, decide exactly what you want. Do you want to be waited on hand and foot? Do you want to lug your own bags around or have someone else do it? Are you working within a budget? Do you need to have oceanview? Do you need family-friendly accommodation?

Hotels & Resorts

Hotel and resorts are great for families and visitors who don't want to cook, clean or worry. Most of the time there's valet parking and a bell desk to help you take your luggage back and forth to the room. Most hotels and resorts are situated on beaches and the personnel can help with activities. You can sometimes find better rates or special packages on a hotel's website. Some hotels have "fifth night free" promotions or honeymoon and/or family packages. You may also be able to get a rental car deal with your reservation.

The hotel room rate you're quoted may sound like a deal, but make sure to ask about additional charges. Some hotels charge up to $17 as a resort fee, which may include a free newspaper and coffee (check hotel info for more). This fee is generally not optional, although they sometimes make it sound that way. Also expect to pay about 11% in taxes, which is usually not included in a price quote.

Condominiums

Condominiums are also great for families, are more like home, and are generally cheaper than hotels and resorts. Most have kitchens, barbecues and washing machines. These are great amenities if you want to cook, if you have a large family or several families visiting together. Most don't have daily housekeeping, although some offer it for an additional fee. Also, a little research can help you find price breaks for those who stay for a week and even better deals if you stay for a month (lucky you!).

Author's Tip: Oceanfront and ocean-view rooms are great but if you don't plan on spending much time in your hotel room or condo, you can save a lot of money by getting a partial ocean-view or garden-view. Check the prices and weigh the options.

Vacation Rentals

Vacation rentals are usually homes that the owner offers to other families. These are for people who want a "home away from home" and want all the amenities. They offer privacy, full kitchens and easy parking. One of the best places to find a vacation rental is on www.vrbo.com.

Bed & Breakfasts

Bed & breakfasts are great for couples and newcomers to the island. They are cozy and, as they only offer breakfast, you have an opportunity to try many O`ahu restaurants for lunch and dinner. Some have small kitchen facilities, mostly capable of making coffee and reheating leftovers. Breakfasts are on a time schedule so if you're not an early riser, you may miss your morning meal. If you're an extra-early riser, some host will prepare your breakfast the night before or make you a togo meal to take with you on your adventures.

Germ Alert: Even the nicest hotels can have a host of germs that will make you or your family ill. The most contaminated objects may be the ones you don't think of – the remote control, the ice bucket, clock radio, doorknobs and telephones. Experts suggest you bring disinfectant wipes to clean these areas. Also, it is suggested that you wear slippers or flip-flops on any floor surfaces and if there is a bedspread on the bed, remove it promptly – they are rarely washed.

Restaurant & Hotel Prices

Restaurant prices are not flexible but keep your eyes open for happy hour or early-bird specials, especially in Waikiki. Hotel room prices are not as set in stone and I always look at the hotel's website for specials. Many hotels have e-newsletters where you can sign up for updates. Also look to see if they have a fifth-night free promotion.

HOTEL PRICE CHART	
Cost per night for two before tax	
$	Under $80
$$	$81-$150
$$$	$151-$225
$$$$	$226-$400
$$$$$	Over $400

DINING PRICE CHART	
Price per person for an entrée, not including beverage, tax or tip	
$	Under $15
$$	$15-$30
$$$	$31-$45
$$$$	Over $45

Eating & Drinking

Flavors of Hawaii

During your visit to O`ahu, you'll be introduced to a lot of foods you normally don't see on the Mainland. There's a lot of Japanese, Chinese and Filipino influence in our cuisines, such as the custom of having white, sticky rice with every meal. Here's a guide to help you discover and enjoy all of Hawaii's unique flavors:

Maui Onion: This sweet juicy onion is mostly grown in Upcountry Maui and is known for its mild taste – real Maui onion lovers have been known to eat them like apples! Large, yellowish with a flattened top, Maui onions are available year-round on all of the islands.

Saimin: A noodle soup with pork slices, egg, green onion and fish cake. Saimin is offered for breakfast, lunch and dinner at many local restaurants and even at McDonalds.

Poi: This thick, paste-like starch made from taro root is a staple in the Hawaiian diet. Poi is low in fat and protein and is usually sold at grocery stores and small markets. It comes in plastic bags or round plastic containers with lids. Poi is an acquired taste, kind of like Vegemite to Australians. In Hawaii, it is often a baby's first food.

Li hing mui: Preserved Chinese plum. Usually sold as a flavored snack or as a flavor of ice cream or shave ice.

Lomilomi salmon: Raw diced salmon mixed with tomatoes and onions, usually served with a plate lunch.

Loco moco: A hearty, artery-clogging breakfast dish consisting of a hamburger patty covered with a fried egg and served over white rice with a generous serving of gravy on top.

Shave ice: (not shaved ice) A Hawaiian snow cone made with shaved (not crushed) ice and then topped with the syrup of your choice. It looks like a snow cone but the difference is that a snow cone has coarse ice shavings that don't allow for the syrups to stick to the ice as well. Pick one flavor – mango, li hing mui, pineapple, lilikoi, guava, Kona coffee or bubble gum, for example – or a rainbow flavor concoction. You can even get a "snow cap" of sweet cream piled on top.

Kalua pig: Tender pork, cooked in an *imu* (underground oven) and frequently served at luaus or with plate lunches.

Plate lunch: A plate lunch consists of a meat such as kalua pig, lomilomi salmon or teriyaki chicken, served with white rice and macaroni salad.

DID YOU KNOW?

Plate lunches are believed to have originated when plantation workers from various ethnic groups took their lunch breaks and discovered they had all brought different cuisines. Japanese workers would bring teriyaki beef with rice and their Filipino coworkers might have brought a pork or chicken stew. Next to them a Korean could be eating marinated ribs or someone from China might be having a rice noodle dish. Once they began sharing their lunches with the Hawaiians, who had Kalua pig lunches, a tradition was born – plate lunches. Plate lunches are traditionally served with "two scoops rice" and "one scoop macaroni."

Poke (pronounced "po-kee"): A raw-fish relish usually made with ahi tuna and then mixed with chopped tomatoes and onions.

Malasada: A Portuguese doughnut found at roadside stands or in bakeries.

Portuguese sausage: A spicy sausage usually served at breakfast as a side-dish or as an ingredient in an omelet.

Haupia: Coconut pudding served as a dessert.

Pupu (pronounced "poo-poo"): This means appetizer or starter. It's always fun to tell newcomers to the island that we love to have "pupu parties."

Pog: A mixture of pineapple, orange and guava juices. This fruity concoction is what they'll probably serve you on the airplane flight over to O`ahu.

White rice: This starch is commonly served with breakfast, lunch and dinner and comes with soy sauce (called shoyu).

Haupia

GREAT CHEFS THINK ALIKE

Many of the finer restaurants serve what is known as Hawai`i Regional Cuisine (shortened to HRC), which incorporates fresh fish, fruits and vegetables into creative and innovative dishes. In 1991, 12 island chefs formed a coalition to promote Hawai`i Regional Cuisine as a way to celebrate and perpetuate the diversity and sophistication of the natural products we have here in the islands. This movement has become very popular and has spread to many of the finest restaurants on the mainland.

TIPS ON TIPPING

Much of the population of O`ahu and the rest of Hawaii is dependent on the tourism industry and much of that market is taken up by the restaurant business. Chances are you'll be eating out a lot during your vacation so here are some guidelines to make your restaurant visit a pleasant experience for you and the restaurant staff.

Tipping for good service is normally 15-20%. Tipping for great service is 20-25%. Servers generally work for minimum wage but if they were especially helpful or informative, why not give them an extra couple of bucks. It will make their day and isn't that a nice feeling?

If the food is horrible, don't punish the server. It's probably not his or her fault and they might not know there is a problem unless you tell them. Then complain to the manager. If nobody tells a restaurant that their food is unacceptable, they might not know. But if it's clearly not the server's fault and his or her service was fine, leave a nice tip. You can ask him or her not to share it with the kitchen, if that is how the restaurant shares tips.

If you're from a state that has a high sales tax, keep in mind that the tax in Hawaii is about 4%. A lot of visitors from places like California (where the tax is 8-9%) will generally just double the tax to figure out the tip. They bring that formula to Hawaii and end up leaving their server an 8% tip! Ouch!

TAXES!! UGGG!

Hawaii has a state sales tax of 4%. Any extra taxes are those added by the city or county. In Honolulu, the lodging tax is 11.42% and rental cars are subject to state tax and a surcharge of approximately $3 a day.

And please don't complain about the prices – everything has to be imported here, including you. Consider how much it costs you to fly here and formulate that into everything you eat and buy. It's not cheap here. But do you see waterfalls, the Pacific Ocean and rainbows from your favorite restaurant at home?

Also, always call to see if you can make a reservation, especially if you have more than four people in your party. It's required at high-end restaurants in high-traffic areas like Waikiki, Kahana, Hawaii Kai and Kailua. Without one, you may be eating dinner after 10 pm.

Fish of Hawaii

Mahimahi is also called dorado or dolphinfish (not the mammal!). It's a moist, flaky, mildly flavored, sweet, light pink fish that turns white when cooked. Mahimahi is mostly available in the spring (March through May) and fall (September through November) and this tasty fish ranges between eight and 25 lbs.

Opah is called moonfish. For a long time, Opah has been thought to be good luck so it was only given away, never sold. Opah is a non-schooling open-ocean fish so this tasty treat is not caught in great quantities. Opah has four types of flesh. The flesh behind the head is orange-tinged, the flesh toward the belly is a pinkish color and the cheeks are dark red. All of these cook to white. The flesh inside the breastplates of the opah is a bright red color that turns brown when cooked. Opah is most frequently available from August through December.

Monchong (also called bigscale pomfret) is becoming more popular in Hawaii restaurants. Monchong ranges in size from four to 25 pounds, with fish over 12 pounds preferred for cooking. Its high fat content makes it an excellent fish for broiling, baking or sautéing. Monchong is mostly available in the months of May through September.

Opakapaka, or pink snapper, is a melt-in-your-mouth fish with clear, pale pink flesh. Most opakapaka caught in Hawaiian waters are between one and five pounds, but can grow up to 12 pounds. Opakapaka are caught all year round in depths of 300 to 500 feet, but are most abundant in the last half of the year.

O`AHU FISH MARKETS

Try out these markets for buying fresh fish or tasting prepared dishes:

Honolulu Fish Auction at Pier 38, ☎ 808-536-2148, opens at 5:30 am when fresh catches of big-eye tuna, yellow-fin tuna, skipjack tuna, albacore tuna, opah, mahimahi, mairagi, ono, monchong, onaga and opakapaka are auctioned off.

Fort Ruger Market, 3585 Alohea Avenue, Kaimuki (northeast of the Ali Wai Canal), ☎ 808-737-4531. This market is famous among locals for its poke (bite-sized pieces of ahi or other fish seasoned with soy sauce, ginger, garlic and sesame)

Tamashiro Market, 802 N. King. Street, (Kalihi) ☎ 808-841-8047 You'll find lots of poke, varieties of freshly-caught reef fish, deep-water tunas and many other types of seafood.

The Poke Stop, 94-050 Farrington Highway E-4 (Waipahu), ☎ 808-676-8100. Grab some poke here or a kit to make your own at home.

Oahu Market, (corner of King and Kekaulike Streets). Founded in 1904, this Chinatown institution has provided O`ahu residents and visitors with a variety of vendors selling fresh island fish.

Yama's Fish Market, 2332 Young Street, ☎ 808-941-9994, www.yamasfishmarket.com. Serving Hawaii since 1980, Yama's Fish Market is located on Young Street near the corner of Isenberg in Metropolitan Honolulu. Their slogan is "Where Every Day is Aloha Friday" and the huge assortment of traditional Hawaiian cuisine will confirm that. Call for daily specials or order off the menu – try local dishes such as Lau Lau, Kalua Pig, Pork Adobo, Shoyu Chick, Squid Luau or Lomilomi Salmon with sides of macaroni salad, rice, poi or soy beans. Yama's Fish Market is open from 9 am to 7 pm Monday through Saturday and 9 am to 5 pm Sunday.

The newest fish market to hit O`ahu is **Tsukiji Fish Market and Restaurant**, ☎ 808-237-5444, on the fourth floor of the Ala Moana Shopping Center. The fish market is just one of the many atrractions here (see the *Ala Moana Shopping Center Restaurants* for more information). At Tsukiji, guests can learn how to fillet fish like a professional. Daily fish filleting demonstrations using fresh island fish are a highlight at the market. There's also a make-your-own-poke station (poke is a Hawaiian raw fish dish). The fish market portion is open from 11 am to 6 pm.

Onaga is also called longtail snapper or red snapper. It ranges from one to eight pounds and, when cooked, is moderately firm and moist. Onaga is most commonly caught from July to December.

Uku, commonly known as grey snapper or jobfish, is also a delicate, moist fish. It is most commonly found in the summer months when other snappers are less available.

Aku, also called skipjack or bonito tuna, is caught all year long and usually weighs between four and 15 pounds. Larger aku, sometimes weighing up to 30 pounds, can be found in the summer months. Aku has a firm flesh that is deep red in color. It can be prepared and eaten raw or, when cooked, the flesh becomes light. Aku can be baked, broiled or grilled and is commonly used in sashimi, sushi or poke.

Shutome (whose Hawaiian name is *A u Ku*) is also called broad-bill swordfish and has a firm texture and mild taste that makes it ideal for broiling, poaching, stir-frying or baking. Shutome is most commonly found from May through October.

Yellow-fin tuna

Ahi is the Hawaiian name for two tunas that are similar in appearance. **Big-eye tuna** is a more plump variety with a larger head, while **yellow-fin tuna** has long, bright yellow fins. Ahi weigh between 10 and 250 pounds. Both fish have firm red flesh that turns white when cooked and are excellent when broiled, baked or sautéed. Top grade ahi has a higher fat content and is considered perfect for sashimi and sushi. Big-eye tuna is most commonly found from October through February, while yellow-fin is seen from April through September. **Toro**, sashimi from the belly portion of the ahi, is oily and succulent. When available, it is a delicacy.

> *Menu Tip:* If you like seafood and see "ahi katsu" on the menu, order it! Ahi katsu is a block of ahi tuna coated with seasonings and rolled in panko (Japanese breadcrumbs). It's deep fried so that it's raw in the middle and cooked on the outside. Yummy!

Tombo is albacore tuna and has light pink flesh. It is the lightest and mildest in flavor of all tunas. Tombo usually weighs in at 40 to 80 pounds, while those over 50 pounds are most desirable. It is available primarily during the months of April through September.

Blue marlin

There are two types of **marlin** (Hawaiian name is *Au*) found in the islands – Pacific blue marlin is called **kajiki** and striped marlin is known as **nairagi**. Kajiki is most frequently caught in the summer and fall months while nairagi is caught mostly in winter and spring. The flesh of marlin varies with each fish but ranges from clear pink to amber or orange-red and they all turn white when cooked.

Hebi is also called shortbill spearfish and usually weighs between 20 and 40 pounds. It has an amber-colored flesh that is similar to marlin but not as firm. Hebi is most commonly found between January and June.

Cooked ono with pineapple

Ono is also known as wahoo and is one of the most common fish you'll see on menus. The ono is a strong, slender fish with a firm yet flaky texture. It is often called the "chicken of the sea" due to its mild taste. People who say they "hate fish" admit to liking ono. It is best sautéed, baked, grilled or broiled and is fabulous as "fish and chips."

Kampachi and **moi** are relatively new to the Hawaiian menu. Both are farmed in open-ocean cages off the shores of the Big Island and O`ahu. Kampachi is similar to hamachi and has a melt-in-your-mouth texture. Moi is often steamed Chinese-style or fried crisp.

O`ahu Farmers' Markets

These aren't your typical neighborhood farmers' markets! Welcome to a cornucopia of exotic fruits and vegetables, brilliant flowers, locally-grown meats and a hodge-podge of other tropical treats. Don't be surprised to see such items as: low fat fruitcake with gogi berries, island ginger ale, Egyptian-style lunch plates, dried snacks like pickled mango, Maui kaki and marlin, sweet Maui onion rings, taro-based products like spreads and wraps and lots of orchids For more information, contact the Hawaii Farm Bureau Federation at ☎ 808-848-2074 or at www.hfbf.org.

There are three major farmers' markets associated with the Hawaii Farm Bureau Federation.

Honolulu

On Saturdays, the **Farmers' Market at Kapi`olani Community College**, 4303 Diamond Head Road, ☎ 808-848-2074, is held from 7:30 am to 11 am. Check out the website at www.hfbf.org/FarmersMarketKCC.html (it changes every week) to see the day's specials along with a detailed list of all participating vendors and their location at the market.

Kailua

Kailua Farmer's Market, www.hfbf.org/FarmersMarket-Kailua.html, is held every Thursday from 5 pm to 7:30 pm at the Kailua Town Center Parking Garage (behind Longs Drugs).

Mililani

Mililani Farmers' Market, www.hfbf.org/FarmersMarket-Mililani.html, is held every Sunday from 8 am to 11 am at the Mililani High School in Central O`ahu.

Made on O`ahu

One of my favorite aspects of traveling is discovering locally made products. It's my way of helping out the local community while obtaining a product that can't be found anywhere else in the world!

Here are some of Oahu's best:

Alan Wong's Restaurant in Honolulu serves Waialua Chocolate, from the only farm in the country that produces chocolate. The delicacy is made on Oahu's North Shore and has a very deep flavor – lots of berry and it's nonacidic. You can pick up your own bars of Waialua chocolate at the Dole Plantation in Central O`ahu.

North Shore Soap Factory, 67-106 Kealohanui Street, ☎ 808-637-8400, www.hawaiianbathbody.com, is located on the North Shore in the town of Waialua. The factory makes body washes, aromatherapy body mists, bath salts, lomi lomi oils and lip moisturizers, all from original recipes using no harsh chemicals, detergents or petroleum-based ingredients. The factory is inside the retail store, so when you're at the North Shore, check out this fascinating shop.

To get to the North Shore Soap Factory from Hale`iwa, head down Waialua Beach road and turn left on Goodale Avenue. Turn right on Kealohanua Street and you are at the front gate of The Waialua Sugar Mill, a.k.a the North Shore Soap Factory. The soap factory is open from 9 am to 6 pm Monday through Saturday and noon to 6 pm on Sunday.

The Soap Box, ☎ 808-284-6170, www.soapboxhawaii.com. Husband and wife duo Steve Cromwell and Jo Ann Takushi began making soap out of their home in O`ahu about nine years ago and their hobby soon became a small business. They make the soap by hand and the translucent glycerin soaps come in many vivid colors and scents. Some have loofahs embedded inside of the soap. Contact them by phone or on the website to find out more about how to get your hands on some special soap and lotions.

The Tea Chest, ☎ 808-591-9400, www.teachest.com, info@teachest.com, opened in 1995 as a distributor and catalog retailer of fine teas and accessories. To promote the business, owners Byron and Satomi Goo went to craft fairs, trade shows and any event that would allow them to set up a booth and promote the tea. Goo discovered that more people were interested in iced tea than hot tea. Eight months later, after much trial and error, the company introduced a Passionfruit iced tea and, later, Mango, Strawberry Guava and `Ohelo Berry teas. In 2001, the company opened a Tea Bar in Downtown Honolulu called Tea Chest Hawaii. If you can't make it back to the islands soon, the teas are available though their Internet site.

Plumeria Rain, www.plumeriarain.com, ☎ 808-391-4443. Tina Ortogero and her son Zachary create handmade tropical-inspired bath and body products from their home in Kailua. Some of their products include a jojoba lotion spray that is infused with Kukui nut oil and is light and easily absorbed. They also offer a Hawaiian-style hand sanitizer. The duo use essential oils from flowers such as pikake, pakalana, pua kenikeni, turberose and plumeria.

Lanikai Bath and Body store

Lanikai Bath and Body, www.lanikaibathandbody.com, ☎ 808-262-3260, is the brainchild of Gloria Garvey and Brook Gramann. They have an impressive selection of body washes, scrubs, soap, bath lotions, oils and a conditioning shampoo made with local ingredients.

The **Honolulu Cookie Company**, ☎ 866-333-5800, www.honolulucookie.com. In 1998, Keith and Janet Sung began baking light, crisp shortbread cookies and, since then, have created a great following. For many locals and tourists, their cookies are a holiday must. Only the best ingredients are used and the cookie company now offers eight flavors: Butter Macadamia Nut, Chocolate Dipped Macadamia, Pineapple Macadamia Nut, Kona Coffee, Triple Chocolate Dipped Chocolate Macadamia Nut, Mango, Lilikoi and White Chocolate Kona Coffee. The Honolulu Cookie Company has nine store locations in Hawaii (seven in O`ahu) or you can purchase goods on their website.

Practical Information

Web Resources

WWW **www.honolulu.com** is more like an advertisement for Honolulu hotels. But it can't hurt to check it out when comparing prices.

www.co.honolulu.hi.us. This is the official website for the City and County of Honolulu.

www.GoHawaii.com is the official website for the Hawaii Visitors and Convention Bureau and offers in-depth, up-to-date information on all the islands, including O`ahu. The site also offers promotional information on a variety of hotel chains, authentic Hawaiian recipes from the "Chefs of Aloha," interactive maps and tools to create your own personal trip planner.

www.GoHawaii.com/waikiki will take you to the Waikiki section of the official website for all of Hawaii.

www.visit-oahu.com is the official site for the island of O`ahu Visitors Bureau. You can also call ☎ 1-877-525-6248 for more information.

www.bestplaceshawaii.com is an independent vacation planner and encompasses all of the islands. It's a good source for out-of-the-way hidden spots, for discounts and maps.

www.andhawaii.com is dedicated to discussion groups asking and answering questions about Hawaii. It has some helpful hints about what to do when you're on the Islands.

www.pubclub.com/hawaii/honolulu/pubclub.htm provides information about Honolulu nightlife.

> **Travel Pink:** The Hilton Hawaiian Village and the Royal Hawaiian Hotel have partnered with the O`ahu Visitors Bureau in a program to benefit the Hawaii Affiliate of the Susan G. Komen Breast Cancer Foundation. For details on how to Travel Pink!, visit www.visit-oahu.com/travelpink.

Print References

The Honolulu Advertiser and the ***Honolulu Star-Bulletin*** are the two daily newspapers in Honolulu and the main newspapers for the state. On Fridays, *The Honolulu Advertiser* publishes a supplement called "tgif" – "The Great Index to Fun," which lists Honolulu and O`ahu restaurants, nightlife, concerts, theater performances, movie reviews and live music venues.

The ***Hawai`i Hochi*** is a bilingual English-Japanese newspaper.

Spotlight and ***This Week*** magazines are available at nearly every street corner in Waikiki and around the island. These thin fully packed brochures offer many discounts and easy-to-read maps.

HAWAII MAGAZINE

Picking up a copy of this magazine before your trip will give you a head start in the excitement department. The articles are well written by mostly Hawaiian authors and promote the best of Hawaii. *Hawaii* magazine is available at the airport bookstore and at many mainland bookstores.

Radio

FM Stations

88.1 KHPR – Classical music & news (National Public Radio)

89.3 KIPO – News, talk, world music & jazz (National Public Radio)

90.3 KTUH – Jazz, Hawaiian, alternative, rock and rap

92.3 KSSK – Adult contemporary

93.1 KQMQ – Contemporary hits

93.9 KIKI – Urban contemporary hits

94.7 KUMU – Adult contemporary music, lite rock

95.5 KAIM – Christian contemporary

96.3 KRTR – Adult contemporary music

97.5 KHNR – Hawaii's FM talk

98.5 KDNN – Island rhythm

99.5 KHUI – Music of Hawai`i

100.3 KCCN – Island music and reggae

101.1 KXRG – Hawaii's dance station

101.9 KUCD – Modern rock hits

102.7 KDDB – Urban contemporary hits

104.3 KPHW – Hawaii's hip hop and R&B hits

105.1 KINE – Contemporary Hawaiian music

105.9 KPOI – Classic rock

107.9 KGMZ – Oldies from the 60's & 70's

AM Stations

590 KSSK – Adult contemporary music

650 KRTR – Easy listening favorites

1270 KNDI – Ethnic programs
760 KGU – Hawaii's Christian talk
1170 KJPN – Asian radio
870 KHNR – Hawaii's FM talk (all news and weather)
690 KORL – Hawaii's local talk & multicultural radio
1370 KUPA – Hawaiian music
1210 KZOO – Japanese music & programming
1460 KHRA – Korean programming
1540 KREA – Korean programming
990 KHBZ – News & talk
830 KHVH – News & talk
1040 KLHT – Religious
1420 KKEA – Sports & talk radio
1500 KUMU – The new talk of Honolulu
940 KKNE – Traditional Hawaiian music

Spas

A spa treatment in Hawaii is a must! Most spas use tropical and local Hawaiian ingredients in their treatments, which make for an unforgettable only-in-Hawaii experience. Most of the larger resorts have in-house spas, but make sure you have a reservation, as they are VERY popular. There are also stand-alone spas, mostly in Waikiki, which also offer wonderful treatment choices. Here's a list of some of the most popular spas:

In Waikiki and Honolulu

Na Ho`ola Spa (at the Hyatt Regency Waikiki Resort & Spa), ☎ 808-237-6330, is a two-story spa filled with Hawaiian atmosphere. There are 19 rooms and treatments include facials, massages, healing stone, body wraps, waxing and treatments for the bride. They also offer packages such as the "Kukui" for the body and hair, which lasts 3½ hours. The spa is also home to the fitness center and offers locker rooms, a retail shop, nail salon and a full workout room. The spa promotes yoga as well and will teach you how to "hula-cise."

Nice Touch: The Hyatt Regency has two special floors just for women that offer added security, upgraded bath amenities and a $50 room credit for food / beverages or a spa visit. It's called the Lehua Floor Ladies Program.

Abhasa Spa (at the Royal Hawaiian Hotel), ☎ 808-922-8200, www.abhasa.com, info@abhasa.com. The spa, in the legendary Pink Palace of the Pacific, offers massage, after-sun treatments, body scrubs, body cocoons, waxing and facials. There are spa packages that mix and specialize treatments. The spa also offers a hair salon, wedding assistance, make-up help and manicures and pedicures.

The **SpaHalekulani**, 2199 Kalia Road, ☎ 808-923-2311, www.halekulani.com, is considered the premier spa in Waikiki. The Halekulani is next to Gray's beach, which was known to early Hawaiians for its healing waters or "*Kawehewehe.*" The SpaHalekulani takes this legend into consideration when offering services inspired by the healing cultures of Hawaii, Asia and the South Pacific. The spa menu is extensive and expensive but the facilities are top-notch and I would highly recommend this spa to anyone. Everything from massages, body scrubs, facials, hair care, nail care and awesome spa package treatments are available. The SpaHalekulani is open daily from 9 am to 8 pm.

Aveda Lifestyle Salon & Spa, 1450 Ala Moana Blvd., Honolulu, ☎ 808-947-6141.

Heaven on Earth, 1050 Alakea Street, Honolulu, ☎ 808-599-5501.

Mandara Spa (inside the Hilton Hawaiian Beach Village & Spa), 2005 Kalia Road, Waikiki, ☎ 808-945-7721, www.mandaraspa.com.

Paul Brown Salon & Day Spa, 1200 Ala Moana Blvd., Honolulu, ☎ 808-591-1881.

Serenity Spa Hawaii, 2169 Kalia Road, Waikiki, ☎ 808-926-2880 or 808-926-2882.

Spa Olakino Salon, 2552 Kalakaua Avenue, Waikiki, ☎ 808-924-2121.

Spa Suites, 5000 Kahala Avenue, Honolulu, ☎ 808-739-8938.

Windward O`ahu

The Spa Suites at The Kahala, 5000 Kahala Avenue, Honolulu, ☎ 808-739-8938, www.kahalaresort.com, spa@kahalaresort.com, is the epitome of lavish living!

Infinity bath at Kahala Spa

Honu You Hawaiian Spa, 122 Oneawa Street, Kailua, ☎ 808-261-1268, www.honuyou.com. Honu You offers spa treatments such as facials, body waxing, lomilomi massage as well as package deals. Appointments are recommended.

In Leeward O`ahu

Ihilani Spa at the JW Marriott Ihilani Resort & Spa at Ko Olina, 92-1001 Olani Street, Kapolei, ☎ 808-679-3321, www.ihilani.com. This world-class spa offers massage therapies (including La Stone Hot Rock treatment), body services (including a scrub bar and body wraps using Hawaiian ingredients), facial and skin care services, and a salon. The facility also offers half-day and full-day packages including the Ihilani Signature Treatment called "Pua Kai," or "flower of the sea," which provides a relaxing soak with rose crystals followed by a 25-minute body scrub. Guests are then given an Aromatherapy Massage and a manicure and pedicure.

Lap pool at Ihilani Spa

To enjoy the spa facilities, hotel guests can pay $20 without a treatment or there is complimentary entrance with the purchase of a treatment. Non-guests can enter the facilities for $15, but must book a treatment. The beautiful locale and fabulous service make the Ihilani Spa a great place to spend the day, whether you're a guest or not.

Lobby of Spa Luana
(Courtesy of Limtiaco Co.)

The North Shore

Spa Luana (at the Turtle Bay Resort), ☎ 808-447-6868, www.turtlebayresort.com. Spa Luana offers massage treatments, body and skin treatments, salon services and package deals. Try one of the indigenous treatments such as a "Pineapple Pedicure," "Kukui Nut Massage," "Coconut Crème Manicure" or a "Hawaii coffee & Macadamia Nut Scrub."

Beach Safety

Never turn your back on the ocean. Use your instinct. Always swim with a buddy. I always tell people that if you don't see anyone swimming at a beach, there's probably a good reason, whether it's a mean rip current that you can't see or a recent shark sighting.

Also, abide by the signs. Most beaches have signs explaining the different hazards you may encounter at that beach. Take these signs seriously – nothing ruins a vacation more than a serious injury or, worse, death. When the surf is high and dangerous, most resorts plaster warning signs around their properties and along the beach. Ocean conditions can change quickly so be aware of your surroundings.

If you're not a confident swimmer but want to snorkel, use a flotation device like a boogie board or a noodle. These are available at most snorkel rental places and, if you're on a tour, most operators have the flotation devices onboard. Also, big surf is seasonal, usually hitting the north-facing shores with monster waves in the winter months, while the south shore gets occasional swells in the summer.

Many of Hawaii's beaches have sharp coral reefs close to the shoreline. Use caution when swimming in shallow reef areas. You can easily brush against the coral and receive painful scrapes and rashes. If a piece of coral should become embedded deeply in your skin, see a physician to avoid the risk of infection. If you're walking on reefs or tide pools, wear protective footgear.

Here are a couple of the terms you might encounter concerning ocean conditions:

Dangerous Shore Break: When waves break directly on the shore, dangerous conditions can occur. Shore breaks are unpredictable and have caused many serious neck and spinal injuries to experienced and inexperienced bodysurfers and swimmers.

Strong Current: These are fast-moving channels of water that make it very difficult to swim if you get caught in them. Strong currents frequently accompany high surf and rapid tide changes. They can sometimes be recognized as a turbulent channel of water between areas where waves are breaking. If you are caught in a strong current, try to keep a level head and, most of all, *don't panic!* Wave one or both hands in the air and scream or call for help. Swim diagonal to the current, not against it.

Waves on Ledge: These are large waves originating from deep water breaking on rock ledges. However, this condition can occur even when the water appears to be very calm. Be very cautious when walking along rocky coastlines when waves are breaking. The rocks can become slippery and are made out of sharp, abrasive lava stone. Don't even try to go into the wet rocky zone. People have been washed away in these conditions.

Small Waves (nicknamed "ankle busters" by surfers) can be very dangerous, too. Check with the lifeguard, as these small yet treacherous waves can be fast and swift.

High Surf: Large, powerful waves are generated by winds and storms at sea, sometimes thousands of miles from the Hawaiian Island chain. Seasonal high surf occurs on all shores of O`ahu and the other islands. Typically, shorelines facing north, east and west receive high surf during winter months. Shores facing southeast and southwest receive high surf during the summer months. During high surf on the North Shore, waves can reach heights over 25 feet, even up to 50 feet. On the west side, they can be as high as 15 feet.

BIG SURF CHECK LIST

- Never turn your back on the ocean! Or, as they say in Hawaiian, *Mai huli `oe I kokua o ke kai!*
- Swim at beaches with lifeguards.
- Communicate with lifeguards about surf conditions.
- Read and observe posted sign warnings.
- Watch children very carefully. Hold on to younger ones at all times.
- Watch the surf for at least 15 minutes before entering the water.
- Never attempt to swim at the water's edge during big surf.
- Never surf or bodyboard in big waves unless you are an **expert**.
- Do not drink alcohol or do drugs before swimming.
- *Keiki* (Hawaiian for children), "Newbies" and "Grommits" (younger surfers) – watch out for them.
- "If in doubt, just stay out."
- Never swim alone.
- Don't dive into unknown water or into shallow breaking waves.
- Rely on your swimming ability rather than a flotation device.

Sharing the Ocean

Show respect for marine life. People entering the water should stay at least 100 yards away from dolphins. Getting closer may drive them away from their habitat.

All marine mammals in US waters are protected by the Marine Mammal Protection Act. Any action that deliberately disrupts their behavior is subject to a fine of up to $25,000, confiscation of your boat or vessel and/or up to one year in prison.

There have also been recent concerns about tour boats hitting whales or vice versa. Approaching humpback whales closer than 100 yards is prohibited by federal and state law and can also result in fines of up to $25,000. For more information visit www.pacificwhale.org.

Whales

The humpback whales are one of Hawaii's greatest tourist attractions (bringing in an estimated $27 million annually) in the winter months when they come to the warm waters of Hawaii to mate, calve and nurse their young. After spending the summers feeding in temperate Alaskan waters, some 60% (about 3,000) of the warm-blooded creatures travel at an average speed of three to six miles per hour during the 3,500-mile migration. Some whales have been known to make the journey is less than 40 days. These amazing creatures use acoustic cues, currents, and temperature changes to find their way to Hawaii – the most isolated chain of islands in the world. The highest concentration of whales in Hawaii is in the four-island area encompassing Maui, Lana`i, Moloka`i and Kaho`olawe where the water is shallow and land masses buffer otherwise strong winds and currents. This migratory cycle ensures that pregnant females and new mothers spend most of their time in warm waters.

A breaching humpback whale
(www.moc.noaa.gov)

Peak of Season Whale Watching, ☎ 808-306-7273, www.sailhawaii.com. Held during the prime whale watching months of January through March, marine biologists share intimate four-hour sails on a sleek 42-foot catamaran. Portions of the proceeds are donated to the Wild Dolphin Foundation.

Humpback calves are conceived in Hawaiian waters and then, after a 10- to 12-month pregnancy, are born in the same warm waters. The calves, which weigh an average of 1½ tons and are 10 to 16 feet long at birth, survive on their mother's fat-rich milk for six to eight months and will double in length during the first year. Males will eventually reach up to 43 feet, while females are slightly larger at about 45 feet long. Mature humpbacks weigh up to a ton per foot, or 80,000 pounds. Female whales can become fertile again soon after giving birth. Male and female whales don't form long-term bonds and their relations typically last for less than a day. Talk about a one-night stand!

Language Tip: Whales are called *kohala* in Hawaiian. The term applies to all whales, not just humpbacks.

Whalewatching is an exciting activity when the whales are active. And it's even more fun if you know what you're looking at. Humpbacks are grayish-black in color and have white markings on the underside of their flukes (the tail area) that are different with each whale. The whales use their tails to swim by moving them up and down, using their pectoral fins to turn and steer. They breathe through a double blowhole on top of their head. Among the interesting behaviors you might witness on a whale-watching tour is a pec slap when the whale rolls sideways to the surface and slaps its pectoral fins against the water. Or you might see a spy hop, where the whale rises straight up out of the water, often turning 90-180 degrees before slipping back down. You may also see a breach, when the whale propels itself out of the water, throws a pectoral fin out to the side and then twists and turns as it heads back down.

Did You Know? Humpback whales can sing. Nobody's quite sure how as they don't have vocal cords, but the long, complex sounds they make generally last between six and 18 minutes.

Fish

Snorkeling is a fun and easy activity for anyone who knows how to swim but try to avoid feeding the fish as it makes them dependent and the more aggressive species tend to take over. During your snorkeling

ing Hawaiian fish wherever snorkeling and scuba supplies are rented.

Monk Seals

There are about 1,300 monk Hawaiian monk seals, most of which live in the Northwestern Hawaiian Islands. Federal and state regulations prohibit disturbing monk seals; people and their pets are required to stay at least 40 yards away from a resting monk seal. It's a real treat to see one of these amazing animals taking a nap on the beach.

Hawaiian monk seal
(www.doi.gov)

Sharks

There are about 40 species of sharks that roam the Hawaiian waters, ranging in size from a deep-water pygmy shark (eight inches) to a whale shark (up to 50 feet or more). They have extremely well developed sensory capabilities and can detect sounds and smells up to two miles away. Tiger sharks, which average 12 to 13 feet in length, are considered the most dangerous. You can recognize a tiger shark by its blunt snout and the vertical bars on its side.

HOW TO AVOID BEING BITTEN BY A SHARK

Your chances of being bitten by a shark are very rare, with only two or three attacks a year on average, a small number considering the number of people who enter the ocean. Here are some guidelines to keep the out-of-this-world odds on your side, just in case:

- Don't swim, surf or dive alone and, if you do, let someone know where you will be.
- Avoid murky waters, especially river and stream mouths where sharks like to feed after a big rain.
- Do not enter the water if you have an open wound or are bleeding, as sharks are attracted to blood and body fluids, even in small concentrations.

- Avoid entering the water at dawn, dusk and night which is when some species move inshore to feed.
- Watch the behavior of fish and turtles in the water. If they start acting erratically, leave the water.
- Look out for fishing boats – sharks, especially tiger sharks, frequent the areas around these boats.

Dolphins

Hawaii is home to 13 species of dolphins, with the three most common being spinner dolphins, bottlenose dolphins and pantropical spotted dolphins. **Spinner dolphins** got their name because of their ability to leap out of the water and spin about. They are fairly small (about six feet in length) and are nocturnal, spending their days resting and then feeding at night. You will most likely see them at dusk when they head out to eat. They are very social creatures and you'll normally see them in a school of 50 to 200 individuals.

Bottlenose dolphin

Bottlenose dolphins (Flipper was one) are larger than spinners and can grow up to 10 feet in length. They are easily recognized by their stubby snout and mouth that curves up, resembling a smile. Bottlenose dolphins are active during the day and can usually be found in schools of two to 12 other dolphins.

Spotted dolphins feed during the day and night and are generally not found as close to shore as other dolphins. They're medium in size (about eight feet long) and, yes, they have spots. These creatures are born without spots but as they get older the number of spots keeps increasing, with males generally having more spots than females.

You'll often see dolphins during boat rides throughout the islands. Most species are attracted to the pressure wave created by moving boats and it's like an amusement park ride for them.

Dolphins are protected under the Marine Mammal Protection Act and it is illegal to harass, hunt, capture, collect or kill any marine mammal, including dolphins.

Just For Kids

In Waikiki

KID FRIENDLY

At the **Moana Surfrider**, A Westin Resort, ☎ 866-716-8112, there is a Westin Kids Club that offers a daily program of scheduled on-site and off-site learning experiences. Activities include trips to the Bishop Museum and the Waikiki Aquarium, local food demonstrations, workouts and local music, language and storytelling performances. The Kids Club is open seven days a week with a daily program from 9 am to 4 pm and a night program from 6:30 pm to 10 pm.

North Shore

Keiki Turtle Club at Turtle Bay Resort, ☎ 808-293-6000, is available on select days and introduces children to the Hawaiian culture with a variety of activities including lei making, reef walks, beach activities and arts and crafts.

Windward O'ahu

Kahala Kids: The Keiki Club children's program immerses kids in the wonders of the Hawaiian Islands through activities such as lei-making, ukulele lessons, hula dancing and lessons about Hawaiian sea life.

Leeward O'ahu

The **JW Marriott Ihilani Resort & Spa**, ☎ 808-679-0079, has a partnership with Aquarium Systems & Ponds, Inc. to provide the *Kahihimanu I Ke Kai* (Reef and Ray Adventure) for children visiting the Ihilani. The program is offered at 9 am and 11 am for children ages 10 and older and at 1 pm for ages four through 10 on Monday, Tuesday, Wednesday, Friday and Sunday. The adventure includes reef shark feeding, a reef safari, Hawaii reef fish feeding and an in-water interactive touch session with adult and young Hawaiian rays and spotted eagle rays.

The resort also has a "Keiki Beachcomber Club" for kids ages five to 12 and provides arts and crafts, Hawaiian games, cultural activities, scavenger hunts and ping pong. A full day at the club runs from 9 am until 3 pm with half-days going from 12:30 pm to 3 pm.

Holidays & Local Festivals

January

Sony Open in Hawaii, Waialae Country Club, ☎ 808-523-7888, www.SonyOpenInHawaii.com. Over 144 of the world's leading professional golfers participate in this weeklong event.

Turtle Bay Championship, www.turtlebaychampionship.com. Visit Turtle Bay Resort or call ☎ 808-545-1588 to find out more about the first full-field event of the PGA Champions Tour on the Arnold Palmer Course at Turtle Bay Resort.

Mike Stewart's International Pipeline Pro, ☎ 808-396-2326. This annual body boarding competition spotlights the worlds best body boarders at Banzai Pipeline on O`ahu's North Shore.

February

NFL Pro Bowl, www.NFL.com, ☎ 808-486-9300. This competition puts the best football players from the NFC and the AFC at the Aloha Stadium.

SBS Open at Turtle Bay Resort, www.SBSOpen.com, or call ☎ 808-792-9333. The tournament is sponsored by the Seoul Broadcasting System.

The **Annual Great Aloha Run** raises money for various charities. This 8.15-mile run/walk features entertainment along the route and a party at the finish. The run starts at Aloha Tower and ends at Aloha Stadium.

Chinese New Year Celebration, ☎ 808-533-3181, www.chinesechamber.com. If you're here in mid-February, come celebrate the Chinese New Year at the only Chinatown in Hawaii.

March

Annual Honolulu Festival, ☎ 808-926-2424, www.honolulufestival.com. This two-day festival includes Japanese plays, street performers, food booths, Sumo, kite making, bon dancing, cultural arts demonstrations and a parade in Waikiki.

Honolulu Festival parade float
(www.honoluluadvertiser.com)

**Waikiki Artfest at Kapi`olani**, ☎ 808-696-6717, www.icb-web.net/haa. This artfest features made-in-Hawaii products from 75-100 artisans and fine artists. Held at Kapi`olani Park near the Waikiki Bandstand, the two-day festival is open from 9 am to 4 pm.

April

Sail With The Stars - Sunset/Full-Moon, ☎ 808-306-7273, www.sailhawaii.com. Held during April and May, Sail With The Stars allows visitors to escape on a 2½- to three-hour semi-private sailing charter.

Annual Hawaii Invitational International Music Festival, www.worldofpagentry.com. Held for two weeks in Waikiki, the festival has participants from Hawaii, the mainland and around the world playing in the largest Spring Break festival on O`ahu. High school, junior high, college band and pageantry units compete.

May

May 1 is **Lei Day** in Hawaii – a very big deal in the islands. Schools hold huge celebrations where students participate in presentations that celebrate the Islands. In Honolulu, thousands of residents convene to celebrate at the Waikiki Shell amphitheatre. Buying and giving a lei can convey congratulations, welcome, gratitude or a simple hello.

The **Annual May Day Concert** with the Brothers Cazimero, ☎ 808-597-1888, is also held on May 1. This concert is arguably the most celebrated May Day festivity on O`ahu, featuring a Brothers Cazimero concert under the stars at the Waikiki Shell.

Another **Waikiki Artfest** at Kapi`olani, ☎ 808-696-6717, www.icb-web.net/haa, is held in April. This artfest features made-in-Hawaii products from 75-100 artisans and fine artists. Held at Kapi`olani Park near the Waikiki Bandstand, the two-day festival is open from 9 am to 4 pm.

> *Historical Lei Day*: Historical references dating back to the late 1700s describe the lei po`o, or head lei, and the lei a`i, which is worn around the neck, as being created by the native people. They used wood, seeds, bones, shells and feathers.

June

Annual Pan-Pacific Hula Festival, ☎ 808-535-9099, www.pan-pacific-festival.com. This festival brings Japanese pageantry, culture and arts to Hawaii with a block party that includes hula and musical performances as well as an arts and crafts fair.

Annual King Kamehameha Hula Competition, ☎ 808-536-6540. Over 20 dance groups from the Mainland, Japan and Hawaii compete for two days in both traditional and contemporary dance styles.

July

Annual Hawaii International Jazz Festival,www.hawaiijazz.com, ☎ 808-941-9974. Four nights of world-class jazz bringing together local, national and international artists and students.

Annual Tinman Triathlon, www.tinmanhawaii.com, ☎ 808-595-5317. This triathlon includes a 750-meter swim, a 40-kilometer bike ride and a 10-kilometer run in and around O`ahu's most spectacular areas.

Prince Lot Hula Festival, www.mgf-hawaii.org , ☎ 808-533-1292. This festival is Hawaii's oldest and largest non-competitive hula exhibition. During this one-day festival, *na halau* (hula schools) perform outdoors at Moanalua Gardens under the monkeypod trees. The festival honors Prince Lot, who revived the hula after missionaries banned it.

The **Waikiki Annual Ukulele Festival**, ☎ 808-732-3739, at Kapi`olani Park Bandstand, brings many of the finest ukulele players in the world to O`ahu. The festival is free to the public.

August

Wild Dolphin Discovery by Sail and Snorkel Charters, www.sailhawaii.com, ☎ 808-306-7273. From May through November, guests sail into the secret underwater world of the Hawaiian spinner dolphins with a marine biologist team on a unique marine safari. The trips are limited to four-12 passengers per charter.

Hawaiian spinner dolphins
(www.swfsc.noaa.gov)

Made in Hawaii Festival, www.madeinhawaiifestival.com, ☎ 808-533-1292.This popular three-day festival, held at the Neal S. Blaisdell Exhibition Hall, has unique made-in-Hawaii items such as books, fashions, plants, arts, crafts and produce. There is also live music and showcases by Hawaii's top culinary artists.

September

`Iolani Palace

Aloha Festivals, www.alohafestivals.com, ☎ 808-589-1771. Opening Ceremonies at `Iolani Palace. Traditional hula and chants introduce the O`ahu Royal Court on the grounds of `Iolani Palace. This is the official beginning of the island-wide Aloha Festival that last from September until October. The 10-day festival is held across the Hawaiian Islands and showcases Hawaii's music, dance, history and culture.

During the Waikiki Ho`olaule`a part of the festival, the streets of Waikiki are closed off and booths offer a variety of local foods and entertainment.

The Downtown Ho`olaule`a kicks off the Aloha Week festivities, offering a variety of Hawaii's best foods and local entertainment.

Aloha Festival History: The first Aloha Festivals took place in 1946 when a group of Jaycees held a grassroots cultural celebration reminiscent of the *Makahiki* season. For nearly 45 years, the festival was called "Aloha Week" but in 1991 the event expanded to its current size, with 300 events on six islands over two months.

October

Princess Kaiulani Commemoration Week, ☎ 808-922-5811. An entire week of festivities in Waikiki is devoted to honoring Hawaii's most beloved princess.

Annual Princes Kaiulani Keiki Hula Festival, ☎ 808-922-5811. Children age five to 12 from *halau* (hula schools) all across the island come to perform in this annual event.

November

The **World International Hula Festival**, ☎ 808-486-3185, www.worldhula.com, is held at the Waikiki Shell in mid-November. More than 400 dancers from Japan, Mexico, Samoa, Alaska, Hawai`i, and other locales prove that hula has become an international phenomenon.

Hawaii International Film Festival, www.hiff.com, ☎ 808-550-8457. This annual festival showcases films from North America, Asia and the Pacific Rim. Events include film screenings, discussions, workshops, symposiums, special awards and media events.

A Birthday Celebration for a King, www.iolanipalace.org, ☎ 808-522-0822. Celebrate with The Friends of `Iolani Palace during the annual commemoration of King Kalakaua's Birthday.

December

The **Vans Triple Crown of Surfing**, www.triplecrownofsurfing.com, is held during November and December and is the pinnacle of professional big-wave surfing.

Annual Honolulu Marathon, www.honolulumarathon.com, ☎ 808-734-7200. This 26-mile scenic course includes spectacular views along world-famous Waikiki Beach and Diamond Head.

Christmas With the Brothers Cazimero, ☎ 808-792-2000, is a festive tradition for those in Honolulu. Held in early December at the Blaisdell Center Concert Hall, the brothers celebrate the holidays with Maestro Matt Catingub and the Honolulu Symphony.

Candy Cane Land, Bishop Museum, www.bishopmuseum.org, ☎ 808-847-3511. The museum turns into a magical Christmas dreamland where children of all ages can get together for train rides, live entertainment, make-and-take crafts, food and beverages and a chance to meet Santa Claus.

Visits from Santa. In early December, Santa arrives at the Outrigger Waikiki beach in an outrigger canoe wearing his Hawaiian attire, including beach shorts and rubber slippers. At 4:30 pm on Christmas Eve, Santa returns and lands on Waikiki Beach near the Halekulani. Arrive early to see him paddle ashore and pass out gifts to the *keiki* (children) and the young at heart. A *keiki* hula performance follows Santa's arrival.

O`ahu Adventures

Surfing

O`ahu is synonymous with surfing, especially on the island's North Shore where some of the world's best hang out during the wild winter months. There are several companies throughout the islands that will teach you to surf if you're a beginner, or show you great surf spots for that time of the year if you're more advanced. Surf shops throughout the island provide equipment (for purchase or rental) as well as maps and tide charts. One of the best references is **Franko's O`ahu Surfing Map**, which is printed on durable, waterproof paper and has elaborate descriptions of O`ahu's surf spots. I will detail some of these in the appropriate chapters.

Golf

Ko`olau Golf Club

Everybody knows that Hawaii has some of the most beautiful and challenging golf courses in the world and O`ahu is home to many of them. On the North Shore, the **Turtle Bay Resort Golf Club** has two fabulous courses, while the **Ko`olau Golf Club** on the Windward side of O`ahu is considered one of the meanest courses in the nation. And the **Ko`Olina Golf Club**, on the island's leeward side, is situated next to the renowned Ko`Olina Resort. There are more details about these courses in the following chapters, but here are some helpful tips to think about before you take off to hit the greens in paradise:

- Many golfers prefer to bring their own clubs but, if you don't feel like lugging them across the Pacific, most courses have clubs for rent. For the prices you're paying, you'll probably be set up with some of the newest models so you'll have a chance to try out the latest and greatest.
- The sun in Hawaii is a lot stronger than on the Mainland due to the island chain's proximity to the equator. Apply and re-apply sunscreen and wear a hat! You'll thank me later!
- Most Hawai`i golf courses don't allow metal spikes (plus they're probably a hassle in airport security these days!), so if you want to bring your own, make sure they're the greens-friendly rubber variety.

Fazio course at Turtle Bay
(Courtesy of Limtiaco Co.)

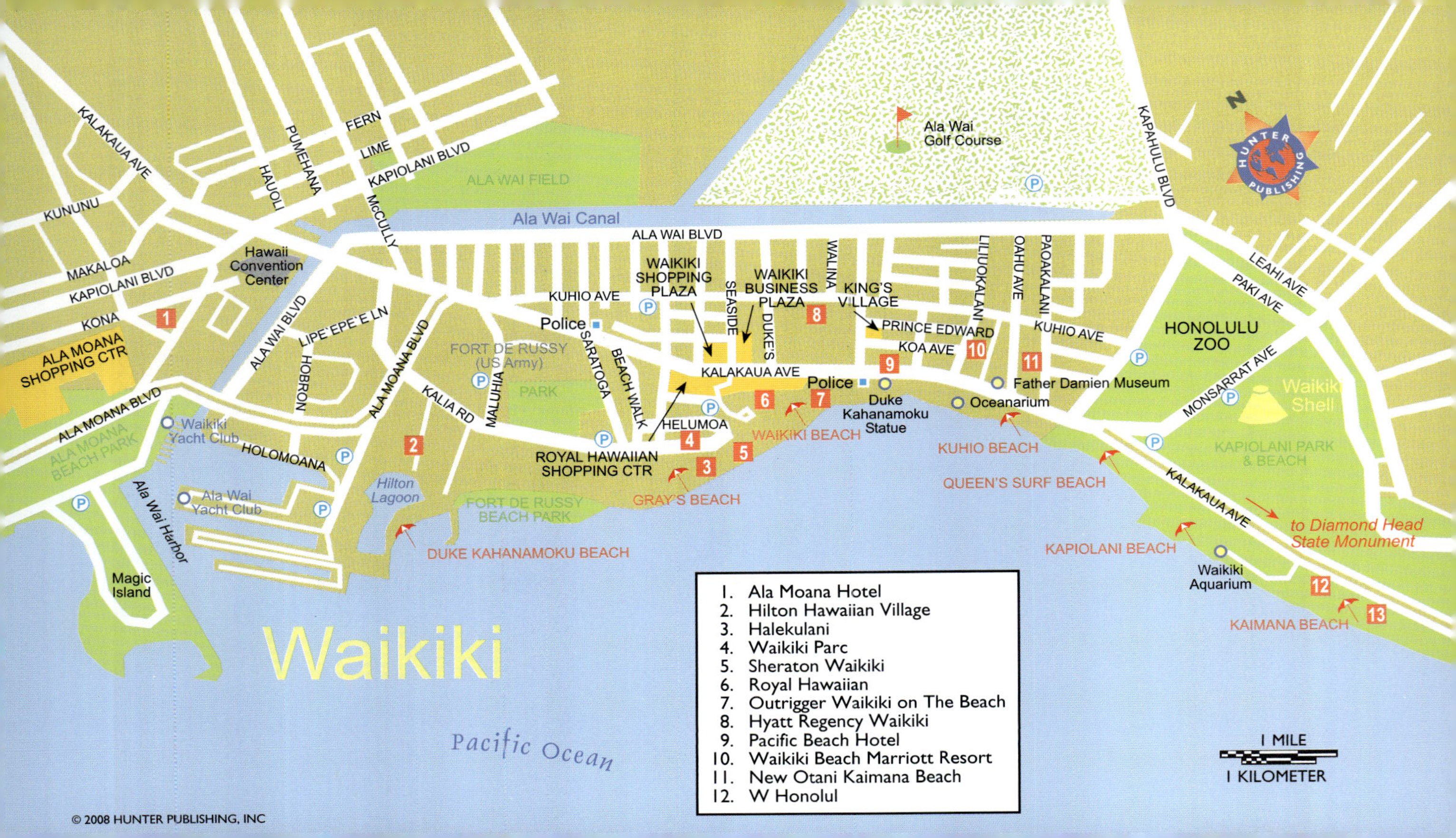
Waikiki
Pacific Ocean
KALAKAUA AVE
KUNUNU
MAKALOA
KAPIOLANI BLVD
KONA
ALA MOANA SHOPPING CTR
HAUOLI
PUMEHANA
FERN
LIME
KAPIOLANI BLVD
McCULLY
ALA WAI FIELD
Ala Wai Canal
ALA WAI BLVD
Hawaii Convention Center
ALA WAI BLVD
LIPE'EPE'E LN
HOBRON
ALA MOANA BLVD
ALA MOANA BLVD
ALA MOANA BEACH PARK
Waikiki Yacht Club
HOLOMOANA
Ala Wai Yacht Club
Ala Wai Harbor
Magic Island
KALIA RD
MALUHIA
Hilton Lagoon
FORT DE RUSSY (US Army)
PARK
FORT DE RUSSY BEACH PARK
DUKE KAHANAMOKU BEACH
Police
SARATOGA
BEACH WALK
KUHIO AVE
WAIKIKI SHOPPING PLAZA
SEASIDE
DUKE'S
WAIKIKI BUSINESS PLAZA
WALINA
KING'S VILLAGE
PRINCE EDWARD
KOA AVE
KALAKAUA AVE
HELUMOA
ROYAL HAWAIIAN SHOPPING CTR
GRAY'S BEACH
WAIKIKI BEACH
Police
Duke Kahanamoku Statue
LILIUOKALANI
OAHU AVE
PAOAKALANI
KUHIO AVE
Father Damien Museum
Oceanarium
KUHIO BEACH
QUEEN'S SURF BEACH
Ala Wai Golf Course
KAPAHULU BLVD
N
HUNTER PUBLISHING
LEAHI AVE
PAKI AVE
HONOLULU ZOO
MONSARRAT AVE
Waikiki Shell
KAPIOLANI PARK & BEACH
KALAKAUA AVE
to Diamond Head State Monument
KAPIOLANI BEACH
Waikiki Aquarium
KAIMANA BEACH
1 MILE
1 KILOMETER
1. Ala Moana Hotel
2. Hilton Hawaiian Village
3. Halekulani
4. Waikiki Parc
5. Sheraton Waikiki
6. Royal Hawaiian
7. Outrigger Waikiki on The Beach
8. Hyatt Regency Waikiki
9. Pacific Beach Hotel
10. Waikiki Beach Marriott Resort
11. New Otani Kaimana Beach
12. W Honolul
© 2008 HUNTER PUBLISHING, INC

Waikiki

At A Glance

Waikiki is experiencing a glorious rejuvenation, mostly due to reconstruction improvements and the addition of the Waikiki Beach Walk, the largest development project ever to be undertaken in Waikiki's history. The beach walk encompasses 7.9 acres and is bordered by Kalakaua Avenue, Lewers Street, Kalia Road, Beach Walk and Saratoga Road. The project cost $535 million and features an outdoor entertainment plaza, 41 new stores, six restaurants and five hotels. For more information visit www.waikikibeachwalk.com.

IN THIS CHAPTER

Where Did All The Hotels Go? The renovation of Waikiki seems to have enlarged Waikiki but, by efficient management, the developer was able to take lots of small hotels with small rooms into larger developments with larger rooms. When the developers started, they had 11 hotels with 3,100 rooms. Now, the Beach Walk has five hotels with 1,996 rooms.

This development has changed the whole look of Waikiki, creating a more energetic and enticing destination in the heart of

Honolulu. An abundance of new restaurants bring a refreshing outlook on cuisine and visitors will delight in the numerous cultural activities and musical events available freely in the center's open-air plaza and center stage. Adults and kids can take part in ukulele lessons, hula lessons, lei making, story telling, wood carving and listening to well-known musical acts. Most of the shops and restaurants are open daily from 9 am to 10 pm.

Orientation

Traveling from the Honolulu International Airport to Waikiki can be an adventure in itself. Try to avoid traveling around busy commuter hours (7 to 10 am and 3 to 6 pm) as the traffic can come to a standstill.

There are basically three ways to get to Waikiki by car once you arrive at the airport. It is almost impossible to miss Waikiki as the routes are clearly marked by road signs.

My preferred route is to take the H-1 Freeway to Punahou (Exit 23) and turn right for one block and then turn right on S. Beretania. Continue for half a block and then turn left on Kalakaua Avenue and you'll head straight into Waikiki.

Another route is to take King Street (Exit 25B) off of the H-1 and go through the first light at Kapi`olani Blvd. Get in the right lane and go under the freeway, then turn right onto Kapahulu Avenue. You'll now be on the eastern side of Waikiki and you can turn right onto Ala Wai Blvd. or Kuhio Ave. to enter Waikiki.

If you want to try a more scenic, oceanfront drive, take the Nimitz Highway Route. You'll pass all of the main shopping centers, Aloha Tower and many other Honolulu landmarks. This route also has the heaviest traffic and many stop lights. From the airport take the H-1 toward Waikiki and then the first off-ramp to Nimitz Highway. The highway eventually turns into Ala Moana Blvd. and then into Kalakaua Ave. where you're forced to turn. Turn right on Kalakaua Ave., which leads to Kuhio Avenue and right into Waikiki.

History

Considered by many to be the most famous island beach in the world, two-mile-long Waikiki Beach (which means "spouting waters") wasn't always about sun, sand and surf.

In Polynesian times, much of Waikiki was off-limits to everyone but chiefs, who had homes here along with taro patches and fishponds. The waters of Waikiki are kept calm by a sheltering reef about a half-mile offshore. This same reef is the one that creates the long waves that have attracted surfers to Waikiki for decades.

In early 2007, Waikiki was in the midst of a sand-replenishing project which encompassed siphoning the equivalent of 1,000 truckloads of sand that has drifted offshore and settled at 2,000-foot depths. Much of the sand was brought to Waikiki by barge from Molokai, and later, from Australia.

Shopping

$ If you're coming to O`ahu to shop, Waikiki is where you'll want to start – it's a shopper's heaven with seemingly endless lanes of shops and boutiques.

It won't take long to notice that there's an **ABC Store**, ☎ 888-703-4222, www.abcstores.com, on every corner. This general store carries all of your basic needs, beach gear, food and beverages as well as aisles full of souvenirs. In fact, the ABC Stores of Hawaii sell more macadamia nuts, sun care products, souvenirs and other visitor-related products than anywhere else in the state. They offer gift packages full of Hawaiian goodies, coffees, Hawaiian-made syrups, dressings and jellies. The ABC Stores also have a huge variety of lotions, soaps, candles, incense and shampoos made in Hawaii. The shops are a great place to pick up plumeria jewelry and the popular casual wear designed for men, women and children.

The Royal Hawaiian Shopping Center, 2201 Kalakaua Avenue, Ste. A500, ☎ 808-922-2299, www.RoyalHawaiianShopping-Center.com, recently embarked on an $84 million renovation, replacing concrete structures with walls and trestles made of wood. A grove of palm trees has been planted and connects the shopping center and Kalakaua Avenue to the grounds of the Royal Hawaiian Hotel. The shopping center consists of more than 310,000 square feet of retail space along a three-block stretch of Waikiki's Kalakaua Avenue and is four stories high. The center has over 60 shops ranging from upscale boutiques like Salvatore Ferragamo, Cartier and Fendi to specialty shops like

Kate Spade, Island Art Gallery and Iolana Designs. Called "Royal Grove," this spot aspires to be the center of Waikiki.

The Hibiscus Court on the second floor is where the entertainment takes place. Depending on the day, you may find a lei-making class, hula lessons, ukulele lessons, Hawaiian quilt making and free musical shows. On an interesting note, the Royal Hawaiian Shopping Center is owned by Kamehameha Schools. The Royal Hawaiian Shopping Center is open daily from 10 am to 10 pm.

Waikiki Beach Walk

The new Waikiki Beach Walk, www.waikikibeachwalk.com, covers 7.9 acres and is bordered by Kalakaua Avenue, Lewers Street, Kalia Road, Beach Walk and Saratoga Road. The project cost $535 million and features an outdoor entertainment plaza, 41 new stores, six restaurants and five hotels. Make sure to check out this trendy, yet impressive development!

For More Information: A Waikiki Visitor Information Kiosk is available along the promenade fronting Mondo Gelato.

Here is a list of some of my favorite shops on the Waikiki Beach Walk:

Alter Ego, ☎ 808-926-1901, is a shop catering to tweens and teenagers. It has popular surf-style clothing lines such as Volcum, Billabong, Hurley, DC Shoes as well as their own original t-shirts.

Banana Wind, ☎ 808-926-1601, www.banawindhawaii.com, is one of my favorite shops. It calls itself a Polynesian trading post and I couldn't agree more. The shop has different sections, each with a common theme. There are housewares, linens, candles and much more tropical stuff. Good stuff!

Blue Ginger, ☎ 808-924-7900, www.blueginger.com. This clothing store has soft cotton and rayon batik fabrics designed in Hawaii, then crafted into easy-care clothing and fabrics for the whole family. If you're looking for matching outfits for your family, this is the place to go.

Crazy Shirts, ☎ 808-971-6016, www2.crazyshirts.com. This out-of-control shirt shop has been a mainstay in Hawaii for 40 years. Besides unique and only-in-Hawaii t-shirts, Crazy Shirts also has outerwear, bottoms, shorts, board shorts, headwear and women's fashions.

Folli Follie, ☎ 808-922-0124, www.follifollie.com. This sophisticated international fashion company offers a full line of jewelry, watches, handbags and accessories.

Freaky Tiki Tropical Optical, ☎ 808-926-3937. This sunglass shop has all of the popular brands – Maui Jim, Oakley, Von Zipper, Prada, Versace and Arnette.

Hawaii Head 2 Toe, ☎ 808-971-2035, has a great selection of resort wear for men and women, including headwear, footwear and accessories.

Malibu Shirts, ☎ 808-923-0306, www.malibushirts.com. This upscale t-shirt shop has an impressive selection of vintage and collectible apparel as well as those honoring surf legends from Hawaii and California. They also carry hooded sweatshirts, women's tops and board shorts. The store contains a fascinating collection of surf legend memorabilia. Check out the website for some fantastic photos of legendary surfers like Duke Kahanamoku. The photos of surfing in the old days are fun to look at.

A Legendary Brew Memorialized: Primo Beer was at one time the top-selling beer in Hawaii. First brewed in the islands by Honolulu's Don Francisco de Paula Marin in 1812, Hawaii's first full-scale brewery, the Honolulu Brewery, opened in 1854. The Hawaii Brewing Company would follow in 1898, introducing Primo. Though Primo would change hands many times – it was bought by Schlitz and then by Stroh – and at one point, it proudly claimed 70% of the Hawaiian market. During the 1960s, Primo Beer was consistently adver-

Waikiki

tised in programs for O`ahu's massive International Surf Championships at Makaha. Sadly, Primo Beer hasn't been produced since 1998, but for 100 years, it was one of the things that united surfers from all over the world. Malibu Shirts has long and short-sleeved shirts and baseball caps with the distinctive Primo Beer logo and are considered a collector's item.

International Market Place

International Market Place, 2330 Kalakaua Avenue, ☎ 808-971-2080, www.internationalmarketplacewaikiki.com. Don't ask me why, but this funky open-air collection of over 130 mostly tacky non-authentic Hawaiian-looking goods has a special place in the heart of longtime Waikiki visitors. Maybe because it has been there forever. And it's conveniently located right in the middle of all the action. There was talk of tearing it down and building a new marketplace but that idea was vehemently shut down. If you must, take a quick stroll through the vendors and then move on to the rest of Waikiki. The International Market Place is open daily from 10 am to 10:30 pm.

King's Village

King's Village, 131 Kaiulani Avenue (right behind the Hyatt Regency Hotel), www.kings-village.com, is home to more than 40 shops and restaurants and is fashioned after a turn-of-the-century Hawaiian neighborhood. Every evening at 6:15 pm the center recreates the "Changing of the Guard" based on the ritual that took place in 1875 when the King's Guard would retire the Hawaiian flag. The guards wear uniforms that are exact replicas of those worn by the Royal Palace Guards of King Kalakaua and perform an entertaining rifle drill exhibition.

King's Village

This funky little shopping center is basically two stories high with the Tanaka of Tokyo restaurant, ☎ 808-922-4233, alone on the third floor. King's Village is a great place to pick up some souvenirs like Aloha wear, Hawaiian quilts and jewelry. Grab one of the free King's Village shopping guides for coupons fast food restaurants KFC, Burger King and Subway Sandwiches. King's Village is open daily from 9 am to 11 pm.

Hawaiian History Lesson: Check out the recently opened King's Guard Museum in King's Village. The museum displays never-before-seen memorabilia, including uniforms, rifles, swords, photos, flags and banners. Admission is free and the museum if open daily from 5:30 to 10 pm.

Sightseeing

It is impossible to be bored in Waikiki! Athletes will find the jogging trails and gentle beach waves a refreshing workout while shoppers will find themselves in a retail heaven, from high-end shops to bargain basements. There are countless activities for kids and their parents and romantic dining and drinking spots where couples can relax and embrace the open-air atmosphere. Walking down the busy Waikiki avenues, you'll see many street entertainers that always seem to have an attentive crowd.

Waikiki Aquarium

View the unique aquatic life of Hawaii and the rest of the Pacific at the Waikiki Aquarium, 2777 Kalakaua Avenue, ☎ 808-923-9741, www.waquarium.org. View more than 350 species and 2,500 aquatic animals and plants, including the popular Humuhumunukunukuapua`a (to the right), which is the Hawaii State Fish. You can also view reef sharks, living corals, endangered Hawaiian monk seals, sea jellies and a multitude of exotic multi-colored fish. There are many programs aimed at kids, including knee-deep-in-the-water quests for indigenous crabs and shrimp as well as lessons about how Hawaii's ocean creatures survive. The aquarium, alongside the vast coral reefs of Waikiki, is the third oldest public aquarium in the United States.

The aquarium is open daily from 9 am to 5 pm (except on Christmas and New Year's Day) and general admission is $9 with discounts for seniors ($6), children 13-17 ($4), children five to 12 ($2) and free for children four and under.

Duke Kahanamoku Memorial Statue

In the heart of Waikiki Beach, this colossal monument honors Hawaii's first Olympian and a legendary Waikiki surfer. Kahanamoku continued his celebrated Olympic career for 21 years and has become a symbol of aloha around the world. You can pay your respects to this amazing legend, nicknamed the "Ambassador of Aloha," by placing a fresh flower lei on the outstretched arms of the Duke Kahanamoku statue.

Waikiki Beaches

Waikiki beaches
(www.student.britannica.com)

What we call Waikiki Beach is actually a series of beaches, starting with the Duke Kahanamoku Beach at the Hilton Hawaiian Village Resort on the western edge to Sans Souci Beach on the Diamond Head end of Waikiki Beach. If you walk the entire stretch of sand, you'll pass Fort DeRussy Beach Park, Gray's Beach, Kuhio Beach Park, Queen's Surf Beach and Kapi`olani Beach.

Duke Kahanamoku Beach is a man-made beach and lagoon named after the famous surfing legend. The Port Hilton Dock, where the Atlantis submarine tours depart, is located here.

Fort DeRussy Beach Park has the widest stretch of white sand in Waikiki and is popular for snorkeling because of an offshore coral reef.

Gray's Beach is in front of the famous Halekulani Hotel and is often very crowded.

Kuhio Beach Park has a sheltered swimming area, making it a popular spot for families.

Queen's Surf Beach, between the Honolulu Zoo and the Waikiki Aquarium, is named after Queen Lili`uokalani as her beach house used to sit on this spot. This is a little-known snorkeling spot.

**Kapi`olani Beach** is next to the Waikiki Aquarium and the expansive Kapi`olani Beach Park.

Sans Souci Beach is also called "Dig Me Beach" and is in front of the New Otani Hotel.

More Sand, More Fun: In early 2007, the state pumped in tons of sand from off-shore deposits onto Waikiki Beach in an attempt to replenish the sand that has slowly disappeared since the last replenishment 31 years ago. In some cases, the crews widened the beach up to 40 feet. This valiant effort has made Waikiki larger from the Kapahulu Groin (a pedestrian walkway extending into the ocean from Queen's Surf Beach and Kuhio Beach Park) to the Duke Kahanamoku statue.

Kapi`olani Park

Part of Kapi`olani Park
(www.kapiolanipark.org)

Travel east on Kalakaua Avenue and you will find Kapi`olani Park, which consist of 500 acres of parkland donated by King David Kalakaua and named after his wife, Queen Kapi`olani. There's plenty of space for picnicking, softball, tennis, soccer, biking and jogging.

Honolulu Zoo

Honolulu Zoo, 151 Kapahulu Avenue, ☎ 808-971-7171, www.honoluluzoo.org. On the grounds of the Kapi`olani Park on Monsarrat Avenue, this 40-acre establishment is home to over 2,000 animals. On weekends, visitors can view the works of local artists and craftspeople at the Honolulu Zoo Art Mart. The Honolulu Zoo is open daily from 9 am to 4:30 pm and closed on Christmas Day. General admission is $8. Children ages six to 12 are charged $1 while those under six are admitted for free. The zoo parking lot entrance is on Kapahulu Avenue and cost 25¢ an hour. Parking at the Waikiki Shell amphitheater in the park is free. Ice chests and outside food are allowed in the zoo so bring a picnic and have a good time! Don't forget to check out the Zootique Gift Shop.

Komodo dragon exhibit
(www.honoluluzoo.org)

Father Damien Museum

Father Damien Museum, 130 Ohua Avenue, ☎ 808-923-2690. This tiny little museum, behind St. Augustine By the Sea Church, on the beach in Waikiki, is devoted to the memory of Father Damien, a Catholic priest from Belgium who is known for his humanitarian work with leprosy (now called Hansen's Disease) on the island of Moloka`i. It is difficult to appreciate the legend of Father Damien without visiting the remarkable Kalaupapa leper colony in Moloka`i. But this museum is next-best.

Leprosy was detected in Hawaii in the 1830s and, as the disease spread, the victims were moved to the isolated peninsula of Kalaupapa, which is cut off from the rest of Moloka`i by 1,600-foot sea cliffs. Father Damien came to Honolulu in 1864 and spent the next 15 years ministering to Hawaiian natives. In 1873 Father Damian arrived in Moloka`i for a short visit but ended up staying until he himself succumbed to the disease in 1889. This museum has an exhibit that includes his glasses, chalice and prayer book. A 20-minute emotionally charged video about the history of the Kalaupapa settlement is available. Admission is free and the museum is open 9 am to 3 pm Monday through Friday, 9 am to noon on Saturday and closed on Sundays. To get to the museum, take Kalakaua Avenue toward Diamond Head and turn left on Ohua Avenue. You'll see the church facing the ocean at the corner of Kalakaua and Ohua Avenues. Metered parking is available on the street beside the church.

Adventures on Land

Golf

Hawaii Prince Golf Club, ☎ 808-956-1111, www.princeresortshawaii.com, has 27 holes with a 72 par. Situated on the Ewa Plain of O`ahu (about 40 minutes west of the Hawaii Prince Hotel Waikiki), the course was designed by Arnold Palmer and Ed Seay and has an all-grass driving range, putting and chipping greens and a pro shop. It's a treat to play here as the course occupies 270 acres of beautiful landscape, including stunning views of the Waianae Mountains. A complimentary shuttle service is available for guests of the Hawaii Prince Hotel Waikiki.

Glow-in-the-Dark Miniature Golf: On the third floor of the Waikiki Shopping Plaza (2250 Kalakaua Avenue), **Big Kahuna's 3D Glow Golf**, ☎ 808-924-3030, is Hawaii's only (and, as far as I know, the world's only) glow-in-the-dark miniature golf course. This is family fun at its best! Big Kahuna's is open daily from 10 am to 10 pm and general admission is $8.50, while *keiki* (children) age 12 and under get in for $5.

Hiking

Diamond Head

Diamond Head, ☎ 808-587-0300, Diamond Head Road at 18th Avenue. In Hawaiian this peak is called "Le`ahi" and it is one of the most famous hikes in Hawaii. Early morning is the best time to attempt this 45-minute hike, which takes you to the top of Diamond Head, a 760-foot extinct volcanic tuff cone and a National Landmark. It's a little steep and can get crowded as the stairways and tunnels narrow. It's worth the effort, though. Once you hit the top, you will be amazed by the wonderful panoramic view of O`ahu's south shore. If the horizon is clear, you can see the islands of Moloka`i, Lana`i and Maui.

View from Diamond Head

The Park is open from 6 am to 6 pm and admission is $1 per person or $5 per car. For further information, contact: Department of Land & Natural Resources Division of State Parks, 1151 Punchbowl Street, Room 310 (PO Box 621), Honolulu HI 96809.

Historical Legend: The name "Diamond Head" originated in the 19th century when sailors mistook the glistening calcite crystal rocks for diamonds.

Hiking Tours

There are several companies that provide tours of Diamond Head. They are competitively priced and usually offer the same benefits, such as a history lesson, pick-up and drop-off from your hotel, bottled water, etc.

I recommend **www.hikingtours.net**. They have an Internet discount ($26.95 as opposed to $31.95). The price includes transportation, tax and admission fee. The company has two tours a day (one at 6 am and another at 9:30 am) and groups are limited to 14 hikers, so be sure to book early. Book online or call ☎ 800-876-3809.

Adventures on Wheels

Segway

Segway ride on the beach

Segway of Hawaii, ☎ 808-941-3151, 2005 Kalia Road (inside the Hilton Hawaiian Village Beach & Spa Resort), www.segwayofhawaii.com. Cruising on a Segway is one of the most amusing ways to maneuver through Waikiki. You'll be amazed at how much territory you can cover and it's fun to see the reactions of other visitors as you glide by. The Segway Human Transporter runs on electricity (so, it's quiet), reaches a top speed of 12 mph and can run for about 24 miles. It only takes a few minutes of training to get used to the body-forward motion needed to make the Segway move ahead. Training is included in the price of the rentals and there are several self-guided tours to choose from – a 2½-hour tour of Waikiki, Kapi`olani Park and Diamond Head, a two-hour history tour along Ala Moana Beach Park and through Chinatown, a 90-minute Waikiki Glide Ride along Magic Island and Ala Moana Beach Park – or a private 2½-hour guided tour where you can create the itinerary.

Prices range from $99 to $125 and up per person. A shorter introductory tryout is available for $49. Prices include a required helmet and the company requests that guests arrive 15 minutes early for training. The minimum age for a Segway Glide Ride is 16, with a maximum weight of 280 lbs.

Cops on Wheels: Don't be surprised to see Honolulu's finest patrolling the area on a Segway. The police department is one of many across the nation that have been using the conveniently light and compact human transporters to protect the public.

Adventures on Water

Boogie Boarding

The Wall in Waikiki is one of the most popular boogie boarding spots in Waikiki beach. The water is not too deep and the waves are consistently good. The Wall is on the eastern side of Waikiki beach where Kapahulu Avenue and Kalakaua Avenue meet.

Aqua Cycling

As you cruise along Waikiki beach, you'll see several beachfront activity stops that rent all sorts of beach equipment, including these huge cycles with gigantic plastic wheels. It's a beach cruiser to beat all beach cruisers.

Snorkeling

Waikiki isn't famous for its snorkeling, but worthwhile spots can be found. **Queen's Surf Beach** in front of Kapi`olani Beach Park is one of those. Tropical fish, lobsters, crabs and eels can be frequently seen at Queen's.

Catamaran Sailing off Waikiki Beach

Dozens of catamaran operations run right off of Waikiki Beach. There are hourly cruises, sunset jaunts and dinner cruises. This is one of the greatest way to photograph Waikiki beach.

Submarine Rides

Surfacing submarine with Diamond Head in the background
(Courtesy of Atlantis Adventures)

Atlantis Submarines, ☎ 808-955-8495 or 800-548-6262 (toll free), www.atlantisadventures.com, offers fascinating tours of underwater Waikiki on a real (retired) submarine where you will see sunken ships, airplanes and reef structures housing colorful marine life. Once inside the submarine, visitors venture more than 100 feet below the surface of the sea – an underwater world where your clothes change colors due to the lack of sunlight and, if you're lucky, you'll even come face-to-face with a shark.

The tours depart throughout the day from the pier next to the Hilton Hawaiian Village Beach Resort & Spa. You can pick up tickets and boarding passes at a small kiosk by the pier. Give yourself plenty of time as the trips will be cancelled if visibility is low – it's no fun to spend the money to see nothing! The tour lasts about an hour and 40 minutes as a small boat takes you from the pier to the actual submarine, which is farther out in the ocean. This is a great family adventure – the kids love it! The ride, though, is limited to children 12 and over and 36 inches or taller. Tours start at $84 for adults and $42 for children but there are many Atlantis Adventure combinations that offer special rates.

Kayaking

Waikiki is one of the least exciting places on O`ahu to go kayaking. If you can, wait until you go to the windward side of the island and head to Kailua.

Surfing

Hans Hedemann Surf School, ☎ 808-924-7778, www.hhsurf.com, is one of the most reliable and esteemed surfing schools in Hawaii. In Waikiki, the company is at the New Otani Kaimana Beach Hotel on the eastern side of Waikiki, the Outrigger Reef on The Beach in central Waikiki and at the Park Shore Waikiki. A two-hour group lesson will cost you $75 and private lessons are also available. Lessons are available for anyone age six and up. The Park Shore Waikiki location offers a year-round surf school and a summer camp (June 1 to August 31) that provides private, semi-private and group lessons.

Hawaiian Fire, ☎ 808-737-3473 or 888-955-7873, www.hawaiianfire.com, surf@hawaiianfire.com, is a surfing company taught by some of Honolulu City Firefighters' finest. These guys know their stuff and as they're already certified in Open Water Rescue, EMT-B, CPR, etc., you can feel safe while trying to "hang ten" in O`ahu. The two-hour classes include transportation from your Waikiki hotel to a quiet beach, surfboards, reef shoes, rash guards, shade 10 and chairs. There are two surf lesson tours a day (one pick-up at 7 am, the second at 9:30 am) and the cost is $99/per person for a group lesson or $169/per adult and $119/per child for private lessons. The session includes a 45-minute safety lesson with beach instruction and then an hour and 15 minutes in the water.

Surf's Up: There are dozens of surf spots along Waikiki Beach, many of them with interesting names – "Rock Pile," "In-Betweens," "Fours," "Threes," "Pops," "First Break," "The Wall," "Old Mans," and "Ricebowl."

Scuba Diving

AquaZone, ☎ 866-923-DIVE, www.aquazone.net, can arrange for beginners to advanced divers and those who need a refresher course to dive in the waters around Waikiki. They offer shore dives, boat dives, day and night adventures, and can take you to some of Hawaii's best wreck dives. The company is set up at two Waikiki locations – at the Outrigger Waikiki on the Beach Hotel, next to the Cheesecake Factory and at the Waikiki Hotel Beach Marriott behind Seattle's Best coffee house.

Waikiki Diving Center, ☎ 808-922-2121, 424 Nahua Street, www.waikikidiving.com, info@waikikidiving.com. Waikiki Diving Center has scuba trips for beginners, novices and experiences divers. On a typical dive tour there will only be five or six divers on their custom dive boat. Morning charters start at 8:15 am and return around 12:30 pm. Afternoon charters begin at 1:15 pm and finish around 5 pm. A two-tank boat dive costs about $99 and if you have a friend who just wants to snorkel, they'll pay $35. Wreck dives are $115. Waikiki Diving Center can also train you to be a certified diver.

Where to Stay & Eat

The two-mile Waikiki Beach stretch is home to more than 31,000 rooms in over 100 hotels. Accommodations range from bare-bones budget bungalows to family fantasy resorts and heavenly honeymoon hideaways. It would be nearly impossible to include every hotel in Waikiki and Honolulu, so I've selected a variety of hotels, some new and fancy; others full of history and legends.

I have divided the Waikiki stretch into three sections. North Waikiki is the first area you'll see after leaving the airport and traveling through Honolulu. Central Waikiki is surrounded on one side by the always-busy street traffic and the beach on the other. East Waikiki is a little quieter and close to many attractions such as the Honolulu Zoo, the Waikiki Aquarium and Kapi`olani Beach Park.

North Waikiki

Hawaii Prince Hotel Waikiki, 100 Holomoana Street, ☎ 808-956-1111 or 866-PRINCE-6, www.princeresortshawaii.com, reservations@prince-hawaii.com. Known for it's architectural design, the Hawaii Prince Hotel has 521 rooms and 57 luxury suites among 28 floors, two towers and a five-story base. All of the rooms have an ocean view with floor-to-ceiling windows. Amenities include a complimentary shuttle to Waikiki, surrounding beaches and to the Hawaii Prince Golf Club, two tennis courts, a pool and whirlpool and a fitness center. $$$$-$$$$$.

Package Deals: The Hawaii Prince Hotel Waikiki and many other resorts on Waikiki have package deals that can save you a lot of money. For example the Prince has a Room and Breakfast package, a Room and Car package, the "Prince Special," which includes a rental car, complimentary parking and daily breakfast buffet for two, the "Romance Package" which includes a convertible rental car, $100 dinner credit, sparkling wine and daily breakfast buffet for two, and the "Unlimited Golf Package," which includes daily unlimited golf for two. Check the websites of the hotels to see what package deals might be appropriate for your vacation.

AUTHOR'S CHOICE

Ilikai Hotel, 1777 Ala Moana Blvd., ☎ 808-949-3811 or 800-468-3571 (toll free), www.ilikaihotel.com. On the northern edge of Waikiki, the Ilikai is one of my favorite hotels on the Waikiki strip. The property overlooks the Ala Wai Yacht Marina and is within walking distance to many popular attractions, including Waikiki Beach. I loved my room here – it was clean, spacious and made me feel at home. The large lanai overlooked the marina and the sunrises were amazing. I'm a sucker for amenities like soaps, coffee and tea and the Ilikai had all my favorites – Kona blend coffee, passionfruit tea, green tea, real creamers, and Bath & Body Works soaps.

Ilikai's Place in Hollywood History: The Ilikai is often recognized as the famous opening shot of the *Hawaii Five-O* television series. The scene depicts Jack Lord as Steve McGarrett standing on the penthouse balcony of the Ilikai, looking out at Waikiki and showing aerial views of the Pacific Ocean and Diamond Head.

The Ilikai has an interesting history – the property opened its doors in February of 1964 with 1,050 guest rooms and condominium apartments and was considered the first luxury high-rise hotel in Hawaii. Chinn Ho, who was born in Hawaii in 1903 and began working in his family's rice fields, which would later be Waikiki, opened the hotel in 1903. A self-made millionaire, Ho was always an entrepreneur – he first earned a living selling *kiawe* (mesquite) beans for 15¢ a bag.

Despite going against the odds in a world in which Asians were excluded from plantation management, corporate boardrooms and prestigious clubs, Ho started his career as a messenger for Dean Witter. He soon became a banker and stockbroker and from 1961 to 1971, he owned the *Honolulu Star-Bulletin* newspaper, a periodical that he had once peddled on the streets. His ambition led him to become the first Asian-American president of the Honolulu Stock Exchange and the first to sit on the board of one of Hawaii's "Big Five" corporations, Theo H. Davies & Co. Ho raised $27 million to create the Ilikai and, in 1961, a ground-breaking ceremony was held where the still-present monkey pod tree at the poolside courtyard was planted. Many, including world-famous surfer Duke Kahanamoku, attended the event.

The building itself is distinctive, with three wings placed in a Y-shape and standing 30 stories high. Back in those days, the glass elevator that overlooks the harbor was one of the highest-reaching glass elevators in the world.

Chinn Ho sold the property in 1974 for $35 million and, in March of 2002, the hotel completed a $27 million renovation, including the addition of a Wyland whale art sculpture that graces the entrance. The hotel has valet parking only, available 24 hours a day. A 24-hour business center, a fitness center and self-service laundry facilities are also available. City view rooms $$. City view with a kitchen or ocean lagoon $$$. Ocean courtyard room $$$. Ocean courtyard with kitchen $$$$. Two-bedroom city view suite and ocean-view suite $$$$$.

Waikiki

Ala Moana Hotel, 410 Atkinson Drive, ☎ 808-955-4811 or 866-448-1396, www.alamoanahotelhonolulu.com. If you plan on doing a lot of shopping, this hotel is the one for you. It's close to the Ala Moana Shopping Center and it's also within walking distance of Waikiki Beach. With a recent multi-million-dollar renovation, the hotel (now part of the Outrigger hotel chain) offers a new pool area, a fitness center, four restaurants, and a nightclub. The expansive Ala Moana Beach Park and Victoria Ward Shopping Center and Cineplex are also nearby. The Ala Moana Hotel has over 1,000 rooms (all non-smoking), 51 suites with kitchen facilities and an exclusive Presidential Suite. Parking is $15 per day. Partial ocean view $$-$$$. Ocean view $$$. One-bedroom suite $$$$.

Waikiki Gateway Hotel, 2070 Kalakaua Avenue, ☎ 800-247-1903, www.waikiki-gateway-hotel.com, is a 17-story hotel at the entrance of Waikiki. The hotel is across the street from the Kalakaua Plaza, which houses the prominently displayed Niketown store and Banana Republic. The rooms are elegantly furnished and connecting rooms are available. They also have a special "Permanent Triple" room with three single beds – perfect for kids or a party of three friends. Standard room $$. Deluxe room $$. Partial ocean view $$. Ocean view $$. Kitchenette $$. Penthouse $$$.

Booking Tip: The Waikiki Gateway Hotel offers several great deals for guests who book directly with them through their website. Recent promotions have included 50% off the $15 a day parking fee and 40% off dinner for two at the fabulous fish restaurant, Nick's Fishmarket, which is on the bottom floor of the hotel.

Hilton Hawaiian Village Beach Resort & Spa, 2005 Kalia Road, ☎ 808-949-4321, www.HiltonHawaiianVillage.com. This enormous all-inclusive beach resort is on the northern end of what is considered the gateway to Waikiki. The resort occupies 22 oceanfront acres on one of the widest stretches of Waikiki Beach.

The Hilton Hawaiian has everything you need right on the property – 22 restaurants (from extravagant to popular to tasty Round Table pizza) and lounges, over 90 shops (from general stores to exclusive boutiques), a spa, five pools, beaches, shows, wildlife, Hawaiian activities, a Polynesian show and a Friday night fireworks and entertainment show called the "King's Jubilee."

With over 3,000 guest rooms, there are always a lot of people meandering around so, if it's privacy you're looking for, keep looking.

The hotel is comprised of six towers, including the exclusive Ali`i Tower. The grounds are immaculate and the décor is very tropical – waterfalls, exotic birds, lots of Hawaiian plants and flowers and a great view of Diamond Head. This is a great place for families and has the Rainbow Express Keiki Club, with whole- or half-day activities for kids ages five-12, ranging from feeding fish to hula dancing or arts and crafts. There is also a Vacation Station Library with books, toys and games for kids. The beachfront "Super Pool" is the largest in Waikiki.

One of the more impressive buildings is the Rainbow Tower, with its rainbow mural painted on the side. The rainbow mural is the tallest in the world at 286 feet high, 26 feet wide and with 8,046 pieces of hand-painted ceramic tiles created especially for this resort by Millard Sheets.

The Rainbow Tower

One of my pet peeves with the Hilton Hawaiian is the cost and seeming pettiness of the services and amenities. Guests are only allowed one coffee packet per morning and have to pay for any additional packets. The in-room safe costs $3.65 per day to use. Another annoyance is the parking fees, although they are high throughout Waikiki. At the Hilton Hawaiian, you will pay $25 a day for valet and $20 for self-parking. So much for a "Hawaii on $100 a day" vacation! Garden view $$$$. Kalia Tower (oceanview) $$$$. Rainbow Towers (oceanview) $$$$. Ali`i Towers (oceanview) $$$$$.

The Mandara Spa at the Hilton Hawaiian Village Resort & Spa is on the fourth floor of the Kalia Tower. The spa includes a state-of-the-art fitness center, a sauna, steam rooms, and indoor whirlpool, a full service salon and an indoor/outdoor spa café. If you're more interested in products, visit the Mandara Spa Shop in the Rainbow Bazaar.

FOR LUCKY MILITARY MEMBERS

The **Hale Koa Hotel**, ☎ 800-367-6027 (toll free), www.halekoa.com, on Fort DeRussy Armed Forces Recreation Center at 2055 Kalia Road, is a resort established for members of the US Armed Forces and their families. The hotel was built and financed by service men and women from their own funds and now operates on a self-sustaining basis. On prime Waikiki property, this is definitely one of the best perks about being in the military! Check out the website to see who is eligible to visit the Hale Koa. The hotel is right on Waikiki and has several restaurants and lounges.

Doubletree Alana Hotel Waikiki, 1956 Ala Moana Blvd., ☎ 808-941-7274 or 808-559-4201 for reservations, www.doubletreealana.com. Just a short walk away from the Hilton Hawaiian Village, this hotel is in more of an intimate setting and considers itself a boutique hotel. The Doubletree Alana Hotel is popular with business and vacation visitors due to its convenient location. The 45 sleek suites and 268 rooms have marble baths, flat-screen TVs and high-speed Internet access. Basic rooms $$$. Suites $$$$.

TRUMP COMING TO WAIKIKI

It was only a matter of time! Mega-developer Donald Trump's first Hawaiian venture is planned for the new Waikiki Beach Walk and all 464 units in the Trump International Hotel & Tower sold out in record time in November of 2006. In just eight hours, all units were sold for more than $700 million in a sale that took place simultaneously in Japan and Hawaii.

Buyers paid an average price of $1.5 million with prices ranging from the mid-$400,000s for studios to more than $9 million for a three-bedroom penthouse. The Trump International Hotel & Tower will be in the space where the OHANA Royal Islander, OHANA Reef Lanai, Malihini Hotel and Hale Pua Nui Hotel used to be – a 49,250 square foot site. Construction started in mid-December of 2006 and is scheduled to finish in mid-2009.

Wyland Waikiki Hotel, 400 Royal Hawaiian Avenue, ☎ 866-346-4679, www.wylandwaikiki.net, is the first artist-inspired hotel by world-renowned marine life artist and part-time Hawaii resident, Wyland. This boutique hotel has over 400 rooms and suites in a modern design with chic interiors inspired by the artists. All guestrooms offer pillow top beds adorned with Wyland-designed motifs on the throw pillows and bed skirts. Amenities include a "chill" room with iJoy massage chairs and Xbox Playstations. The complimentary business center has two 24-inch screen iMac computers with high-speed Internet and printers. The lobby has a feeling of tranquility with its ocean-hued color scheme and contemporary furnishings. The hotel is managed by the Outrigger Enterprises Group and recently underwent a multi-million dollar transformation in 2007. Standard room $$$. City view $$$. Partial ocean view $$$. Kitchenette $$$. City view with kitchenette $$$. Partial ocean view with kitchenette $$$$. One bedroom $$$$. One bedroom with kitchenette $$$$. One bedroom with partial ocean view and kitchenette $$$$.

BUDGET ACCOMMODATIONS

Hawaii Hostels Management, www.hokondo.com, ☎ 808-923-9566, 2556 Lemon Road, St. B101, manages several hostels in O`ahu. These accommodations are usually sold by the bed rather than the room and usually incorporate a dormitory-style room with shared bathrooms and kitchen. The hostels are most popular with backpackers, usually 18 to 30 years old.

The **Waikiki Beachside Hostel** (O`ahu's largest), ☎ 808-923-9566 or 866-478-3888 (toll free), is half a block from Waikiki Beach. Nightly rates range from $29 to $75. Large dormitory $. Small dormitory $. Semi-private $.

Outrigger Waikiki on the Beach

The Outrigger, ☎ 1-800-outrigger, www.outrigger.com, chain of inexpensive (for O`ahu!) and fun-for-the-younger crowd hotels has four properties in Waikiki. My favorite is the **Outrigger Waikiki on the Beach**, 2335 Kalakaua Avenue, www.outriggerwaikikihotel.com, which is adjacent to Duke's Canoe Club, an ultra-popular spot in the midst of Waikiki Beach. Across the street from the International Marketplace, the Outrigger is also in the midst of Waikiki's somewhat crazy nightlife.

The others include **Outrigger Reef on the Beach**, www.outriggerreef.com, with the relaxing Serenity Spa, **Outrigger Waikiki Shore**, a condominium resort, and the **Outrigger Luana Waikiki**, which has studios and one-bedroom condominium suites along Kalakaua Avenue. The company is offering free high-speed Internet in all rooms, free high-speed wireless access in public areas and free domestic long-distance calls to the Mainland and Canada and free inter-island calls within Hawaii.

Recently opened is the **Outrigger Regency on Beachwalk**, a boutique-style condo collection in the heart of the reconstructed Waikiki. They have 48 one- and two-bedroom deluxe condominiums designed in a contemporary and chic style. Each unit has floor-to-ceiling windows, an outdoor lanai and plasma TVs. The property also has a sundry shop and three restaurants. One-bedroom units $$$. Two-bedroom units $$$$.

Embassy Suites Waikiki Beach Walk, ☎ 800-Embassy, www.waikikibeach.embassysuites.com, is a brand new all-suite prop-

Embassy Suites pool area

erty situated on 1.3 acres in the midst of the new Waikiki Beach Walk. Waikiki Beach is half a block from the hotel. Amenities include a 24-hour-fitness center, high-speed Internet, a nightly Manager's Reception and a full cooked-to-order breakfast daily. All rooms are either one- or two-bedroom suites, and the hotel contains two towers: the Hula Tower and the Aloha Tower. Standard one-bedroom suite $$$$. Ocean-view one-bedroom suites and all two-bedroom suites $$$$$.

The **Breakers at Waikiki**, 250 Beachwalk, ☎ 808-923-3181, www.breakers-hawaii.com, is one of the few "under $200" and is a great deal as it is just half a block from Waikiki Beach. The Breakers will give you a straight reminder of Hawaii in the 60s with its six two-story ranch-style buildings, attractive interiors and kitchenettes. The guest rooms have Japanese-style *shoji* doors that open to the lanai. The rooms also have kitchenettes and shower-only bathrooms. A Big Bonus: Parking is free (although limited). Singles.$$. Doubles $$. Garden suites $$$ to $$$$.

The Ambassador Hotel of Waikiki, 2040 Kuhio Avenue, ☎ 808-941-7777 or 800-923-2620 (toll free), www.ambassador-waikiki.com, reservations@ambassadorwaikiki.com, has great Internet specials (under $100/night!) for their studio and one-bedroom condos with full kitchens. There are many good dining options around the Ambassador, including Keo's Thai restaurant, which is on the ground floor of the hotel. $$.

Waikiki Sand Villa Hotel, 2375 Ala Wai Blvd., ☎ 808-922-4744 or 800-247-1903, www.waikikisandvillahotel.com. A few blocks away from the main strip, the 12-story, 214-room Waikiki Sand Villa Hotel is a good deal if you want to stay away from all the chaos. The hotel also promotes itself as being one of the "greener" hotels around as they recycle glass, plastic, paper and ink cartridges. They also use energy-efficient lights and timers.

The hotel has a 70-foot swimming pool and is very Internet-friendly, with complimentary access in every room as well as WI-FI service available in the pool area. The Sand Bar & Grill also has two high-speed Internet computers for bar patrons. Parking is $15.50 a day. Standard room $$. Pualeilani studios $$$.

If you book a room at the Waikiki Sand Villa Hotel through their website, you can save 50% on parking (a $7.85 per-day discount). Check the website for more discounts.

Aloha Punawai, 305 Saratoga, ☎ 866-713-9694 or 800-923-5211, www.alohapunawai.com, is a family-owned apartment hotel a block from Waikiki Beach. Calling itself "a little treasure in a sea of choices," each apartment at Aloha Punawai has a fully equipped kitchen and a private balcony. Monthly discounts are available. Studio $$. One bedroom $$. One bedroom deluxe $$$.

Aqua Bamboo & Spa

New to Waikiki are the **Aqua Hotels and Resorts**, ☎ 866-406-2782, www.aquaresorts.com, a trendy and budget-oriented chain that has five boutique hotels and five "Aqua Lite" hotels in the heart of Waikiki.

This chain includes the **Aqua Aloha Surf**, **Aqua Bamboo & Spa** (inspired by Southeast Asia), **Aqua Palms & Spa**, **Aqua Waikiki Wave**, **The Equus** (with Ralph Lauren-inspired rooms), **Aqua Coconut Plaza**, **Aqua Continental**, **Aqua Island Colony**, **Aqua Marina** and the **Ocean Tower Hotel**. Amenities include a daily continental breakfast, free high-speed Internet and Wi-Fi, an in-room safe, daily newspaper, local calls, mini-fridges, coffeemakers and microwaves. The chain of hotels has a good reputation for thorough service and a pleasant staff. Check the website for bargains. Most properties have bargain rooms from $80 to deluxe rooms for $400. $$-$$$$$.

Mid-Waikiki Accommodations

Sheraton Waikiki, 2255 Kalakaua Avenue, ☎ 808-922-4422 www.sheraton-waikiki.com. Situated on a half-mile of Waikiki Beach, the Sheraton has fantastic views of the Pacific Ocean, the Ko`olau mountains and Honolulu's spectacular city lights. Over two-thirds of the rooms directly face the ocean.

The Sheraton Waikiki originally opened in June 1971 but went through a $20 million renovation in 1995 and then a $55 million room renovation in 2007. The hotel has dozens of package deals, so, whether you're focused on family, the beach, golf, romance, honeymoon or spas, there is a specialized vacation for you. See the website or call the Sheraton for more information. City view $$$$. Ocean front $$$$. Deluxe ocean front $$$$. Partial ocean view $$$$. Ocean front (package deal) $$$$$. Partial ocean view (package deal) $$$$$. Ocean front suite $$$$$. Ocean front premier suite $$$$$.

AUTHOR'S CHOICE

Halekulani, ☎ 808-923-2311 or 800-367-2343 (toll free), www.halekulani.com. This hotel deserves the raves it gets for the superior service it provides and the unmatched ambiance. In 2007, *Travel & Leisure* magazine named the Halekulani the number-one hotel in O`ahu. It's the special touches that make a property number-one and the Halekulani is all about the little perks. A pool attendant takes you to your beach chair (the most comfortable I've found). They also continually replenish the ice in your room. I met a rough-around-the-edges couple who stayed at the Halekulani and asked the bellman to go get them dinner from Taco Bell. He did and they tipped him $70!

The oval-shaped pool has the design of a hibiscus on the bottom – a nice touch. The SpaHalekulani is one of the state's top-rated facilities and oceanfront La Mer restaurant at the Halekulani is the only restaurant in the state to receive the AAA Five Diamond rating. The SpaHalekulani was rated #2 in *Condé Nast Traveler's* roundup of "Top 50 Best Resort Spas."

The Halekulani is comprised of five interconnected buildings containing 455 rooms with unfettered views of Diamond Head. If you're going to go all out, reserve one of the Diamond Head Suites on floors nine and above for fantastic ocean views. $$$$$.

In My Dreams: The Vera Wang Suite at the Halekulani is simply spectacular. The one-bedroom suite, entirely designed by Wang, features 2,135 square feet of interior space and a 642-square-foot oceanside lanai. The famous designer has personally picked some of her favorite movies to put in the DVD collection. Guests can watch them on state-of-the-art 50-inch plasma screen TVs that can't be bought in the United States. The amenities are endless – a private concierge, private pool butler, 24-hour in-room dining, etc. The toilet seat even opens up automatically when you enter the bathroom. All this and more for only $5,000 a night!

My mom and dad stayed at the Halekulani 30 years ago and I have inherited some of the souvenirs from that trip. It's a funny trip back in time to see the room service menu where a Budweiser is $1.40, Heineken is $2.25, Tab is $1 and a bucket of ice costs 50¢. For breakfast, a papaya cost $1 and sliced pineapple is 90¢. French toast is $1.70 and a fresh tomato, ham, cheese or jelly omelet is $3.50. For lunch, guests enjoyed a ground tenderloin steak sandwich for $2.50 and a mahimahi burger for $2.50. Dinner room service included fresh mahimahi with macadamia nut butter for $8 or teriyaki steak dinner for $8.25. A double room went for $35 to $45 and a suite was between $50 and $90. Someone please call me when time travel becomes available!

Waikiki Parc Hotel, 2233 Helumoa Road, ☎ 808-921-7272 or 800-422-0450, www.waikikiparc.com, has recently become the chicest place to be in Waikiki, thanks to the opening of the highly-anticipated NOBU Waikiki restaurant and a newly-revitalized design of this "hidden gem." Chef Nobuyuki "Nobu" Matsuhisa is considered the world's master of eclectic Japanese cuisine. The Waikiki Parc Hotel is associated with the Halekulani Corporation and the property is a block away from the famous Halekulani.

The 297-room hotel, in a modern boutique setting, has a rooftop outdoor heated swimming pool and a pool-view fitness room. The guest rooms are decorated in a contemporary and modern style with plantation shutters and a signature design of the orange and white abstract "Swoon Pillow" created by Los Angeles artist Gabrielle Jennings and exclusive to the Waikiki Parc Hotel. All rooms have flat screen TVs, high speed Internet access and compact refrigerators. A big plus for guests at Waikiki Park Hotel is the hassle-free restaurant signing privileges at the neighboring oceanfront Halekulani. $$$$-$$$$$.

ResortQuest, ☎ 866-77-Hawai, www.ResortQuest-Oahu.com, has an assortment of hotels, boutique hotels, condominiums suites, villas and cottages in Waikiki. They offer some great incentives such as a

Waikiki Joy Hotel

fifth-night free promotion and a "Kids Stay, Play & Eat Free!" deal for families.

The ResortQuest rooms are decked out with a fun, nostalgic Hawaiian/Tiki-type décor. Check out the website to see ResortQuest's condominium resorts (**ResortQuest at the Waikiki Banyan**, **Pacific Monarch**, **Waikiki Beach Tower**, **Waikiki Sunset** and the **Executive Centre Hotel**), Waikiki-themed hotels (**Coconut Plaza Hotel**, **Waikiki Circle Hotel**, **Waikiki Joy Hotel**, **Waikiki Beachside Hotel**, **Waikiki Beach Hotel**) and the company's Waikiki hotels (**Aston Coral Reef Hotel** and **Aston Honolulu Prince**). There's something for everyone at ResortQuest and a little research will help you find the perfect spot for your vacation needs. Condominiums $$$-$$$$$. Hotels $-$$$.

Ohana Hotels Resorts, ☎ 800-462-6262, www.ohanahotels.com, reservations@ohanahotels.com, is another Waikiki chain. The company has six resorts in Waikiki and you can choose from the **Ohana East**, **Ohana Islander Waikiki**, **Ohana Waikiki Malia Sky Court**, **Ohana Waikiki West** and **Ohana Waikiki Beachcomber**.

Ohana Waikiki West

The Waikiki West is two blocks away from Waikiki Beach and a great spot for families.

It's a little corny but I like the *Ohana Flash*, a daily newsletter for guests of the hotel filled with information about the Hawaiian language, the different islands and other little tips. Simple rooms $$. Standard $$. Kitchenette $$. City view with kitchenette $$.

Did You Know? *All guests of Ohana Hotels & Resorts receive a valuable Ohana Waikiki Connection amenities package that includes free rides on the Waikiki Trolley's Pink Line that runs through Waikiki and Ala Moana Center, free local and long-distance phone calls to the United States and Canada, free Internet service and a free local newspaper. An added bonus is the Ho`okipa Host, an in-lobby manager who provides guests with valuable tips on hidden local eateries, off-the-beaten-path attractions and where to go to experience local customs.*

Renovation News: The Ohana Waikiki Beachcomber, a Waikiki landmark where Don Ho performed in his final years, is undergoing a $12.1 million renovation. All 493 guest rooms will be redecorated to reflect a modern take on vintage Hawaii décor inspired by the Waikiki of the 1950s and 60s. The first phase of the renovation was completed in late 2007 and the final room renovations should be completed by February 2008.

AUTHOR'S CHOICE

Pacific Beach Hotel, 2490 Kalakaua Avenue, ☎ 808-923-4511 or 800-367-6060 (toll free), www.pacificbeachhotel.com, is a favorite of mine – partly because of the fantastic three-story, 280,000 gallon indoor oceanarium with over 50 different species of marine life. Across the street from Waikiki Beach, the Pacific Beach Hotel is a good value, with convenient shopping at the hotel, and a pool and whirlpool on a sundeck. A convenient ABC Store is on the hotel's ground level. The hotel has 837 rooms spread out between two towers – the 17-floor Beach Tower and the 38-floor Oceanarium Tower, which lies behind the Beach Tower. The main entrance to the hotel is off Lili`uokalani Avenue, a one-way street that fronts Kalakaua Avenue by Waikiki and heads inland. $$$$-$$$$$.

Pool area at the Queen Kapiolani

Queen Kapiolani Hotel, 150 Kapahulu Avenue, ☎ 808-922-1941 or 800-367-2317, www.queenkapiolani.com, is near the foot of Diamond Head yet still just steps from Waikiki Beach. The hotel has 315 room on 19 floors, ranging from studios with kitchenettes to one-bedroom suites. The hotel overlooks the 108-acre Kapi`olani Park and Diamond Head. With Internet discounts, the Queen Kapiolani is a good deal but don't forget about the extras – parking ($15 and limited), in-room dial-up Internet (for a fee), and an in-room safe (for a fee). Standard room $$. Standard ocean view $$. Standard city view $$. City view $$. Diamond Head view $$. Ocean view $$. Diamond Head Studio with kitchenette $$$. Ocean-view studio with kitchenette $$$. Penthouse with city view $$$$. Penthouse with ocean view $$$$.

Internet Discount: The Queen Kapiolani Hotel, www.queenkapiolani.com, and the Ocean Resort Hotel Waikiki, www.oceanresort.com, offer substantial discounts for those who book through their websites.

Ocean Resort Hotel Waikiki, 175 Paoakalani Avenue, ☎ 808-922-3861 or 800-367-2317 (toll free), www.oceanresort.com. The resort has two towers – the Pali Tower and the Diamond Tower) – with a total of 450 rooms.

As the hotel can be a little tricky to find, here are directions from the airport. Take the H-1 freeway East for approximately 10 miles. Take Exit 25A (King Street Exit) on the right side of the

freeway. You'll pass through a four-way intersection. Get into the right lane, which will take you onto Kapahulu Avenue. Stay on Kapahulu Avenue for approximately two miles. Proceed through the intersection of Kapahulu Avenue and Kuhio Avenue and then turn right on Lemon Road. Lemon Road is a one-way street that ends at Paoakalani Avenue. Turn right onto Paoakalani Avenue, which is also a one-way street. The Ocean Resort Hotel Waikiki is on the right hand of the street. City view $$. City view studio $$. Diamond Head view studio $$. Penthouse city view junior suite $$$$. Penthouse city view one-bedroom suite $$$$. Penthouse with Diamond Head view one-bedroom suite $$$$$.

Hyatt Regency Waikiki Resort & Spa, 2424 Kalakaua Avenue, ☎ 808-923-1234 or 808-237-6300 (reservations), www.waikiki.hyatt.com. In the midst of busy Waikiki, the Hyatt Regency has twin 40-story towers connected by a three-story open-air atrium with tropical flowers, exotic birds and cascading waterfalls. Not what you expected to see in Waikiki! The resort has 1,230 guest rooms, including 18 suites. Inside the resort are more than 60 shops and boutiques selling sundries, jewelry, sporting goods and art. There's also a freshwater swimming pool, and twin Jacuzzis at the Elegant Dive (the pool bar on the third floor).

The Na Ho`ola Spa, Waikiki's largest luxury spa, features 19 treatment rooms, a sauna, fitness center, steam showers and a relaxation area.

Parking is $15 a day or valet parking is $19 a day. I say – "Always valet."

Don't Miss: From the Elegant Dive you should be able to see the nightly torch-lighting ceremony at Kuhio Beach at the site of the can't-be-missed statue of legendary surfer Duke Kahanamoku.

The resort has coin-operated laundry machines, a business center, computer and fax connections in each room, a concierge and currency exchange. $$$$-$$$$$.

Just So You Know: The Hyatt offers many specials – golf packages, spa packages, family plans and romance getaways. Just check out the website at www.waikiki.hyatt.com or call ☎ 808-923-1234 for more information.

Royal Hawaiian Hotel, 2259 Kalakaua Avenue, ☎ 808-923-7311 or 888-488-3535 (toll free), www.royalhawaiian.com, is a Waikiki landmark with its pink towering design, vaulted Spanish archways and a prolific history in the story of O`ahu and Waikiki (the land where the hotel sits once served as King Kamehameha I's playground).

Situated on 10 prime acres along Waikiki, the hotel is affectionately known as the "Pink Palace of the Pacific" and captures the glamour of Old Waikiki. Built in 1927, the landmark hotel has 538 rooms and suites decorated with historical replicas and the resort has lovely gardens. It is also home to the 7,000 square-foot Abhasa Spa and guests have access to the Sheraton Waikiki's fitness center.

The Royal Hawaiian has two restaurants, a Royal Hawaiian Luau and a legendary beachfront lounge called the "Mai Tai Bar."

Bad News For Tourists: The Mai Tai Bar will close on June 1, 2008 for seven months as the Royal Hawaiian shuts down for a $110 million renovation. The Surf Room will also be closed. This is the most extensive renovation in history for the Royal Hawaiian. The 528-room hotel will reopen in January 2009.

If you're really dying for one of their mai tais visit www.royal-hawaiian.com/de_mairecipe.htm for their secret recipe to tide you over until they return bigger and better.

In the 1930s, the Royal Hawaiian earned a solid reputation for quality and service. Hawaii was the place to stay and be seen and anyone who could afford a trip on a Matson steamer was off to Hawaii.

The Royal Hawaiian is a Starwood Resort, which means you can take advantage of the "Stay at One, Play at All" feature in which you have access to facilities at the four other Sheraton Hotels in Waikiki.

Aerial view of the "Pink Palace"

Service is of the utmost importance and guests are greeted with leis and freshly baked Hawaiian banana bread. $$$$$.

Self-Guided Garden Walking Tour: Pick up a copy of the very detailed Royal Hawaiian Hotel's self-guided walking tour of exotic flora and fauna on the property. You will see the beautiful flowers that make Hawaii so special – the bird of paradise, red and yellow hibiscus, red ginger and monkey pod trees.

ROYAL HAWAIIAN HISTORY

In 1924, Castle & Cooke pledged $200,000 for construction of a new hotel. A corporation was then created and proposed to build a hotel on a 15-acre parcel on Waikiki Beach for $2 million.

Construction began in October 1925 and would take almost 18 months to complete. 35,000 barrels of cement, 75 miles of wire, 50 tons of stucco and 9,000 gallons of paint, stain and lacquer where used in what was, at the time, the largest building project in the Pacific.

The design of the hotel is considered Spanish-Moorish, unusual for Hawaii at that time but popular due to the Spanish style in demand on the Mainland, partly as a result of Rudolph Valentino movies. Movie stars and other celebrities flocked to the Royal Hawaiian.
On July 14, 1934, President Franklin D. Roosevelt stayed in the hotel's Presidential Suite. The same year, Peter Lawford and his family stayed at the hotel. George Burns and Gracie Allen were photographed at the hotel, as was Shirley Temple, who visited in the mid-1930s.

Moana Surfrider, A Westin Resort, 2365 Kalakaua Avenue, ☎ 808-922-3111, www.moana-surfrider.com. Built in 1901 and called "The First Lady of Waikiki," the Moana Surfrider offers a turn-of-the-century take on modern-day Waikiki. You can't help but be impressed with the grand columns on the porch, the Palladian windows overlooking the ocean and the Banyan Veranda. On June 7, 2007 the Moana Surfrider was transferred from Sheraton to become a Westin Resort (with the fabulous Westin Heavenly Bed!) The re-opening included a traditional Hawaiian blessing and a release of 106 butterflies, signifying the age of the Moana.

FIRST LADY OF WAIKIKI HISTORY

With an increase in steamship travel to Honolulu, the inflow of tourists soon followed. In 1896 Walter Chamberlain Peacock, a wealthy Waikiki homeowner proposed to build Waikiki's first resort. His corporation, The Moana Hotel Company, Ltd, commissioned architect Oliver G. Traphagen to draw up plans for the hotel. The Lucas Brothers, who also built the I‘olani Palace, were the prime contractors. The Moana Hotel officially opened on March 11, 1901 and became the catalyst for the new era of tourism in Waikiki. Using the old colonial architecture of the period, the Moana Hotel had 75 rooms and was the costliest, most elaborate and modern hotel building in the Hawaiian Islands. They were also trailblazers with modern commodities – each room on the three upper floors had a bathroom and a telephone. The first floor was home to a billiard parlor, saloon, main parlor, library, and an office and reception area. The hotel's first guests in 1901 were a group of 114 Shriners hosted by the local Aloha Temple Shriners. They paid a costly $1.50 per night for the rooms. In 1905, Peacock sold the hotel to Alexander Young and, after Young's death in 1910, his estate continued to operate the hotel until Matson Navigation Company bought it in 1932 for $1.6 million. As tourism continued to grow (by 1918, there were 8,000 visitors annually), the hotel expanded with two floors added along with concrete wings on each side, doubling its size.

Today, it takes its place among America's leading hotels listed in the National Register of Historic Places. A historical tour of the property is offered at 11 am and 5 pm every Monday, Wednesday and Friday. The tour originates on the second floor of the Banyan Wing where the hotel has constructed its own historical room, with memorabilia dating back to the early 1900s.

The Moana Surfrider is the first Westin Resort to open on O`ahu. In the afternoon, guests can take advantage of the Westin's new take on happy hour – "Unwind: A Westin Evening Ritual." The resort is also planning on creating Waikiki's first and only beachfront spa, which is scheduled to open in 2008. $$$$-$$$$$.

Waikiki Beach Marriott Resort & Spa, 2552 Kalakaua Avenue, ☎ 808-922-6611 or 800-367-5370 (toll free), www.marriottwaikiki.com. With 1,310 rooms in two towers (named Kealohilani and Paoakalani after Queen Lili`uokalani's two homes), the Waikiki Beach Marriott Resort & Spa is across the street from Waikiki and just minutes away from the International Marketplace, Waikiki Aquarium, Honolulu Zoo and Kapi`olani Park. Each room at this resort has a private balcony and the rooms are decorated with a pleasant Hawaiian motif. The resort has two heated freshwater swimming pools and a 24-hour fitness center. $$$$-$$$$$.

Historical Note: A century ago, the land on which the Waikiki Beach Marriott Resort & Spa now stands was once the summer home of Hawaii's last reigning monarch, Queen Lili`uokalani.

The Embassy Suites Waikiki Beach Walk, 201 Beachwalk Street, ☎ 808-921-2345 or 800-362-2779 (toll free), www.embassysuites.com. Owned by Outrigger Enterprises, this property has one- and two-bedroom suites in two 22-story towers, the Hula Tower and the Aloha Tower. Amenities include a nightly Manager's Reception, a 24-hour fitness center, a business center and high-speed Internet. $$$$$.

Sheraton Princess Kaiulani, 120 Ka`iulani Avenue, ☎ 808-922-5811 or 800-782-9488 (toll free), www.princess-kaiulani.com, is just a crosswalk away from Waikiki Beach. The hotel also has historical significance – it's at the former entrance to the royal of estate of Ainahau, once home to Hawaii's beloved Princess Victoria Kaiulani.

The Sheraton Princess Kaiulani opened on June 11, 1955 (King Kamehameha Day) at a cost of $4.5 million. At the time, it was the largest hotel built in Hawaii since the Royal Hawaiian was constructed in 1927. When it opened, the hotel's Princess Wing was the tallest building in Hawaii at 11 stories. Historic photos of the Princess and the royal family are displayed throughout the hotel. In 1959, the hotel added 12 luxury suites and the Diamond Head Wing (now the Kaiulani Wing) was opened in September of 1960. Upgrading continued through the decades and in 1970 the Ainahau Tower was added. The Sheraton Princess Kaiulani celebrated its 50th anniversary on June 11, 2005.

HISTORY LESSON

This 10-acre oasis with its Victorian-style home was where Princess Victoria Ka`iulani, the last princess of Hawaii and her father Archibald Cleghorn, the Governor of O`ahu, lived. When tourism in Hawaii hit a peak in the mid-1950s, the Matson company constructed its third hotel, named the Princess Kaiulani, in 1955. The entrance to the hotel's parking lot marks the site of the arched entrance to Governor Cleghorn's `Ainahau garden, filled with island flora. Because the hotel stands on the former royal Ainahau Estate, the hotel was named in honor of Hawaii's most beloved monarch, Princess Kaiulani. Born on October 16, 1875, she was named Victoria Kawekiu Lunalilo Kalaninuiahilaplapa Ka`iulani (what a mouthful!). Ka`iulani's godmother, Princess Ruth, gave the young princess part of her royal estate – `Ainahau – meaning "land of the hau trees." Princess Kaiulani would enter the estate from Waikiki through her private driveway near the arched entrance. She winded through rows of palm trees to reach the white Victorian-style house set deep within the grounds.

The hotel offers a complimentary history tour at 1:30 pm every Wednesday. The tour takes guests back to the late 19th century, when the `Ainahau graced the hotel's premises. Guests will learn about the legacy of Princess Kaiulani – her history, education, interests and her love of the Hawaiian Islands. One of the highlights of the tour is an original life-sized portrait of the princess, which was dedicated to the hotel on its opening day. The tour also shows visitors an unusual stone bench where the princess shared stories with Robert Louis Stevenson and *Island Rose*, a touching poem Stevenson penned in Princess Ka`iulani's honor.

The hotel has 1,152 rooms and 14 suites, which offer views of the Pacific Ocean, Diamond Head, Honolulu city lights and the Ko`olau mountains. The hotel is also close to Kapi`olani Park, the Honolulu Zoo, Waikiki Aquarium and the International Marketplace.

The rooms reflect the Hawaiian heritage with traditional prints. All rooms are equipped with high-speed Internet access and a wireless network is available throughout the complex. $$-$$$$$.

Dinner Show: The Sheraton Princess Kaiulani hosts "Creation – A Polynesian Journey," a theatrical excursion through the South Pacific islands. This dinner and cocktail show has live music, ancient drums, authentic costumes, special effects, and start-of-the-art sound and lighting.

Celebrity Resorts Hotel Waikiki, 431 Nohonani Street, ☎ 808-923-7336 or 866-507-1428 (toll free), www.celebrityresorts.com, is a pleasant, budget-oriented resort with a total of 80 studios and one-bedroom suites. The resort has three three-story buildings but there are no elevators! Parking costs $10 a night. But be aware of the $3.99 resort fee applied nightly to your bill. This is "for your convenience" and covers local calls, use of the business center, in-room safe and coffee. Like many of Waikiki's resorts, Celebrity is part timeshare so there will be timeshare presentations at the resort and you may actually be staying in someone else's timeshare. This is often a benefit as they make it homier, with beach equipment and kitchen necessities easily available. Studio for two people $$. Studio for four people $$.

Miramar At Waikiki, 2345 Kuhio Avenue, ☎ 808-922-2077 or 800-367-2303 (toll free), www.MiramarWaikiki.com. The Miramar is behind the Princess Kaiulani Hotel and is one block from the beach and next to the popular International Marketplace. Included in the 358 rooms are six suites and a variety of room choices, from mountain and city views to the more expensive ocean-view rooms. HBO is free but Internet access and the in-room safe come with a fee. Parking is $10 per day. $$$$.

Hilton Waikiki Prince Kuhio, 2500 Kuhio Avenue, ☎ 808-922-0811, recently had a name-change and a $65 million renovation. The hotel is situated on the Diamond Head end of Waikiki and is one block from the beach, within walking distance of central Waikiki. The rooms are decorated nicely with exotic Zebrano and Wenge wood from South America, combined with vibrant island colors. $$$$$.

East End of Waikiki

ResortQuest Waikiki Beach Hotel, 2570 Kalakaua Avenue, ☎ 877-997-6667. Directly across from the best stretch of Waikiki Beach, 85% of the guest rooms at ResortQuest have partial or full ocean views. The rooms and lobby are impressive with a trendy display of surfboards at the Porte Cochere in the lobby. Much of the room décor is endearing Hawaiiana, such as red Hawaiian flowers on the bed covers. Standard room $$$$. Partial ocean view $$$$. Ocean view $$$$. Ocean front $$$$$. Junior suite $$$$$.

Royal Grove Hotel, 161 Ulunlu Avenue, ☎ 808-923-7691, www.royalgrovehotel.com, is in the heart of Waikiki. This six-story pink concrete building is about 200 yards from Waikiki Beach. Rooms start at $46.50. The Royal Grove is kid-friendly with a great pool. The parking garage next door is relatively cheap at $12 per night and weekly rates for rooms are offered, from April through November, for seven consecutive night stays. $-$$.

Park Shore Waikiki, 2586 Kalakaua Avenue, ☎ 866-282-4773, www.parkshorewaikiki.com. This can be a great deal if you do your research. Look for Internet discounts and make your plans far in advance of your trip. The Park Shore overlooks Diamond Head and sits across from the Honolulu Zoo. It has 226 guest rooms and an outdoor swimming pool and deck along Waikiki Beach. A Starbucks coffee shop is in the lobby. City view $$. Partial ocean view $$. Poolside lanais $$$. Ocean view $$$. Ocean front $$$. Diamond Head suite $$$.

Holiday Surf Hotel, 2303 Ala Wai Blvd., ☎ 808-923-8488 or 888-923-8488 (toll free), www.holidaysurfhotel.com, holiday.surf@hawaiiantel.net, is a small condominium hotel property that has been owned by the same family for 40 years. The Holiday Surf Hotel offers a "room with a view" from every unit. This waterfront hotel faces the Ala Wai Canal and is on the corner of Ala Wai Blvd. and Nohonani Street. Each of the units has a view, whether it be the Ala Wai Canal, the Ko`olau Mountain Range or Diamond Head. The property has studio and one-bedroom units (some are connecting) that include full kitchens. Studios $$. One-bedroom suites $$.

The New Otani Kaimana Beach Hotel, 2863 Kalakaua Avenue, ☎ 808-923-1555 or 800-356-8264 (toll free), www.kaimana.com, rooms@kaimana.com. On Sans Souci Beach and close to the Waikiki Aquarium, this 125-room hotel is between hectic Waikiki and Diamond Head. The main tower has 86 rooms and 23 suites while the smaller Diamond Head Wing has 16 rooms. There is a small fee for high-speed Internet and for access to the fitness center. $$$$.

W Hotel Honolulu, 2885 Kalakaua Avenue, ☎ 808-922-1700, www.starwoodhotels.com/whotels. W Hotels are known for their modern design and luxurious furnishing. Their motto is "Whatever, Whenever" which alludes to the 24-hour concierge service, meaning "Whatever you want, whenever you want it." At the foot of Diamond Head Crater and Kapi`olani Park, W Honolulu is nestled between two beaches and is a short walk to the Honolulu Zoo. The hotel's Living Room is a perfect place to unwind – board games are available as well as newspapers and beverages. The hotel has 50 guest rooms and who can resist such names as the "Wonderful Room," "Spectacular Room," "Fabulous Room" and the "Extreme Wow Suite." $$$$.

The Ewa Hotel Waikiki, 2555 Cartwright Road, ☎ 808-922-1677 or 800-359-8639 (toll free), www.ewahotel.com, is a little-known gem one block from Waikiki Beach and next to Kapi`olani Park. A sundeck is on the 8th floor and is a nice spot to watch the sunrise or sunset. The hotel also has a WebsIte Story Café with a full-service bar, snacks and espresso. Standard (single) $$. Standard (twin/double) $$. Studio superior $$. Studio deluxe $$$. One-bedroom suite $$$. Two-bedroom suite $$$$. Three bedroom suite $$$$$.

Gay Accommodations: **The Cabana at Waikiki**, 2551 Cartwright Road, ☎ 808-926-5555 or 877-902-2121 (toll free), www.cabana-waikiki.com. This four-story, 15-unit property is off the beaten path but still close to Queen's Surf Beach, Kapi`olani Park and many restaurants and shops. Aloha suite $$$. Ali`i suite $$$.

Vacation Rentals

VRBO (Vacation Rentals by Owner), www.vrbo.com, is a great spot to look for vacation rentals in Waikiki and the rest of O`ahu.

One of the houses on VRBO is a three bedroom, two-bathroom house that sleeps six. It's near Diamond Head and between Waikiki and Kahala. Newly remodeled, the house has a washer, dryer, stove and there is a shady mango tree in the front yard. $$$$$.

Where to Eat

The prices for meals are for a standard breakfast and lunch. For dinner, I included an appetizer (called a *pupu* in Hawaiian) and the price of a dinner for one. None of the prices reflect drinks.

Best View of Waikiki: Head up the glass elevator to the Hanohano Room on the 30th floor of the Sheraton Waikiki. Day or night, this is one of the most stunning views of Waikiki.

At the Sheraton Waikiki

The Hanohano Room at the Sheraton Waikiki, ☎ 808-922-4422, 2255 Kalakaua Ave. can be reached by zipping up 30 stories in a glass elevator.

Dinner is served nightly from 5:30 to 9 pm in this fine dining establishment (translation – no shorts, slippers, beach wear, baseball hats or t-shirts). The cuisine is also upscale with a combination of continental flavors and Hawaiian essences. Appetizers include escargot and oysters followed by a salad-for-two prepared tableside. Dinner entrées include a number of seafood dishes like jumbo prawns, steamed onaga, pancetta wrapped monchong as well as chicken, prime rib and rack of lamb. Three signature desserts – bananas Foster, cherries jubilees and a seasonal fruit flambée – are prepared tableside and are meant to be shared. $$$$.

Holiday Alert: The Hanohano Room has special menus for Thanksgiving, Christmas and New Year's Eve. New Year's Eve is one big night at the Hanohano Room, with three seatings and the final seating including champagne and party favors!

The **Cobalt Room** is in the Hanohano Room of the Sheraton Waikiki and this lively lounge features drinks and appetizer specials from 5 to 7 pm. On Fridays and Saturdays, the lounge features "live action" stations featuring a chef preparing savory appetizers from 5:30 to 8 pm and flambée desserts from 8 to 9:30 pm.

The Ocean Terrace, ☎ 808-921-4600, serves breakfast, lunch and dinner, including breakfast and dinner buffets. The breakfast buffet is offered from 6 am to 11 am and varies from day to day. A continental breakfast is served from 7 am to 11 am daily. The buffet is $23 for adults and $10.80 for children ages six-12 and the continental breakfast is $18.50 for adults and $10.80 for children. (Hint: Go for the buffet!). Lunch is served from 11:30 am to 2:30 pm and offers burgers, wraps, fish tacos and salads. At dinnertime, the Ocean Terrace serves a different dinner buffet every night with an early bird special from 5:30 to 6 pm and regular prices from 6 to 9:30 pm. Buffet $$$.

Sand Bar. Located directly on Waikiki Beach, this is the Sheraton's poolside bar where you can enjoy a yummy tropical drink while taking in the beach and water. Cocktails are served from 10:30 am to 9 pm and live music is performed nightly from 6 pm to 8:30 pm nightly. $.

ing views of Diamond Head, Waikiki Beach and the famous Honolulu skyline. Reservations are recommended and Sarento's has a dress code – slacks, covered shoes and a shirt with a collar for men and upscale resort attire for women.

Cuisine is regional Italian with a Mediterranean flair including award-winning homemade pastas, Hawaiian seafood, prime steaks, veal, lamb, chicken and pork. Sarento's is also known for its fabulous and extensive wine list including wine by the glass, half-bottle and bottle. This restaurant will not disappoint you!

Open Sunday through Thursday from 5:30 pm to 9 pm and Friday and Saturday from 5:30 to 9:30 pm. $$$.

For a quick bite before exploring Waikiki, stop at the **Trivial Deli & Ice Cream Parlor**, ☎ 808-441-7942, on the lobby level of the Ilikai. They offer a large selection of sandwiches, plate lunches, salads, quickie breakfast entrées, ice cream and shave ice. The deli is open Monday through Saturday from 8 am to 9 pm. $.

For Diners not staying at the Ilikai: Valet service is available at the front entrance Porte Cochere of the Ilikai Hotel. Self-parking is also available in the hotel parking lot and in the Marina Parking on Hobron Lane. Go for the valet which costs $2 per hour, while validated self-parking is also $2 per hour. It's a no-brainer!

FAST FOOD SUSHI

Right across from the Ilikai is **Aloha Sushi**, ☎ 808-955-5223, in the Discovery Village. Aloha Sushi has dozens of sushi and sashimi combinations and a colorful to-go menu is available to help you decipher the menu. There are so many mixes and combinations that only the most experienced sushi connoisseur will know exactly what they want. They also offer party platters with 30-piece plates to 54-piece combinations. Free delivery is available with orders of $40 or more. Aloha Sushi is open from 9 am to 9 pm Monday through Saturday and from 11 am to 4 pm on Sundays. $$.

At the Hilton Hawaiian Village Beach Resort & Spa

Of the 50-odd restaurants inside this huge resort, the Rainbow Lanai in the Rainbow Tower is one of my favorites for casual dining while award-winning Bali By The Sea is the perfect spot for a romantic or special evening. Here are some of my favorites:

Bali By the Sea, ☎ 808-941-2254 or 808-949-4321 ext. 43, is in the Mezzanine Level in the Rainbow Tower. Serving dinner 6 to 9:30 pm Monday through Saturday, the chef uses only the freshest and local ingredients to make the restaurant a fantastic showroom for Hawaii cuisine. The restaurant has a well-considered wine list and fantastic combinations of ingredients for the rest of the menu – sugar cane crusted scallops and a sashimi platter with fresh ahi and Kona kampachi (farm raised on the Big Island) make for great pupus. Maui onion soup or a salad made with roasted island beets and goat cheese are also great starters. Besides wonderful seafood entrées like sautéed opakapaka and orange miso-glazed Kona kampachi, Chef Adam Hightower also serves a "curry style" breast of chicken and oven-roasted Colorado rack of lamb. $$$$.

Oyster appetizer

Sergio's Italian Restaurant, ☎ 808-951-6900, has recently been reopened and is in the Rainbow Bazaar. Sergio's serves tableside presentations of some dinners and flambée desserts in a Tuscan farmhouse setting. $$$.

Round Table Pizza, ☎ 808-955-0137. This is my favorite pizza chain in California so I'm happy to see it in Hawaii. Of course, the Hawaiian Pizza is good (ham and pineapple) and they have lunch specials from 11 am to 5 pm, as well as specialty sandwiches. $.

At the Ala Moana Hotel

☎ *808-955-4811*

The **Plantation Café** has scaled down its services. It no longer offers lunch or dinner – just a breakfast buffet daily from 6:30 to 10 am. $$.

The **Moana Lanai** offers poolside lunch options such as light sandwiches, salads and smoothies from 11 am to 6 pm daily. $$.

Tsukasa is a Japanese restaurant open for lunch and dinner. Check it out from 11:30 am to 2:30 pm and 5:30 to 10 pm. Lunch $$. Dinner $$$.

If you're in the mood for Chinese cuisine, the **Royal Garden Restaurant** is open for lunch from 11 am to 2 pm Monday through Friday. On Saturday and Sunday, the restaurant is also open for dinner from 5:30 to 10 pm. Lunch is served from 10 am to 2 pm on the weekends. $$$.

The wannabe Aussies have hit Waikiki with the **Waikiki Outback Steakhouse**, 1765 Ala Moana Blvd., ☎ 808-951-6274, www.outback.com. The food and service are reliable and the portions are huge (as in Australia!). They have great steaks, a fantastic "Bloomin' Onion" appetizer, salads, pasta, chicken entrées and some surf n' turf. The Outback Steakhouse is open Monday through Saturday from 3:30 pm to 11 pm and on Sundays from 3:30 pm to 10 pm. $$$.

If you're staying in Waikiki, do not miss an opportunity to eat at the **Shore Bird Restaurant & Beach Bar** at the **Outrigger Reef Hotel**, 2169 Kalia Road, ☎ 808-922-2887. It's a short walk along the beach from the north side of Waikiki and the food, although not legendary, is hearty and affordable. The Shore Bird has an amazing breakfast buffet served daily from 7 to 11 am and offers basic buffet fare as well as Hawaii favorites such as steamed mahimahi, Hawaiian sweet bread French toast, mango bread and even *poi,* a Hawaiian staple made of taro root and mashed into a pudding-like consistency. Believe me, it's an acquired taste but you have to give it a shot.

Live Hawaiian music is performed during the breakfast service and, if you're lucky, get an oceanside table with a fantastic view of Waikiki and all of its craziness. Lunch is served from 11 am to 1 am and dinner is from 4:30 to 10 pm. The Shore Bird also has live local entertainment daily from 4:30 pm to 1 am. Dinner specialties include lobster tail, steak and lobster, the "paniolo" rib eye steak and teriyaki beef kabob. Lunch is basic burgers, sandwiches and favorites such as fish & chips, calamari & chips and coconut shrimp & chips. The restaurant also has a "healthy lunch buffet" for $11.95 and is an all-you-can-eat feast of island fruits, salads, chili, rice pasta, soup and Hawaiian beef stew. Breakfast $. Lunch $$. Dinner $$.

About five feet away from the entrance to the Shore Bird is the **Ocean House Restaurant**, ☎ 808-923-2277, which serves dinner from 5 to 10 pm. A bit more elegant than the Shore Bird, this oceanfront restaurant is known for its "Hawaiian Salt" slow-roasted prime rib, fresh fish entrées, steak and pastas. If you're looking for a fantastic fish dinner, I recommend the parmesan-crusted opah picatta in a caper wine lemon butter sauce, served with Maui onion mashed potatoes. $$$.

Brew Moon Restaurant & Microbrewery, ☎ 808-955-9045, recently opened its second location in Waikiki (the first is in the Ward Centers in Honolulu). This popular spot is next to the Local Motion store on the second floor at 1958 Kalakaua Avenue. The Brew Moon menu is huge – and that's without even looking at the beers. There are dozens of pupus, lots of sandwiches, gourmet pizzas and salads. For a true splurge, try the Moon Feast – a full slab or ribs, BBQ chicken breasts, marinated shrimp, charbroiled skirt steak and grilled jalapenos for $58.

If you're not sure which beer to try, order the lunar sampler with six four-ounce samples of handcrafted beer. Beers include the Moonlight (an American-style light lager), the German-style North-Star Lager, the MoonBerry Wheat, Big Band Pale Ale,

Orian's Red Ale and Black Hole Lager. Brew Moon Waikiki is open daily from noon until 10 pm. Lunch $$. Dinner $$$.

Cheeseburger in Paradise, 2500 Kalakaua Avenue, ☎ 808-923-3731, www.cheeseburgerland.com. This "little" burger shack that began in Lahaina, Maui has now expanded into a burger empire with shops in Key West, Las Vegas, Wailea (Maui), Waikiki Beach and Waikiki. It is home to the "5-napkin cheeseburger" and the décor is fun tiki-style. The food is consistently good and includes all of your "vacation splurges" from yummy pupus to fantastic tropical drinks. Cheeseburger in Paradise is open from 7 am to 11 pm. $$.

California Pizza Kitchen, 2285 Kalakaua Avenue, Space E, ☎ 808-924-2000, www.cpk.com. Open every day 11 am to 11 pm. This is the newest California Pizza Kitchen to pop up on O`ahu (the others are at the Ala Moana Center and the Kahala Mall). As it is in the midst of Waikiki, expect lines and a wait. The pizzas and ambiance are worth the wait. Choose from over 25 specialty pizzas (like their famous BBQ chicken pizza or perhaps the mango tandoori pizza), chicken entrées, pastas, focaccia sandwiches and desserts. $$.

The Cheesecake Factory, 2301 Kalakaua Avenue, ☎ 808-924-5001, www.thecheesecakefactory.com. This is on the ground level of the Royal Hawaiian Shopping Center. Two hours of complimentary validated parking are available at the Royal Hawaiian Shopping Center garage. The restaurant is open from 11 am to 11 pm Monday through Thursday and 11 am to midnight on Friday and Saturday. On Sunday the restaurant is open from 10 am to 11 pm and offers a fabulous Sunday Branch. The menu here is huge – if you're not a good decision maker, take a togo menu home with you! Portions are huge and you can get anything from pizzas to pastas, salads, fish and seafood, sandwiches, eggs & omelets and, of course, cheesecake. $$$.

At the Hyatt Regency Waikiki Resort & Spa

The Colony, ☎ 808-923-1234 ext. 59, is open daily from 5 to 10 pm. The Colony, on the second floor in the Diamond Head Tower, has won several awards at the annual "Taste of Honolulu" competition. It's pricey but you pay for what you get – fresh lobster and fish and prime cut-to-order steaks grilled over a kiawe wood grill. For dessert, try the Chocolate in Paradise or the Oreo Cookie Cheesecake. $$$$.

Ciao Mein, ☎ 808-923-2426 or 808-923-1234 ext. 59, is open nightly from 6 to 10 pm and has the unique combination of Chinese and Italian cuisine. Dishes are served "family-style" and the restaurant has won several awards, including many "Taste of Honolulu" honors as well as those from *Zagat*, *Gourmet Magazine* and *Honolulu Magazine*. $$$$.

Musashi, ☎ 808-923-1234 ext. 59. on the third floor of the Diamond Head Tower. Musashi serves breakfast and dinner. They offer four kinds of authentic Japanese cuisine – teishoku (table dining), teppanyaki (counter dining in the presence of a chef), hibachi (barbeque prepared at the table) and sushi. For dessert, try the pineapple cheesecake or the mango custard. Breakfast is served from 5 to 10:30 am and dinner from 5:30 to 10 pm nightly. $$$.

For small gatherings, Musashi has a Japanese dining area that can be reserved for parties of six to 10. The setting is a Japanese garden with a view of Waikiki Beach. The menu must be pre-arranged 72 hours in advance but you can choose from a seasonal seven-course French-style with a Japanese influence or a seven-course kaiseki menu. There is also a private room that accommodates 18 people.

Terrace Grille, ☎ 808-923-1234 ext. 59, on the third floor of the Diamond Head Tower, serves breakfast and lunch daily. This is a more casual approach to dining and the breakfast buffet is a great way to start the morning. Breakfast is served from 6 to 11:30 am and lunch is from 11:30 am to 4 pm daily. $$$.

The Elegant Dive is on the third floor near the pool and Jacuzzis. Open from 11 am to 11 pm, the Elegant Dive overlooks Waikiki Beach and serves casual snacks and yummy tropical cocktails. Nightly live entertainment seals the deal in making this an excellent sunset spot. $$.

At the Royal Hawaiian

The Surf Room is situated along Waikiki and is popular for its wonderful brunches. Sunday brunch is served from 11 am to 2:30 pm. Don't wait until 2 pm to show up or you may not have much to choose from. My philosophy for brunch is to pace yourself and drink lots of champagne. The price is $46 for adults and $23 for children ages five to 12. The Surf Room also has a daily buffet during the rest of the week which is served from 6:30 to 11:30 am. Lunch is served à la carte daily from 11:30 am to 2 pm. Dinner is from 6 to 9:30 pm, with the fabulous Friday night Seafood Buffet from 5:30 to 9:30 pm. Reservations are strongly suggested for this popular event. The Seafood Buffet is $50 for adults and $25 for kids aged five to 12. An à la carte dinner menu is served from 6 to 9:30 pm Saturday through through Thursday. $$$.

The Mai Tai Bar is a wonderful spot to have a drink and people watch along Waikiki Beach. Open from 10:30 am to 12:30 am, this is a spectacular place to try a tropical drink and one of the many appetizer offerings. The bar is set up outdoors with umbrellas on the tables for shade. Service is great and the drinks even better. $$.

Renovation Alert: *The Mai Tai Bar will close on June 1, 2008 for seven months as the Royal Hawaiian shuts down for a $110 million renovation. The Surf Room will also be closed. The hotel will reopen in January 2009.*

The Royal Hawaiian Beach Club by the pool serves breakfast, lunch and afternoon snacks. Open from 7 am to 4:30 pm, the beach club offers sandwiches, pizzas, snack and beverages $$.

At the Royal Hawaiian Shopping Center

Okonomiyaki Chibo Restaurant, ☎ 808-922-9722, is on the third level of Building A and has been around for 17 years. Authentic Japanese cuisine from dishes originating in Osaka, Japan can be custom-made to please all customers. Okonomiyaki is basically a Japanese pancake cooked with the ingredients of your choice and then served with a thick mayo sauce and a Worcestershire-based sauce. The restaurant has private tatami rooms that are ideal for large parties. Call for hours. Lunch $$. Dinner $$$.

Coming Soon! At press time, the Royal Hawaiian Shopping Center was planning on opening an ultra-popular franchise of Maui Tacos and Wolfgang's Steak. I can't wait to try those out!

Restaurant Suntory, ☎ 808-922-5511, has been serving authentic Japanese cuisine for 27 years. The recently renovated 6,393-square-foot restaurant is on the third level of Building B and overlooks the Royal Grove. Entrées include fresh fish, shellfish, shabu-shabu and teppan-yaki in an authentic contemporary Japanese setting. Lunch is served Monday through Friday from 11:30 am to 1:30 pm and Saturday and Sunday from noon to 2 pm. Dinner is nightly from 5:30 to 9:30 pm. Lunch $$. Dinner $$$.

Beijing Chinese Seafood Restaurant, ☎ 808-971-8833, has also gone through an extensive renovation. On the third level of Building C, the restaurant has 5,992 square feet of dining space with an authentic Chinese décor including a gold-plated Emperor Chair display room. Lunch includes Dim Sum and there is a prix fixe dinner menu. Lunch $$. Dinner $$$.

Villa Paradiso, ☎ 808-926-1717, is in Building B on the third floor and features the cuisine of Northern Italy. Pastas, risottos, pizzas, antipastos and seafood dishes are elegantly served at this popular restaurant. Lunch is served Monday through Friday 11:30 am to 2 pm. Dinner is 6 to 10 pm. Lunch $$. Dinner $$$.

Internet Savings: Visit www.ecouponshawaii.com to print out coupons for many of the restaurants you may visit while in O`ahu!

Nick's Fishmarket, 2070 Kalakaua Ave., ☎ 808-955-6333. Nick's is at the bottom level of the Waikiki Gateway Hotel. There are dark booths, dim lighting, velvet chairs... But the seafood, though pricey, is some of the best on the island. The service is professional and formal and the ambience is romantic. Besides lobster tails, Alaskan crab legs and various fresh fish dinners, Nick's also serves chicken, veal, rack of lamb, New York steak and filet mignon. Daring and experienced seafood eaters will enjoy appetizers like Beluga caviar, escargot and oysters Rockefeller. Nick's is open nightly from 5:30 to 9:30 pm and every evening includes live entertainment. $$$$.

Keo's Thai Cuisine, 2028 Kuhio Avenue, ☎ 808-951-9355, www.keosthaicuisine.com. Keo's has been around since 1977 and has been a favorite of tourists and locals since the beginning. Keo's serves breakfast, lunch and dinner, with breakfast being

an affordable option in an otherwise expensive Waikiki. Breakfast is typical American with eggs, pancakes, cereal, French toast and Belgian waffles. Lunch returns to Thai cuisine with dishes like Evil Jungle Prince (Keo's most famous dish) and curries. Plate lunches are also available and include a vegetarian plate, beef or chicken plate and a seafood plate. Dinner features the traditional Thai dishes as well as set dinner menus that include an appetizer, salad, entrée, rice and dessert. Breakfast is served daily from 7 am to noon; lunch from 11 am to 2 pm; and dinner is from 5 pm to 10:30 Sunday through Thursday and 5 to 11 pm Friday and Saturday. Breakfast $$. Lunch $$. Dinner $$$.

At the Waikiki Shopping Plaza

Tanaka of Tokyo, 2250 Kalakaua Ave., ☎ 808-922-4702, www.tanakaoftokyo.com, offers the best of Japanese cuisine. The Shogun Special is to die for – choice tenderloin, whole lobster tail and deep sea scallops. Other entrées include chicken, shrimp, salmon and utage – considered to be the rarest and tastiest cold water lobster in the world. The mouth-watering *pupus* (appetizers) include Alaskan king crab, calamari, blackened ahi and a vegetarian tofu steak with teppanyaki vegetables. Tanaka of Tokyo is open nightly from 5:30 to 9:30 pm. $$$.

At the Waikiki Business Plaza

Top of Waikiki, 2270 Kalakaua Avenue (on the top floor of the Waikiki Business Plaza), ☎ 808-923-3877, www.topofwaikiki.com. This three-tiered restaurant makes a full 360-degree rotation every hour. The dining room is centered around an open sit-down bar that revolves independently and provides guests with an additional level perfect for viewing the city skyline.

The restaurant opened in October 1965 and has hosted well over a million guests. The menu is varied and offers delicious pupus such as Thai-spiced marinated catfish with coconut shrimp and a sweet potato-mango guacamole and seared furikake-wonton crusted ahi sashimi with honey mustard soy and edamame.

The Top of Waikiki also serves vegetarian entrées along with fish dinners and meat and poultry entrées. Two prix fixe menus are available for those who want to rely on someone else to coordinate their dinners. Early Bird specials are available for $14.95 and lobster and steak dinners for $23.95, if you come early.

Dinner is served nightly from 5 to 9:30 pm. Free validated parking is available. $$$.

At the Outrigger Waikiki Hotel

Duke's Canoe Club Waikiki, 2335 Kalakaua Avenue, ☎ 808-922-2268, www.hulapie.com. This is what almost everybody comes to Hawaii for – oceanside dining, umbrella drink and surf, surfers and major surf attitude. Yet, Duke's will also take you back to Old Hawaii and remind you of simpler times. Duke's Waikiki is right over the site of the original Outrigger Canoe Club, where legendary Duke rode the biggest wave of his life. The restaurant is a virtual museum, with old-fashioned photos of Duke, the koa outrigger canoes, surfboards and posters of Old Hawaii.

The "Barefoot Bar" is open from 11 am to midnight and is consistently good with menu items including nachos, sashimi, shrimp cocktail with a guava sauce and Waikiki hot wings. For bigger appetites, the Baja fish tacos are excellent. Fish sandwiches, cheeseburgers and salads are also on the casual menu. Dinner is a bit more upscale and is served in the open-air dining room. Steaks, prime rib, fresh fish dinners and various seafood dishes (including a seafood luau with fish, shrimp, scallops) are available. For fresh fish dinners I recommend the "Seven spice ahi" with a papaya mustard sauce or the "Ti Leaf Steamed Opakapaka." Duke's is also known for is generous salad bar. Dinner is served from 5 to 10 pm. Lunch $$. Dinner $$$.

WHO WAS DUKE?

Duke's is named for Duke Kahanamoku (1890-1968), a man considered the father of international surfing and a six-time Olympic medalist in swimming and water polo. Duke was a local Waikiki beach boy who became a hero, a legend and a leader of the Hawaiian people. In fact, he is considered Hawaii's official Ambassador of Aloha as he personified and preached the spirit of genuine hospitality and true "Aloha Spirit." Kahanamoku is also known as Hawaii's most famous citizen and the "Father of International Surfing." Those are some titles hard to live up to! Duke Paoa Kahanamoku was born August 24, 1890 in Honolulu and was the first of six sons and three daughters of Duke and Julia Kahanamoku. The younger Duke grew up in a carefree Waikiki, before the appearance of hotels and resorts, with the ocean as his playground. He loved swimming, surfing, canoeing and bodysurfing. The handsome Hawaiian was one of the few people allowed onto Shangri La, the personal property of heiress Doris Duke who shunned publicity to live a simple life in Honolulu.

At the age of 21 Kahanamoku won his first Olympic gold medal, then went on to represent the United States in the Olympics for 20 years, winning not only medals but fans all over the world. He is remembered not just as a swimmer, but for his grace in the water, his good humor and his sportsmanship. Duke is considered one of the pioneers of surfing with his legendary longboard and his exploits on a surfboard which catapulted the sport to new heights.

Duke was a handsome fellow – tall, athletic with bronze good looks that attracted the Hollywood film industry. He appeared in over 28 movies, including "*The Wake of the Red Witch*," which also stared the other "Duke" – John Wayne.

As Duke acquired medals, trophies and worldwide fame, he mostly practiced surfing purely for enjoyment in an era before it was a competitive sport. He truly lived the "Aloha Spirit."

Duke's Creed

"In Hawai`i we greet friends, loved ones or strangers with Aloha, which means with love. Aloha is the key word to the universal spirit of real hospitality, which makes Hawai`i renowned as the world's center of understanding and fellowship. Try meeting people or leaving people with Aloha. You'll be surprised by their reaction. I believe it and it is my creed.
Aloha to you."
Duke Paoa Kahanamoku

Hula Grill, 2335 Kalakaua Avenue, ☎ 808-923-4852, www.hulapie.com. You will definitely see the Hawaiian influence on the menu at Hula Grill – there are macadamia nuts, corn from Kahuku, Moloka`i sweet bread, coconut, pineapple, Maui onions and even Spam! Hula Grill serves breakfast (6:30 to 10:30 am) and dinner (5 to 10 pm), not to mention pupus served in the Plantation Bar (4 to 11 pm). This is the kind of place where you could linger all day and people-watch while enjoying great drinks and food. P.S. Happy Hour is 4 to 6 pm. Breakfast $. Dinner $$$. Pupus $$.

At the Waikiki Beach Marriott Resort & Spa

☎ *808-922-6611*

Kuhio Beach Grill offers continental cuisine with a focus on Hawaiian and Pacific Rim flavors. On Friday, Saturday and Sunday evenings, a prime rib and crab leg buffet is offered. Kuhio Beach Grill is open daily from 5 to 11 am and 5 and 10 pm. Breakfast $$. Dinner $$$.

Restaurant RUN is a casual Japanese noodle shop and sushi bar. It is open daily from 11:30 am to 3 pm and 5:30 to 10 pm. $$.

Moana Terrace has casual dining and delicious cocktails along the beach. Guests can take in the breathtaking views of Waikiki and watch gorgeous sunsets nightly. The Moana Terrace is open daily from 11 am to 11 pm for lunch, dinner and pupus. $$.

Arancino di Mare, ☎ 808-931-6273. On the ground level of the Kealohilani Tower, this 4,500-square-foot restaurant has lots of room for people who enjoy good food! They don't take reservations, so don't wait till the last minute to drop in to this Italian delight. Arancino di Mare is open daily for breakfast from 7 am to 10 am, lunch from 11:30 am to 2:30 pm and dinner from 5 to 10:30 pm. Breakfast $$. Lunch $$. Dinner $$$.

The **d.k. Steak House** at the Waikiki Beach Marriott Resort & Spa, 2442 Kalakaua Avenue, ☎ 808-931-6280, www.dksteakhouse.com. d.k, is open nightly from 5:30 to 10 pm. It is considered one of Oahu's best steak houses. The restaurant has O`ahu's only dry-aging room, which imparts a sweeter, fuller and more robust flavor while tenderizing the meat. The restaurant's signature items include Steak House Crab Cakes, Monster Shrimp Cocktail, Filet Mignon and Crab Oscar. $$$-$$$$.

At the Waikiki Beach Walk

www.waikikibeachwalk.com

Roy's Waikiki, Corner of Lewers Street and Kalia Road, ☎ 808-923-7697. Open daily from 11 am to 11 pm. Famous chef Roy Yamaguchi brings his Hawaiian cuisine empire to Waikiki where he blends fresh local ingredients with European sauces and bold Asian spices. The focus is on seafood. The wine list includes Roy's signature cuvées created by some of the world's best-known winemakers. Diners can order one of "Roy's Classics" (such as a macadamia nut crusted mahi mahi or Roy's classic trio of hibachi grilled salmon, blackened island ahi and misoyaki butterfish), which are served at Roy's nationwide. Or try one of the innovative specials. $$$.

Ruth's Chris Steak House, 226 Lewers St, #L-233, ☎ 808-440-7910, www.ruthschris.com. This new 5,500-square-foot restaurant is the chain's second O`ahu venture. Renowned for its premium choice cuts of beef, this eatery can seat up to 180 customers for dinner only. The steak house is open nightly from 5 to 10 pm and you can make reservations online. $$$.

Holokai Grill, 226 Lewers Street, ☎ 808-924-7245, www.holokai-grill.com. On the upper level of the new center along the Waikiki Beach Walk, the 152-seat Holokai Grill serves contemporary island cuisine in a relaxed South Pacific setting. They serve breakfast, lunch and dinner and have live entertainment every morning. This is the place to try one of those fun tropical drinks with an umbrella! The menu contains tasty, affordable cuisine catering to the casual diner. Appetizers include nachos, calamari and pizzas while lunch consists of salads, sandwiches, burgers and plate lunches. For dinner, the menu is more upscale, with fresh fish dinners, steaks, ribs and pastas. Holokai Grill is open daily from 6:30 am to midnight. Breakfast $. Lunch $$. Dinner $$$.

Yard House, 220 Kapuni Street, ☎ 808-923-9273, www.yardhouse.com. I usually avoid suggesting chain restaurants but Yard House is an exception. Their restaurants have opened everywhere from Arizona to California, Florida and Colorado. The décor is totally un-Hawaiian – dark, trendy, rock and roll-ish – and the food and drinks are delicious. Everything is huge – the extensive menu, the beer selection and other drinks. Besides over a hundred beers on tap, Yard House also has a large selection of wine and martinis. The pupus are excellent. Try the signature deconstructed California roll or the Hawaiian poke stack. They also offer a very satisfying selection of salads, sandwiches, burgers, pizzas, steaks and seafood. Lunch $$. Dinner $$$.

> *Art Lesson:* Yard House contains a spectacular art collection created by Jerome Gastaldi. The works were created to reflect the regional environment as well as the energy in the Yard House restaurants. To find out more about the artist, check out www.jeromegastaldi.com or call ☎ 949-702-1800.

Kaiwa Waikiki, 226 Lewers St, ☎ 808-924-1555. This Japanese restaurant has a twist – combining traditional and contemporary tastes into innovative dishes. Guests will also enjoy the original creations from the teppan counter and the sushi bar. The interior is also impressive with one tiled wall showcasing a shimmering cascade of water. Kaiwa is open daily for lunch from 11 am to 2:30 pm and dinner from 5 to 10 pm. The lounge and cocktail bar is open from 10 pm. to 1:30 am. Lunch $$. Dinner $$$.

Giovanni Pastrami, 227 Lewers St, Suite 118, ☎ 808-923-2100, www.giovannipastrami.com. Surrounded by 18 50-inch plasma TV screens, this is comfort food at its best. The restaurant serves breakfast, lunch and dinner all day and includes 24 kinds of omelets. Giovanni's has New York-style sandwiches and salads as well as Waikiki's largest breakfast selection. Park at the Wyndham garage on Lewers Street on the Waikiki Beach Walk. Validated valet parking is $6 for four hours. Breakfast is served from 7 am to midnight and includes an impressive selection of omelets, a meatloaf loco moco, pancakes, eggs benedict and a lox and bagel platter that serves three. Lunch consists of Round Table Pizza, deli sandwiches and burgers. For dinner, try the fish and chips, fresh fish dinner or baby back ribs and chicken. The interior is also impressive, with Peruvian tile floors, Italian beveled glass columns and African wood wallpaper. Breakfast $$. Lunch $$. Dinner $$$.

Taormina Sicilian Cuisine, 227 Lewers Street, ☎ 808-926-5050, www.taorminarestaurant.com. This Sicilian-style trattoria is a new concept from the owners of Tony Roma's Hawaii and Capricciosa. The restaurant offers traditional southern Italian fare with an indoor/outdoor café setting in a prime location at the corner of Lewers Street and Don Ho Lane. The menu is very Sicilian with antipasti, pastas, fish entrées, veal and lamb. Expect lots of garlic and be sure to check out the wine list, with its over 125 selections. Taormina is open Friday to Saturday from 11 am to 11 pm and Sunday to Thursday from 11 am to 10 pm. Lunch $$. Dinner $$$.

Beard Papa's Sweets Café, 227 Lewers St, Suite 126, ☎ 808-926-8247, www.beardpapahawaii.com. One of Japan's favorites,

Beard Papa's cream puffs are made fresh daily and are baked, not fried. The shells are made of a double layer of soft French "choux" and outside "pie crust." Each puff is filled with a whipped-cream custard when the order is placed to ensure optimum freshness and quality. Open daily from 7 am to 9 pm. $.

The Coffee Bean & Tea Leaf, 227 Lewers St, Suite 115, ☎ 808-926-4951, www.coffeebeanhawaii.com, offers 32 varieties of the finest grades of Arabica coffee from specially selected estates around the world and more than 30 varieties of full leaf teas. Fresh baked goods and light meals are available for breakfast, lunch and dinner. Ask the cashier about getting a free hour of Wi-Fi access with any purchase. The Coffee Bean & Tea Leaf is open Sunday to Thursday from 5:30 am to 10 pm and Friday and Saturday from 5:30 am to 11 pm. $.

Honolulu Cookie Company, 227 Lewers St, ☎ 808-924-6651, www.honolulucookie.com. What more can I say? Pineapple-shaped shortbread cookies made with the exotic – pineapple, lilikoi, mango, Kona coffee and macadamia nut – flavors of Hawaii. Grab some gifts for your friends on the Mainland. They'll love you for it! Open daily from 9 am to 10 pm. $.

Mondo Gelato, 226 Lewers St, Suite #L130, ☎ 808-926-6961, www.mondogelato.com, is an Italian gelateria café which specializes in authentic artisan-style gelato (Italian ice cream) and gelato products (sorbetto, soya gelato, yogurt gelato) using fresh ingredients, a natural production process and following the highest quality Italian recipes. The result is a gelato free of any stabilizers or preservatives. Mondo Gelato also has espresso, pastries and a small selection of panini grilled sandwiches. The café is open daily from 8 am to 11 pm. $.

Also in Waikiki

It might not look like much from the outside but the **Wailana Coffee House**, 1860 Ala Moana Blvd., ☎ 808-955-1764, has an upstanding reputation among residents and visitors for great food at great prices. It's conveniently located across from the Hilton Hawaiian Village and is open 24 hours a day. Best known for its hearty breakfasts, the Wailana Coffee House also has a cocktail lounge and impromptu entertainment from locals who have been visiting the Wailana for decades. An appetizer menu is served all day and night and lunch and dinner come with an all-you-can-eat salad bar. Entrées include fried chicken, hamburgers and their famous meatloaf. $.

L & L Drive Inn, 909 Kapahulu Avenue, ☎ 808-735-5505, www.hawaiianbarbecue.com. L & L is a popular fast food Hawaiian-style restaurant chain. For an authentic take on Hawaiian cuisine, try one of the combination plates (served with rice and salad). The "mixed plate" has hamburger steak, teriyaki beef and your choice of beef curry, beef stew or chili. The "seafood combo" contains mahimahi, fried shrimp and your choice of teriyaki beef, BBQ chicken or BBQ short ribs. Most plate lunches offer a mini-portion (one scoop of rice and one scoop of salad) or a regular one (two scoops of rice and one of salad). Then there are sandwiches ranging from hot dogs and hamburgers to mahimahi burgers, a katsu burger or a shrimp burger. They also serve saimin and ramen as well as bowls of chili, beef curry and beef stew. Brave diners should try the Spam omelet for breakfast or the loco moco (a hamburger patty with gravy and an egg served over rice). $.

At the Miramar At Waikiki

2345 Kuhio Avenue, ☎ 808-922-2077, www.miramarwaikiki.com

If you're craving a bit of comfort food with a familiar menu, there's a **Denny's Family Restaurant** on the Lobby Level. It's open 24 hours a day and can get very busy. $.

Sammy's Restaurant serves breakfast, lunch and dinner daily and is on the fifth floor. $$.

Also on the Lobby Level is **Fatty's Chinese Kitchen**, offering Chinese fast food from 10:30 am to 10:30 pm daily. $.

Mika Won II Korean Restaurant, on the Lobby Level, serves Korean fast food from 10 am to 10 pm daily. $.

There are also two lounge/bar areas at the Miramar. During the day visit the **Poolside Bar** which serves drinks and light snacks from 11 am to 5 pm Thursday through Monday. $.

In the evening, check out the **Banana Patch Lounge** on the Lobby Level, open from 6 pm to 2 am Wednesday through Sunday. $.

At The Wyland Waikiki

400 Royal Hawaiian Avenue, ☎ 808-954-4000, www.thewylandwaikikihotel.com

KiMOBEAN is a local company that provides 100% premium Hawaiian-grown coffee. The company has several outlets throughout the Hawaiian Islands and this premium coffee and espresso bar is the second franchise to hit O`ahu. KiMOBEAN also offers locally baked pastries, sandwiches, desserts as well as logo items, teas and chocolates to go. Open daily from 6 am to 9 pm. $.

At the ResortQuest Waikiki Beach Hotel

Award-winning **Tiki's Grill & Bar** ☎ 808-923-8454, www.tikisgrill.com, tiki@tikisgrill.com. Inside, Tiki's looks like a throwback to the tiki bars from the 1950s and 60s, with hand-carved masks, fish nets hanging from the ceiling and palm wood flooring. A 30-foot, man-made volcano is the main showpiece in the bar area. The open-air atmosphere is very inviting and there is lanai seating overlooking Kuhio Beach.

For lunch, try the Kalua pig quesadilla for an appetizer and their famous fish & chips, with fresh fish encrusted with panko, cilantro and green onion. The grilled ahi sandwich is served with a wasabi mayonnaise, lettuce and tomato. At dinner, try Pele's bottle rockets, which are spicy Thai spring rolls served on skewers with two dipping sauces. For entrées, try the guava glazed ribs, the grilled portobello mushroom, or the macadamia nut-crusted mahimahi. Lunch is served from 10:30 am to 4 pm and dinner from 4 to 10:30 pm. Lunch $. Dinner $$.

At the Halekulani

2199 Kalia Road

AUTHOR'S CHOICE

La Mer, ☎ 800-367-2343, is the only AAA Five Diamond Restaurant in Hawaii and has been for 17 consecutive years. La Mer Chef de Cuisine Yves Garnier creates legendary menus featuring Neoclassic French cuisine that are served along with majestic ocean views.

I had the pleasure of enjoying Chef Yves Garnier's "Menu Degustation," which is a gastronomical tour of the cuisine at La Mer. It was a night I will never forget! Imagine nine amazing courses perfectly timed and precisely paired with exotic wines. This unforgettable experience takes about four hours and costs $150 per person.

The regular menu has French-inspired fish entrées as well as meat and poultry dishes. The restaurant is small (it only seats up to 16 guests) and recommendations are highly recommended. Long-sleeved collared shirts or jackets are required wear for gentlemen. La Mer is open nightly from 6 to 10 pm. $$$$.

Orchids serves breakfast, lunch and dinner in an elegant oceanside setting. Sunday brunch, served 9:30 am to 2:30 pm, is a spectacular, not-to-be-missed event. The rest of the week, breakfast is from 7:30 to 11 am and lunch is from 11:30 am to 2 pm. Dinner is served nightly from 6 to 10 pm. The food is extraordinary and the prices reflect the care that is put into each meal. Breakfast $$. Lunch $$$. Dinner $$$$.

House Without a Key is an informal indoor/outdoor gathering spot for breakfast, lunch, cocktails and appetizers. Free entertainment is usually available and spending an afternoon out here is a great way to relax. House Without a Key (named after a 1925 Charlie Chan novel) is open daily from 7 am to 9 pm. Lunch $$. Dinner $$.

At the Waikiki Parc Hotel

2233 Helumoa Road, ☎ *808-921-7272, www.waikikiparc.com*

Waikiki Parc Hotel has recently become the chicest place to be in Waikiki thanks to the opening of the highly anticipated **Nobu Waikiki**, ☎ 808-237-6999, www.noburestaurants.com, restaurant. Chef Nobuyuki "Nobu" Matsuhisa is considered the world's master of eclectic "new style" Japanese cuisine. The much-anticipated restaurant opened May 28, 2007 and the restaurant's décor is almost as prolific as the food itself. Running water, bamboo, fish nets, island foliage and stone structures adorn the restaurant, which has a full-service sushi bar and private dining areas for special events. Nobu Waikiki serves dinner from 5:30 to 11 pm and the Bar Lounge is open from 5 pm to midnight. Complimentary valet service is available at Waikiki Park Hotel's

Helumoa entrance. Reservations for dinner at Nobu Waikiki are strongly recommended.

Offered exclusively for Waikiki Parc Hotel guests is the "PARC am" breakfast in the stunning dining room of Nobu Waikiki. The daily breakfast is offered from 6 to 9:30 am at $16.50 and up, featuring an assortment of American, healthy, sweet and Asian favorites.

Waikiki Parc Hotel guests can also enjoy an enhanced 24-hour room service menu that features a custom Halekulani Trans-Fat-Free menu with selections such as Oriental chicken salad, jumbo shrimp and an artisanal cheese plate. $$.

At the Pacific Beach Hotel

2490 Kalakaua Ave., ☎ 808-921-6111, www.pacificbeachhotel.com

It's hard to think about food at the **Oceanarium Restaurant** when you're seated next to a three-story 280,000-gallon indoor aquarium right in the middle of the restaurant. It definitely gives guests something to talk about! Open for breakfast, lunch and dinner, the Oceanarium also has fantastic buffets, including a weekend brunch buffet and nightly dinner buffets. The weekend brunch is offered from 11 am to 2:30 pm Saturdays and 10 am to 2:30 pm on Sundays. Bring your appetite as the buffet includes prime rib, snow crab legs, seafood specialties, omelets-to-order and a pupu and salad bar. On Sundays, a dim sum station, roast duck and roast suckling pig are added to the menu.

The dinner buffets have a different theme every night – king crab legs and shrimp scampi on Monday and Thursday, black bean, seafood and lobster alfredo on Tuesday, black bean, seafood and Cajun cream lobster on Wednesday, maki sushi and Louisiana BBQ shrimp on Friday, roast suckling pig and shrimp & scallop Alfredo on Saturday and dim sum and Louisiana BBQ shrimp on Sunday. And this is all in addition to the nightly servings of prime rib, snow and Dungeness crab legs, island fish, sashimi, poke and a pupu and salad bar.

Saturday brunch is $22 for adults and $11.50 for children ages five to 10; Sunday brunch is $27 for adults and $11.50 for children. The nightly buffets are held from 4:30 to 10 pm and cost $35 for adults and $15.25 for children ages five to 10. A la carte breakfast $$. Lunch $$. Dinner $$$.

Neptune's Garden, ☎ 808-921-6112, serves a breakfast buffet daily from 7 to 11 am and dinner from 5:30 to 9:30 pm Tuesday to Saturday. The dinner menu has a huge variety of smaller-portion tapas and then an amazing selection of fresh fish and several steak dinners. Breakfast $$. Dinner $$$.

For a quick bite to eat and perhaps a relaxing tropical drink, check out the **Aloha Center Café**. Open daily from 6 am to 7:30 pm, the café has coffee, espresso, smoothies, pastries, sandwiches, beer and cocktails. Happy Hour is from 4 to 6 pm and includes beer specials as well as a tropical drink selection of the day. $$.

At the New Otani Kaimana Beach Hotel

2863 Kalakaua Avenue, ☎ 808-923-1555

The Hau Tree Lanai, ☎ 808-921-7066, serves breakfast, lunch and dinner in an open-air oceanfront setting. The menu has a Pacific Rim theme and specializes in fresh island fish. On Sundays, the Hau Tree Lanai has an "East Meets West" brunch. Breakfast is served daily from 7 am to 11 am and lunch is from 11:30 am to 2 pm Monday through Saturday. Dinner is nightly from 5:30 to 9 pm. Breakfast $$. Lunch $$. Dinner $$$.

Miyako, ☎ 808-921-7077, offers traditional Japanese cuisine in an oceanview setting on the second floor of the hotel. The restaurant features Japanese service in a comfortable setting with fantastic sunset views. Western and Tatami-style seating is available. on the second floor of the hotel, Miyako serves dinner every night from 5:30 pm. $$$.

For lighter fare, try the **Sunset Lanai Bar** which serves island favorites (both drinks and food) with a spectacular sunset view. They're known for their delicious mai tais! The Sunset Lanai Bar is open daily from 11 am to 11 pm. $$.

If you're dying for a really good steak, **Chuck's Steak House**, 2335 Kalakaua Avenue, ☎ 808-923-1228, www.chucks-steakhouse.com, is upstairs from Duke's. The restaurant opens at 4:45 pm for cocktails and Happy Hour (which lasts till 6 pm) and dinner service runs from 4:45 until 10 pm, with an Early Bird special from 4:45 pm to 6 pm. This large restaurant chain spans the United States but its Waikiki location might be the most scenic – it overlooks Waikiki Beach and has a view of Diamond Head. Known for their USDA prime-grade steaks, Chuck's also serves great portions of seafood and has a fine salad bar. $$$.

At the Sheraton Princess Kaiulani

☎ *808-921-4600, www.princess-kaiulani.com*

Pikake Terrace, ☎ 808-931-8383. This casual restaurant serves breakfast and dinner daily with a breakfast buffet. The continental breakfast and breakfast buffet are offered from 6 am to 11 am, while dinner is from 5:30 to 9:30 pm, with live music performed poolside by some of Hawaii's premier entertainers. Breakfast $$. Dinner $$$.

Pikake Lounge serves tropical drinks poolside from 11 am to 11:30 pm. Nightly entertainment is scheduled from 6:15 to 11 pm. $.

Momoyama, ☎ 808-931-8383, serves traditional Japanese cuisine including an extensive selection of sushi and dinner combinations. Momoyama is open nightly from 5:45 to 9:30 pm and is also available for private parties. $$$.

At the W Hotel Diamond Head

The **Diamond Head Grill** serves breakfast (7 to 10:30 am) and dinner (6 pm to midnight). This award-winning restaurant offers the "Flavors of Hawai`i" with innovative and local, tropical cuisine. The hotel describes its cuisine as an exotic blend of Asian, Euro-American and Polynesian flavors. Breakfast $$. Dinner $$$.

Dinner Shows/Luaus/Magic Shows

South Pacific Cultural Center, ☎ 808-922-3705, www.spccwaikiki.com, bookings@spccwaikiki.com, is an independent dinner show/luau that caters to larger parties and conventions. The dinner show is held from 6 to 8:30 pm and showcases the dance and art of Hawaii, Tahiti, Tonga, Samoa, Fiji and Aotearoa

(New Zealand). The center also provides two daily shows that include free entrance to the Waikiki Aquarium and Waikiki Zoo. These shows are held at 8:30 and 11 am and provide guests with lessons in hula, coconut husking, basket weaving and tiki carving.

The cultural center also offers an assortment of tours, including full- and half-island tours of O`ahu and a combination of a Polynesian show following a trip on the *Atlantis Submarine*. Private limousine charters are available for parties of eight to 12 people. There is a two-hour minimum on all charters.

The "**Magic of Polynesia**" show, starring John Hirokawa, has been entertaining audiences nightly for more than five years. It is held nightly in a $7.5 million showroom at the Ohana Waikiki Beachcomber Hotel and mixes Polynesian legend with death-defying stunts. The show is sponsored by Roberts Hawaii and tickets can be reserved by calling ☎ 808-971-4321 or 800-831-5541 (toll free), www.robertshawaii.com. There are three options: a 7 pm dinner show, a 7 pm deluxe dinner show and an 8 pm show. Online discounts can save you 20% so get on your computer.

Nightlife

Waikiki is all about nightlife – it's a 24-hour seven-day-a-week party. For a current listing of what's happening, check out the "tgif" – The Great Index to Fun – section of Friday's *Honolulu Advertiser.* The supplement contains a complete list of music venues, nightclubs, movie theaters and restaurants. When you're deep inside Waikiki, you can't walk 10 feet without running into a nightclub.

Following is a condensed list of some awesome nightspots in Waikiki.

The Wy-Bar, 400 Royal Hawaiian Avenue, ☎ 866-346-4679, www.thewylandwaikikihotel.com, at the Wyland Waikiki is a

new, chic place to grab a drink after a day at the beach or, for locals, a great place for a *pau hana*. The Wy-Bar is open nightly from 5 to 10 pm. It offers a cool and contemporary setting with views of the garden swimming pool and its cascading waterfall.

W Honolulu Bar is inside the Diamond Head Grill Restaurant. Wednesday and Thursday nights are reserved for the talents of Zannuck Kapala Lindsey playing contemporary favorites from 9 pm to midnight. The W Honolulu Bar is open from 5:30 pm to midnight.

Lewers Lounge (in the Halekulani, 2199 Kalia Road), ☎ 808-923-2311, is an upscale lounge with a drink menu created by master mixologist Dale DeGroff. The lounge was recently revamped – soda guns and pre-made mixes were 86'd and the staff was re-trained on how to make fantastic drinks with fresh, natural ingredients. Some of the more exotic elixirs include a blackberry julep with a real berry marinade, the ginger lychee caiprissima and your basic martinis, Manhattans and mai tais. Lewers is open nightly from 7:30 pm to 1 am with entertainment from 8:30 to midnight, Sunday through Thursday and 8:30 pm to 12:30 am Friday and Saturday. Valet parking or complimentary self-parking is available.

ALOHA DON HO

Famous Hawaiian crooner Don Ho passed away on April 14, 2007 from heart failure at his Diamond Head home. Ho was born in the little Honolulu neighborhood of Kaka`ako and was of Hawaiian, Chinese, Portuguese, Dutch and German heritage.

In 1962, Ho began playing at Duke's in Waikiki and he became a legendary performer in Hawaii and abroad. He is immediately associated with his hit, *Tiny Bubbles*. Ho, who was called "The King of Waikiki," had 10 children. His family held a memorial service on May 5, 2007 and his ashes were scattered off of Waikiki Beach after a tribute at Kapi`olani Park. A new book, Don Ho's autobiography, called *Don Ho My Music, My Life*, written by the crooner himself and Jerry Hopkins can be ordered at www.bookshawaii.net.

On Friday nights the **Hilton Hawaiian Village** in Waikiki presents "**King's Jubilee**" – a condensed version of Hawaiian history that includes a fire-knife performance and a fireworks display that can be seen throughout much of Waikiki. The Hilton Hawaiian Village's own Hula O` Kapo hula group performs at the event. At press time, the cost was $12 per person for poolside seating and includes one cocktail or beverage. The "King's Jubilee" is held at 6:30 pm at the resort's Super Pool and you may want to get there early as I have seen long lines waiting to get in.

At the **Ala Moana Hotel**, ☎ 808-955-4811, **Rumours Nightclub** is open for dancing on Thursdays (5 pm to 2 am), Fridays (5 pm to 4 am) and Saturdays (9 pm to 4 am). For something more subdued, head to **Aaron's Atop the Ala Moana** cocktail lounge, which is open from 5 to 10 pm Sunday through Thursday and 5 pm to 11 pm on Friday and Saturday nights.

The Cellar, 205 Lewers Street, ☎ 808-923-9952. This club for guests age 18 years and older is one of Waikiki's top dance clubs and has miraculously survived all of the construction of the past couple of years. Catering to college-aged students, The Cellar is open on Tuesday through Saturday until 4 am. Each night has a theme, such as $2 Tuesday, which offers $2 domestic beers, standard cocktails and select wines from 9 pm to closing.

The Wave Waikiki, 1877 Kalakaua Avenue (between Ala Wai Blvd. and Ena Road), ☎ 808-941-0424, www.wavewaikiki.com. The Wave Waikiki is one of Hawaii's top dance clubs. If you're young (but over 21), beautiful and looking to meet someone, this club is for you. It's been around for a while but is consistently busy. They open nightly at 9 pm but most people show up around midnight. The bar closes at 4 am.

Pipeline Café, 805 Pohukaina Street, ☎ 808-589-1999, www.pipelinecafe.net. This is another popular dance club which also has sports events playing on many large screen TVs. Live bands play occasionally. The rules state that after 8 pm no open-toed shoes or tank tops are allow. Happy Hour drink specials start at 9 pm. Open Monday through Saturday 4 pm to 4 am, Sunday 10 pm to 4 am.

Club Femme Nu, 1693 Kapiolani Blvd., ☎ 808-947-3444, calls itself a "gentleman's club," which I guess is a nice way of describing a strip club. The club is legendary among all males in Hawaii. Bachelor parties are not complete without a stop at Femme Nu. Established in 1988, Femme Nu is open daily from 2 pm until 2 am.

Metropolitan Honolulu

At a Glance

This section is divided into two areas – Chinatown and then the rest of Honolulu (excluding Waikiki and Pearl Harbor – those areas have chapters of their own). The "rest of Honolulu" takes the reader from the western section of Waikele and then through Pearl City and `Aiea before hitting the heart of Honolulu. We'll then head to the hills and visit the inland areas of Manoa, Nu`uanu, up the Pali Highway before going down to the ocean again to visit the Kapi`olani area and Diamond Head. There you'll be on the Windward Coast of O`ahu (another chapter!).

IN THIS CHAPTER

Chinatown

Home to some of the best restaurants this side of Hong Kong, Honolulu's Chinatown is the hot spot of the moment – for food, shopping and nightlife. It is definitely worth your time to take a

Incense burning in Chinatown

walking tour of historic Chinatown and visit one of its fabulous restaurants for lunch, dinner or both.

Ensconced between Beretania Street, Nimitz Highway Nu`uanu Avenue and Nu`uanu Stream, Chinatown was first known as the "Chinese Quarter" when Chinese immigrants began to arrive in 1855. The immigrants got jobs as plantation workers for the growing sugar industry. By 1876, there were a total of over 3,900 Chinese immigrants living in Hawaii and that number surpassed 5,000 by 1884.

Following a devastating fire in 1886, the Chinatown that exists today was constructed between 1910 and 1920 and is comprised of many Victorian-style two-story buildings.

The whole area underwent a complete renovation in the 1990s, with millions of dollars invested in making it a more desirable destination. The investment has paid off, as Chinatown is one of the top attractions in Honolulu.

Tours: The Chinese Chamber of Commerce, 70 N. King Street, Suite 202, ☎ 808-533-3181, www.cchi.org, offers guided tours of the area, including the hot acupuncture spots, herbal stores, dim sum parlors and noodle shops. The tour is a great introduction to this fascinating part of O`ahu. Tours begin promptly at 9:30 am every Tuesday at the chamber's headquarters on 42 N. King St. If you have a party of 10 or more, call to see if your group can have an individual tour.

Full of open-air markets, traditional Chinese herb shops and fragrant lei stands, Chinatown also has many historic monuments, trendy bars and lounges with live music, film screenings and art exhibitions. The area is filled with celebrations at the beginning of the year when the Chinese New Year takes place.

For Art Lovers: From 5 to 9 pm on the "First Friday" of every month, Chinatown turns into an art lover's dream where the galleries are open late and the local merchants offer receptions, refreshments and live entertainment. For more details, check out www.firstfridayhawaii.com.

You can download a *Chinatown Walkabout Map* from the Chinatown website, www.chinatownhi.com, which marks all of the points of interest and places to park.

The **Bethel Street Gallery**, 1140 Bethel Street, ☎ 808-524-3552, www.bethelstreetgallery.com, info@bethelstreetgallery.com, can provide you with a very informative brochure, *Gallery Walk & Chinatown*, showing the way for a self-guided tour.

Parking

Parking in Chinatown can be tricky but your best bet may be one of the municipal lots near the King Kamehameha Statue on South King Street between Mililani Street and Punchbowl. There is also parking between Maunakea and Smith Streets and between Bethel Street and Nu`uanu Avenue.

Shopping

Galleries

Chinatown's galleries offer a multitude of shops that you can't find on the Mainland. Some of my favorites include:

The Bethel Street Gallery, 1140 Bethel Street, ☎ 808-524-3552, www.bethelstreetgallery.com, has one of Hawaii's largest artist-owned and -operated galleries with a rotating presentation of local art.

rRed Elephant, 1144 Bethel Street, ☎ 808-545-2468, www.rredelephant.com, is a funky gallery, café and live music venue. rRed Elephant is open from 7 am to 9 pm Monday through Saturday and 9 am to 9 pm on Sundays.

Honolulu
Moanalua Golf Club
Honolulu Country Club
Oahu Country Club
Lyon Arboretum
Queen Emma Summer Palace
Royal Mausoleum State Monument
Bishop Museum
Tenet Art Foundation
Foster Botanical Garden
Dole Cannery Square
CHINATOWN
Aloha Tower
Maritime Museum
Fishermans Wharf
University of Hawaii
Ali Wai Golf Course
Waikiki Aquarium
WAIKIKI
SAND ISLAND
SAND ISLAND PARK
MOKAUEA ISLAND
KEEHI LAGOON BEACH PARK
Keehi Lagoon
KAKA'AKO WATERFRONT PARK
AINA MOANA REC AREA
KAPIOLANI PARK
DIAMOND HEAD STATE MONUMENT
HONOLULU INTERNATIONAL AIRPORT
Mamala Bay
N
HUNTER PUBLISHING
SALT LAKE BLVD
AHUA ST
KAUA ST
SCHOOL ST
LIKE LIKE HWY
MIDDLE ST
LUNALILO HWY
KING ST
KAMEHAMEHA HWY
DILLINGHAM
MAUKA VIADUCT
NIMITZ HWY
SAND ISLAND ACCESS RD
LILIHA ST
NUUANU AV
PALI HWY
ALAKEA ST
PROSPECT
WILDER AVE
BERETANIA ST
KAPIOLANI BLVD
ALA MOANA BLVD
KALAKAUA AV
ALA WAI BLVD
MANOA AVE
UNIVERSITY AVE
DOLE ST
WAIALAE AV
DATE ST
PALOLO AVE
10TH AVE
WILHELMINA RISE
PAHOA AVE
KILAUEA AVE
ALOHEA AV
DIAMOND HEAD RD
H1
61
63
64
66
78
92
I MILE
I KILOMETER
© 2008 HUNTER PUBLISHING, INC

The ARTS at Marks Garage, 1159 Nu`uanu Avenue, ☎ 808-521-2903, www.artsatmarks.com, is a community exhibit and performance space.

Details Gallery, 1142 Bethel Street, ☎ 808-546-8000, has local art as well as hand-knotted rugs by Hanalei Bay Designs.

THIRTYNINEHOTEL, 39 Hotel Street, ☎ 808-599-2552, www.thirtyninehotel.com, is not a hotel, but serves as a community space featuring modern and alternative exhibits, as well as a bar and music at night.

The Pegge Hopper Gallery, 1164 Nu`uanu Avenue, ☎ 808-524-1160, www.peggehopper.com, has original paintings, drawings, posters and limited editions by artist Pegge Hopper. The gallery occasionally displays other artists.

New Life Gallery, 1190 Nu`uanu Avenue, ☎ 808-531-0303. This gallery of paintings, sculpture and crafts celebrating Hawaii is open on First Friday and then by appointment only.

Shops

Bad Sushi! Inc. Boutique, 935 River Street, ☎ 808-548-7874, www.badsushihawaii.com. For cutting-edge and daredevil fashions, check out this funky boutique. Much of the wares are Ninja and Kung-Fu-based, which adds to the fun of browsing this shop. Where else can you find arm strap throwing daggers, throwing star necklaces, lipstick knives and Ninja clocks? Also, ladies, don't forget to pick up some pepper spray (either jogger or lipstick versions). Open daily from noon to 8 pm and until midnight on First Fridays.

Hasr Wine Co., 31 N. Pauahi St 1B, ☎ 808-535-9463, www.hasrwineco.com. This fine wine shop specializes in boutique California wines and also displays local art. It is open Monday through Friday from 11 am to 8 pm.

Simply Grape, 41 Bishop Street, Suite 153 (on Queen Street between Bishop and Alakea), ☎ 808-447-9000, www.simplygrape.net. This wine boutique/store has a large selection of wine and has occasional wine tastings. Check out the website for a coupon and specials.

Into Inc., 40 N. Hotel Street, ☎ 808-536-2211, www.into-honolulu.com. This upscale specialty store offers top-notch traditional home accessories, furnishing and lighting fixtures. They also have an impressive collection of specialty books. Into Inc. is open Tuesday through Saturday from 10 am to 6 pm.

M P Lei Shop, 1145 Maunakea Street, ☎ 808-531-3206. Check out this small 200-square-foot shop for the freshest and most authentic leis on the island.

Maunakea Marketplace, 1120 Maunakea Street, ☎ 808-524-3409, has a little bit of everything crammed into two stories. It's like a local bazaar full of crafts, clothes, jewelry and souvenirs. If you want a real "local" experience, check out this marketplace. The food court is very popular and CHEAP! All sorts of cuisines can be found – Vietnamese, Thai, Italian, Chinese, Japanese and Filipino. Don't be surprised to see fish heads or chicken and goat feet for sale – remember, this is local-style.

Sightseeing

Hawaii Theatre Center, 1130 Bethel Street, ☎ 808-528-0506, www.hawaiitheatre.com. This historic theatre first opened its doors September 6, 1922 and was a popular spot in downtown Honolulu for vaudeville, plays, musicals and silent films until 1984 when the building fell into disrepair and the owners abandoned the land lease. In 1986, the Hawaii Theatre Center, a non-profit corporation was formed to save the theatre from the wrecking ball. After a labor-of-love $20.8 million renovation, the Hawaii Theatre reopened its doors as a 1,400-seat, multi-purpose, state-of-the-art facility in May of 1996. Since then, the theatre building is back to its original grandeur and has become a sightseeing delight in its own manner. In 2005, the theatre was recognized as the "Outstanding Historic Theatre in America" by the League of Historic American Theatres and in 2006, was awarded an Honor Award by the National Trust for Historic Preservation. The Hawaii Theatre is also listed on both the State and National Registers of Historic Places.

Docent-guided tours of the theatre are offered from 11 am to noon every Tuesday of the month. Price is $5. The box office is open from 9 am to 5 pm Tuesday through Saturday. You can also purchase tickets and view the calendar of events anytime on the website.

The **Hawaii State Art Museum** (HiSAM), 250 S. Hotel Street, ☎ 808-586-0900, www.hawaii.gov/sfca. Located on the 2nd floor of the No. 1 Capitol District Building, Hawaii's newest museum is open from 10 am to 4 pm Tuesday through Saturday. The museum highlights exhibitions celebrating the rich artistic history of Hawaii. Wander through the three galleries – the Diamond Head Gallery, the Ewa Gallery, and the Sculpture Gallery. Entrance is free.

GETTING HUNGRY?

Downstairs from the museum is a new restaurant called **Downtown @ the HiSAM**, ☎ 808-536-5900, brought to you by Ed Kenney, the proprietor of the fabulous "town" restaurant in Kaimuki. "Organic first" is the approach Kenney has taken with both restaurants. Downtown @ the HiSAM serves breakfast Monday through Friday from 7 am to 11 am and lunch Monday through Saturday from 11 am to 2 pm On the special "First Friday" art celebration, it's open from 5:30 pm to 8:30 pm.

Where to Eat in Chinatown

Duc's Bistro, 1118 Maunakea Street, ☎ 808-531-6325, www.ducsbistro.com. Duc's is considered the chicest restaurant in the chicest part of Honolulu. The trendy yet affordable bistro serves French and Vietnamese cuisine in a pleasant setting surrounded by contemporary art from Balcony Gallery. Lunch is served from 11:30 am to 2 pm on Monday through Friday and offers such delicacies as escargot, traditional deep-fried spring rolls, noodle dishes pastas and unique entrées. Dinner is served nightly from 5 to 10 pm and Duc's offers the same style appetizers as lunch but adds salads and main courses with a French flair – Seafood Feuillete Joinville in a puff pastry, Delice of Chicken Olympic, fish entrées and interesting "Meals in a Bowl" with soft rice noodles with your choice of fresh fish, spring rolls and Lemongrass Prawns or beef. Validated parking is available. Lunch $$. Dinner $$$.

soul de cuba café (across from the Hawaii Theatre), ☎ 808-545-CUBA, 1121 Bethel Street, www.souldecuba.com. There's more than just Cuban cuisine at this Honolulu hot spot – it's got a small but comfortable and warm setting with refreshing food made from fresh ingredients and "Cuba-inspired" cocktails using the finest premium spirits. Cuban flavors immersed throughout the menu include white, yellow and moro rice, sweet plantains, mangoes, capers, black beans and much more.

Happy Hour is from 4 to 5:30 pm and there are $3 sangrias and $4 mojitos. soul de cuba café is open from 5:30 to 10 pm Monday through Thursday and 5:30 to 10:30 pm Friday and Saturday. $$.

Indigo, 1121 Nu`uanu Avenue, ☎ 808-521-2900, www.indigo-hawaii.com. Indigo opened in 1994 and become a mainstay in Chinatown and, some would say, marked the beginning of the emergence of Chinatown as the trendy spot it has become today. Chef Glenn Chu serves an Eurasian menu in an inviting dining spot with three bars and nightly entertainment. The lunch menu offers dim sum, soup and salads and entrées that include Wokked Buddhist Vegetables, Grilled Dragon Fire Shrimp and Black Mustard- and Black Pepper-crusted Ahi Steak. Dinner includes dim sum, soup, salad, sashimi, entrées similar to the lunch menu, followed by some dim sum smaller plates including a tempura ahi roll and lumpia-wrapped shrimp. Indigo also offers a wine list with over 100 varieties from around the world.

For dessert, don't miss Madame Pele's Chocolate Volcano, which is announced with the banging of a gong! Lunch $$. Dinner $$$.

Bar 35, 35 N. Hotel Street, ☎ 808-537-3535, www.bar35hawaii.com. Open Monday through Saturday 4 pm to 2 am Happy Hour is from 4 to 8 pm Monday through Friday, with any 12 oz. bottle of beer or draft $3. Bar 35 is one of the most happening hot spots in Chinatown with seating for 150 customers, an outdoor garden bar and rock-n-roll background music. Their specialty, though, focuses around the bar as Bar 35 has 110 beers to choose from as well as a full cocktail menu with tropical drinks and lots of wines, ports and sherries. The bar menu is satisfying for the drinking crowd – personal pan pizzas, oyster shooters and oysters on the half-shell. If you want more they'll direct you to Indigo which is around the corner and serves a much larger and more upscale menu. $.

Brasserie Du Vin, 1115 Bethel Street, ☎ 808-546-1115, www.brasserieduvin.com. This premiere wine and tapas bar promises to bring "a little bit of Paris" to Honolulu and it certainly delivers. Everything – from the architecture to the décor with it's dark wood furniture, to the outdoor garden patio – reminds me of my many trips to Paris (but with better weather). Lunch consists of typical Parisian cuisine – olives, tomatoes, exotic cheeses, pommes frites and escargot in a garlic green butter. Lunch is served daily from 11:30 am to 4 pm Dinner is served from 4 pm to closing and the cuisine is similar to lunch offerings. Ask about the day's special and check out the website for special wine and cheese events. Lunch $$. Dinner $$.

Escargot

CHINATOWN GEM

The Green Door Café, 1145 Maunakea Street, ☎ 808-533-0606, is a tiny 12-seat café that offers authentic Singaporean and Malaysian Nonya cuisine, which is full of flavor and spices that will bring you back again and again (if you're lucky enough to have the time!). The wait is worth it, but be sure to bring cash as the café doesn't take credit cards, checks or reservations. The Green Door Cafe is open for lunch from 11 am to 3 pm Tuesday through Sunday and dinner is served from 5:30 to 8 pm. Lunch and Dinner $.

Sushi Sasabune, 1419 S. King Street, ☎ 808-947-3800, is open Monday thru Saturday from 5 to 10 pm and closed on Sundays. This Japanese restaurant and sushi bar has a stellar reputation for excellent fish, great values and friendly service. The sushi is served omakase-style where the chef gives you what he wants – you don't order. Reservations are highly recommended. $$.

Cassis, 66 Queen Street, ☎ 808-545-8100, www.cassishonolulu.com, res@cassishonolulu.com. At the corner of Queen Street and Bethel in Chinatown, this is the newest establishment from famous chef George Mavrothalassitis, who owns Chef Mavro restaurant in Honolulu. Cassis is a fantastic new bistro serving lunch and dinner that brings the chef's signature French-island fusion cuisine to the Chinatown crowd. The sophisticated structure was designed by Mary Philpotts and includes a bar, a private dining room that holds 50 people, and the 295-seat main room. The restaurant is inspired by four places – Cassis (a picturesque harbor village on the Mediterranean), Paris, Alsace and Honolulu, according to Mavrothalassitis. The cuisine contains familiar down-to-earth bistro classics with a contemporary Hawaii regional spin, including a tako-green papaya salad, rotisserie chicken with plum wine sauce, steak frites with curried fries, Manoa salad and li hing mui tarte tatin. Besides lunch and dinner menus, Cassis has a wine bar and pupu menu as well as a "plat du jour." A bonus: From Cassis, you can see the sun setting over Honolulu. It is open for lunch Monday-Friday from 11 am to 2:30 pm. The restaurant serves dinner Monday-Thursday from 5 to 9:30 pm and Friday and Saturday from 5 to 10 pm. The restaurant is closed on Sundays. $$$.

Mei Sum Chinese Dim Sum Restaurant, 65 N. Pauahi Street (at the corner of Smith Street), ☎ 808-531-3268. Try the dim sum at this unremarkable-looking diner that is always full. It is open daily from 7 am to 9 pm. $.

The Rest of Metropolitan Honolulu

Shopping

ONLY IN HAWAII

Na Lima Mili Hulu Noeau, 762 Kapahulu Avenue, ☎ 808-732-0865, is open Monday through Friday 9 am to 9 pm, Saturday 9 am to 5 pm. It is called "The Feather Aunties' Shop." Mary Lou Kekuewa and her daughter Paulette Kahalepuna are the proprietors of Hawaii's only specialty feather shop. The name translates to "skilled hands touch the feathers."

The women have been working for more than 30 years to preserve the ancient art of feather craft. In ancient Hawaii, feathers were a sign of royalty and esteem as birds were in short supply. Capes, cloaks and helmets made from the tine feathers of five or six indigenous birds were used as the sacred insignia of the highest male chiefs in ancient Hawaii.

Auntie Mary Lou is qualified for the job – she was queen of the 1975 Aloha Festival, a statewide cultural event. Mary Lou and her daughter occasionally teach classes in the creation of feather art. Classes are available by appointment at the shop or you may be lucky enough to watch them work their magic during different cultural events held throughout the state.

To see a historic feather art collection, check out the Hawaiian Hall in the Bishop Museum, www.bishopmuseum.org, ☎ 808-847-3511.

Waikele Premium Outlets, 94-790 Lumiaina Street, ☎ 808-656-5656, www.premiumoutlets.com. This is one of the most popular destinations for shoppers as they can find discounted clothes and other attire from such brands as A/X Armani Exchange, Banana Republic, BCBG Max Azria, Barneys New

York Outlet, Brooks Brothers, Calvin Klein, Coach, LeSportsac, MaxMara, Michael Kors, Polo Ralph Lauren, Saks Fifth Avenue, Skechers, Tommy Hilfinger and more. Shopping hours are 9 am to 9 pm Monday through Saturday and 10 am to 6 pm on Sunday. Labor Day, Columbus Day, Thanksgiving and Christmas holiday hours may vary.

To get to the Waikele Premium Outlets, take the H-1 Freeway west from downtown Honolulu past Aloha Stadium. Turn off at exit 7 onto Paiwa Street and head north one block to Lumiaina Street. Turn right on Lumiaina Street, then left into Waikele Premium Outlets. Waikele is about 15 miles west of Honolulu. This outdoor shopping center is huge, so if the heat is getting to you or you have a lot of baggage, a free trolley travels frequently through the center. The Waikele Premium Center's headquarters is next to the Information Center.

The Shops at Dole Cannery Square, 650 Iwilei Road, ☎ 808-548-3700, www.dole-cannery.com. Wondering what to do with an abandoned former pineapple cannery? How about turning it into a shopping center with an 18-screen multiplex movie theater! Located between the airport and Waikiki, this relatively new shopping center contains retail offices, restaurants and a variety of shops. It's not too crowded, has a variety of shops and restaurants and a Longs Drugs. Open daily from 8 am to 6 pm.

Author's Note: There is a K-Mart next to The Shops at Dole Cannery Square. K-Mart is a great place to pick up vacation necessities such as ocean toys or something you may have forgotten, like sunscreen!

Aloha Tower Marketplace, 1 Aloha Tower Drive, ☎ 808-566-2337, www.alohatower.com, is anchored around the Aloha Tower, which was once the tallest building in the islands. The striking, Gothic structure includes four seven-ton clocks from the Howard Clock Company in Boston, one on each of its sides. The shopping center offers more than 70 harbor-front shops and restaurants. This is one of my favorite stops in

Waikiki. The restaurants are fun (I LOVE dining along the ocean) and shops are more personalized and unique. There are no large department stores anchoring the shopping center, just a huge variety of smaller shops.

The tower is open daily and admission is free. Parking is usually easy if you park in the lot fronting the center. If you purchase anything in the center, validate your parking ticket and you'll save some money. Or, on busy nights, it's convenient to valet park. The center has frequent free cultural activities, including ukulele lessons and live entertainment. Taxis are easily available at the Aloha Tower. Or, if you're staying in Waikiki, take the Waikiki Trolley Red Line. If you're coming by bus, ride TheBus numbers 19 or 20 from Waikiki and get off downtown at Nimitz Highway and Alakea Street. You can also take bus routes 2 or 13 and get off at Bishop & Hotel Streets. Walk toward the ocean and cross Nimitz Highway.

Ward Centers, 1200 Ala Moana Blvd., ☎ 808-591-8411, www.wardcenters.com. Containing some 125 shops, 22 restaurants and a 16-screen megaplex, the Ward Centers are one block from Ala Moana Center and are spread out over four blocks. Some of the main shops include Borders Book & Music (where this and my other book *Adventure Guide to Maui* are available), Pier 1 Imports, Nordstrom Rack, Nordstrom Shoes and Sports Authority. The complex actually is composed of several mini-centers: the Victoria Ward Centre, Ward Warehouse, Ward Village Shops, Ward Gateway and Ward Farmers Market. Most shops are open until 10 pm on Fridays and Saturdays. Parking is free and plentiful.

Ala Moana Center, 1450 Ala Moana Blvd. (between Waikiki and downtown O`ahu), ☎ 808-955-9517, www.AlaMoanaCenter.com, has more than 260 shops, restaurants and kiosks. This is the big Kahuna of shopping malls in Hawaii and encompasses over 50 acres, making it the largest open-air shopping center in the United States. The center is a Mecca for all – big spenders can find luxury brands like Chanel and Louis Vuitton, while local favorites include The Gap, Old Navy and several surf shops. The Makai Market Food Court offers fast and cheap cuisine from all corners of the world. Parking is relatively easy (and free!) with several entrances to the mall from Ala Moana Blvd.

Tucked away in a little corner of the Ala Moana Center is **Bonheur** (happiness or good luck in French), ☎ 808-944-8744, a cutting-edge boutique that resembles the Parisian subway. Bonheur is on the mall level and is next to the Patisserie and Quiznos. Besides edgy clothing lines, Bonheur also sells sunglasses, shoes, swimwear and lingerie.

GETTING TO ALA MOANA CENTER

From Waikiki, you can take TheBus routes 8, 19, 20, 42 or 58; from the North Shore take TheBus route 52 and from Honolulu International Airport, take TheBus route 19 or 20. The Ala Moana Shopping Shuttle provides transportation between the center and Waikiki seven days a week, every eight minutes. Look for the Pink Line trolleys throughout Waikiki. It costs $2 each way.

Reyns, ☎ 808-949-5929, www.reyns.com, is located in Ala Moana Center and is one of the locals' favorite spots to get high-quality Aloha wear.

The Ala Moana Center is open from 9:30 am to 9 pm Monday through Saturday and 10 am to 7 pm on Sunday. Ala Moana is closed on Thanksgiving Day and Christmas Day.

ONLY IN HAWAII

One of my favorite shops on the islands, **Martin & MacArthur**, www.MartinandMacArthur.com, is a small chain unique to Hawaii and definitely not to be missed. The upscale home furnishings marketplace offers a fascinating array of items that represent the best of island living. They offer a great variety of Hawaiian-made items from heritage quilts to homemade wooden gifts made of exotic Hawaiian woods. In O`ahu, the company has a shop in the Ala Moana Center as well as a branch at the Hyatt Regency Waikiki. They also have a furniture showroom, ☎ 808-845-6688, at 1815 Kahai Street in Honolulu. There are also two shops in Maui.

Hilo Hattie's – The Store of Hawaii, 700 North Nimitz Highway, ☎ 808-535-6500, www.hilohattie.com. Hilo Hattie's is an institution among visitors to Hawaii and few people leave the islands without visiting one of their several outlets across the state. Hilo Hattie's makes it very accessible since they provide shuttles that venture through Waikiki, picking up and dropping off customers. This is the spot you want to hit to pick up souvenirs and gifts for friends and family. Hilo Hattie's has a huge selection of Hawaiian-made goods, aloha apparel, T-shirts and jewelry. In fact, it is the largest retailer of Hawaiian island lifestyle products in all of Hawaii. The "aloha spirit" is alive and well here from the moment you walk in and are greeted with a shell lei to the final "mahalo" as you leave the store with your goods.

FARMERS' MARKET

The island's largest farmers' market is held Saturdays from 7:30 to 11 am at Kapi`olani Community College, 4303 Diamond Head Road, ☎ 808-848-2074, www.hfbf.org/FarmersMarketKCC.html. The market is sponsored by the Hawaii Farm Bureau Federation, a non-profit organization supporting Hawaii's farmers and ranchers. Check out the website (it changes every week) to see the day's specials along with a detailed list of all participating vendors and their location at the market. A big plus – parking is free! A local-style breakfast is usually offered by one of the vendors for a small price. And if you want to take a little bit of the Farmers' Market home, you can purchase *The Hawaii Farmers' Market Cookbook* for $13.

Aloha Stadium Swap Meet, 99-500 Salt Lake Blvd., ☎ 808-486-6704, www.alohastadiumswapmeet.net. This is Hawaii's largest swap meet with over 700 vendors, crafters and artists displaying a serious hodge-podge of products. The swap meet is held from 6 am to 3 pm on Wednesday, Saturday and Sunday and, with an admission price of only $1, it's an easy way to kill an hour or so. To get there from Waikiki, take the H-1 Freeway west to the Stadium Exit 1E.

Aloha Rag, 1221 Kapi`olani Blvd., ☎ 808-589-2050, www.aloharag.com/highseas/assets/images/home/htm#shop. Don't be fooled by the name – the duds here are hardly rags. The boutique has men's and women's brands like Badgley Mischka, John Galliano, Mark Jacobs, Tom Ford and Alexander McQueen. Aloha Rag also carries shoes and accessories of the same caliber. The boutique is open Monday through Saturday 11 am to 8 pm and Sundays from 11 am to 6 pm.

Lai Fong, 1118 Nu`uanu Street, ☎ 808-537-3497, is a family-owned antique store that specializes in Chinese antiques and other collectibles from around the world. The store has been owned by the Lai Fong family for nearly 80 years. This is a fabulous place to view or buy authentic Chinese silk, brocades and custom dresses. They also carry everything from rare antiques to turn-of-the-century postcards.

★★★**Bailey's Antiques & Aloha Shirts**, 517 Kapahulu Avenue, ☎ 808-734-7628, www.aloha-shirts.com, has one of the largest vintage aloha-shirt collections in Honolulu, as well as nearly new aloha shirts and many other vintage treasures, from clothing and sheet music to jewelry and household items. Altogether they have over 15,000 aloha shirts that are divided into four sections – used, new, vintage and specialty. This is the place to look for Hawaiiana – the staff is friendly and the store is stuffed with goods. Bailey's Antiques & Aloha Shirts is open daily from 10 am to 6 pm.

The Closet Chick, 2013 S. King Street, ☎ 808-942-2442. For the vintage-loving wahine (girl or woman in Hawaiian!), this shop has high-end items at low-end prices. Discover great vintage clothing in this nicely organized shop or grab some fantastic jewelry, handbags and other accessories. Check out the $5 rack or look for the 50%-off sale held monthly. Park off of McCully Street in the former McCully Chop Suey parking lot.

The Butik,1067 Kapi`olani Blvd., Suite A-3 (at the base of the new Public Storage building), ☎ 808-593-4484. This trendy shop is known for its collection of dresses – lots of dresses. Co-owner Lan Chung is also one of the popular Fighting Eel clothing line designers. The shop also has teeny bikinis, handmade jewelry and handbags.

Rockabella, 510 Pi`ikoi Street, Suite 200, ☎ 808-597-8715. This chic boutique has high-end items like Dior sunglasses, a wide selection of trendy jeans and a refreshing collection of t-shirts. Free parking is at the back of the store and you can enter from the Kona Street side. Rockabella is only a five-minute walk from Ala Moana Shopping Center.

Sightseeing

★★★**Bishop Museum**, 1525 Bernice Street, ☎ 808-847-3511, www.bishipmusuem.org. Do not miss this museum! Businessman Charles Reed Bishop founded the Bishop Museum in 1889 to honor his late wife, Princess Bernice Pauahi Bishop, the last direct descendant of King Kamehameha I. Completed in 1890, the museum is considered the preeminent keeper of the natural and cultural history of the Pacific islands. The museum's collections reach far back into ancient Hawaiian and Polynesian history and contain some 24 million items. Don't miss the glorious royal feather capes, each made with hundreds of thousands of red and gold feathers and worn by the great kings. The museum's newest exhibit is the Science and Adventure Center where visitors can explore 30 state-of-the-art interactive exhibits, including a man-made, walk-in volcano that erupts several times a day and a wave-making tank.

From Waikiki, you can get to the Bishop Museum by heading southeast on Kalakaua Avenue (toward Diamond Head) for about 1½ miles and then turning left on Kapahulu Avenue. Follow the signs for H-1 West and get onto to the Highway. Exit at exit 20A and merge onto HI-63 North/Likelike Hwy, then turn right at Bernice Street.

To get to the Bishop Museum from the Honolulu Airport, merge onto H-1 Eastbound via the ramp to Waikiki/Honolulu. Take exit

20A at the Likelike Highway (Hwy 63) and follow the Likelike Highway for a few hundred yards, then turn right at Bernice Street.

The Bishop Museum is open from 9 am to 5 pm every day of the year except Christmas Day. Admission is $15.95 for adults, $12.95 for ages four to 12 and seniors age 65 and over. Members of the Bishop Museum and children age three and under are free. The Bishop Museum is on TheBus (take the #2 or City Express B "School St/Middle St" bus and exit at the intersection of School and Kapalama Streets) and the Waikiki Trolley routes.

Located across from the Aloha Tower Marketplace is the **Hawaii Maritime Center**, ☎ 808-536-6373, at Pier 7 of the Honolulu Harbor, www.bishopmuseum.org. Open daily (except Christmas Day) from 8:30 am to 5 pm, the center offers an interesting view of Hawaii's maritime heritage, from the voyages of ancient Polynesian mariners to the ramifications of the jet age upon the islands. The site itself is a historical monument as it is located on the spot where King David Kalakaua once had his Royal Boat House.

Built in 1988, the museum contains a replica of an ancient sailing canoe (named the *Hokule`a*) and visitors have an opportunity to explore the 266-foot *Falls of Clyde*, the world's only four-masted iron-hulled sailing ship. A rare skeleton of a humpback whale hangs in the central atrium. The center caters to kids and has a series of interactive computer sites where kids (and adults!) can learn about voyaging. The atmosphere of the museum is pleasant, with large window views of Honolulu Harbor and the Aloha Tower. Admission is $7.50 for adults; $4.50 for children ages four to 12 and free for children under age four. The Center is open daily from 8:30 am to 5 pm.

UNDER RENOVATION

The popular *Falls of Clyde*, the world's only four-masted, full-rigged ship left remaining afloat, has been under renovation and is expected to be opened by the time you read this.

With the help of a $300,000 grant from the Save America's Treasures program, the project began in 2002 with the goal of stabilizing, restoring and maintaining the ship in accordance with standards approved by the National Park Service and the State of Hawaii Historic Preservation officer.

Built in 1878 in Port Glasgow, Inverclyde, Scotland, the *Falls of Clyde* was launched as the first of eight iron-hulled four-masted ships built for Wright and Breakenridge's Falls line. She was named after a waterfall up the River Clyde. The *Falls of Clyde* was 266.1 feet in length, with a 40-foot beam and a 23.5-ft depth of hold. The ship registered at 1,807 gross tons.

In 1963, the bank holding the mortgage on *Falls of Clyde* decided to sell her to be sunk as part of a breakwater at Vancouver, British Columbia. After much haggling, the ship was bought by a private company. The ship arrived in Honolulu on November 18, 1963. The *Falls of Clyde* was given to the Bishop Museum and opened to the public in 1968. In 1973, it was listed on the National Register of Historic Places as a National Historic Landmark.

**`Iolani Palace**, 364 S. King St, ☎ 808-522-0832 or 808-538-1471, www.iolanipalace.org. `Iolani Palace is one of Honolulu's most honored landmarks and holds the distinction of being the one and only Royal Palace on United States soil. The royal residence, in downtown Honolulu, was built in 1882 by King David Kalakaua and last occupied by Hawaiian royalty in 1893 by deposed Queen Lili`uokalani.

A tour of the two-story American Florentine-style palace takes you back more than a hundred years to the days when King David Kalakaua and Queen Lili`uokalani entertained European royalty. In fact, King Kalakaua was the first monarch to circumnavigate the globe and the palace displays many of the treasured gifts bestowed on him by other monarchs. The palace had indoor plumbing, electric lights and telephones – high-tech luxuries in those days. On the down side, `Iolani Palace was the official residence of Hawaii's last two reigning monarchs, King Kalakaua and his sister Queen Lili`uokalani.

In 1895, the Queen was imprisoned for nearly eight months for her alleged role in a failed coup attempt. The tour immerses visitors into the trials and tribulations of King Kalakaua and Queen Lili`uokalani and shows you where the Queen spent her time in a modest second-floor bedroom while being exiled in the palace. A large quilt made out of remnants of gowns, hat bands and other bright fabrics is displayed in the "famous" bedroom where the Queen spent her days in exile.

From 1893 to 1968, the palace served as Hawaii's official capitol.

`Iolani Palace is open Tuesdays through Saturday and the first Sunday of the month.

A 90-minute docent-guided tour is held every 20 minutes from 9 to 11:15 am. The tour includes a visit to the first floor where the state apartments are located, the second floor, which is home to the private quarters, and the basement, containing the exhibit gallery.

The Exhibit Gallery: A tour of the gallery is a rare chance to see ancient regalia, royal crowns, jewelry, diplomatic orders, the Chamberlain's Office, the China Storage Room, the Palace Kitchen and a history gallery.

Self-guided audio tours are available every 10 minutes from 11:45 am to 3:30 pm and include entrance to the first floor, the second floor and the basement. Self-guided tours of the gallery are available from 9 am to 4:30 pm.

The grand tour costs $20 for adults and $5 for children five to 12. Reservations are highly recommended and children under five are not allowed. The audio tour costs $12 for adults and $5 for children. Kids under five are not allowed. The self-guided gallery tour is $6 for adults and $3 for children five to 12. Children under five are welcome at no charge. Metered parking is available on the grounds and vehicles can enter the museum at Likelike Street.

The original statue of Kamehameha the Great, so named as the first warrior to unite all of the Hawaiian Islands, was temporarily lost at sea during its transport from Europe and now stands in front of the Kapa`au Courthouse in North Kohala on the Big Island. The replica on King Street, across from `Iolani Palace, is a popular photographic attraction, especially on June 11 – King Kamehameha Day – when the statue is draped with dozens of 30-foot leis. King Kamehameha Day is a state holiday in Hawaii.

Mission Houses Museum, 553 S. King Street, ☎ 808-531-0481, www.missionhouses.org. Visitors interested in the history of missions in Hawaii will appreciate an escorted walking tour of the original frame homes of the Protestant missionaries who settled in Hawaii in 1820. On the tour, visitors can view three of the original homes that were built in New England between 1821 and 1841 and then shipped to Hawaii. The tour is a great way to see the lifestyles and hardships of the missionaries. In those days, the buildings served as the Sandwich Islands mission, Hawaii's first Christian mission.

The museum was established in 1920 by the Hawaiian Mission Children's Society, a private, non-profit organization and genealogical society. It includes the three beautifully restored houses and a research library that provides a unique glimpse into 19th-century Hawaii.

The three houses are called the Frame House, the Printing Office and the Chamberlain House. During your visit, you'll see a working replica of the printing press and take a historic walking tour that follows the footsteps of missionaries, Hawaiians and merchants in the downtown district.

The general hours for the museum are Tuesday through Saturday 10 am to 4 pm. Daily tours at 11 am, 1 and 2:45 pm show visitors how these 19th-century pioneers lived as they shared their faith with the native tribes from the village of Honolulu. The Museum Shop is open Tuesday through Saturday from 10 am to 4 pm. General admission is $10, with $2 discounts for senior citizens and members of the military.

The **Hawaii State Capitol**, renowned for its fascinating architecture, is a short walk from `Iolani Palace. Head toward the mountains and you'll run into the Capitol building. In-depth tours of the palace interior can be arranged by making reservations at ☎ 808-522-0832. If you don't have time for the full tour, stop by the gift shop, called the Palace Shop, ☎ 808-532-1050, for some souvenirs.

For recorded exhibition information about the **Honolulu Academy of Arts**, call ☎ 808-532-8700 or 808-532-8701 or visit www.honoluluacademy.org.

The Academy, at 900 South Beretania Street, contains six garden courtyards with over 30 galleries highlighting Asian, American and European art. It was founded in 1927 and contains Hawaii's largest collection of fine arts with more than 35,000 diverse pieces ranging from ancient Greece in the third millennium BC to contemporary American and European masterpieces.

To reach the Academy, get on the H-1 freeway from Waikiki and take the Lunalilo St exit and then a left at Ward Avenue. Take another left on Kinau Street and you'll see the Academy. For parking, the Art Center Lot is open from 7 am to 11 pm Monday through Saturday and 10 am to 6 pm on Sunday. Another lot at 1035 Kinau Street is closed to the public, but open for Academy patrons, during regular museum hours. Parking fees are $3 for every four hours with validation or a $4 flat fee in the evenings.

The Honolulu Academy of Arts is open Tuesday through Saturday 10 am to 4:30 pm and Sunday 1 pm to 5 pm. Admission is $10 for adults, $5 for students, seniors and military and free for Academy members and children 12 and under accompanied by an adult. Guided tours are available at 11 am Tuesday through Saturday and at 1:15 pm on Sunday.

First Wednesdays: Many of O`ahu's museums and art galleries offer one day a month where admission is free. At the Honolulu Academy of Arts, the doors are open to all on the first Wednesday of the month.

SHOP THE ACADEMY

The Academy Shop, ☎ 808-532-8703 or 800-829-5211, at the Honolulu Academy of Arts is in the Luce Pavilion Complex and, with 1,500 square feet of showroom, provides a huge selection of gifts, books, stationery, prints, posters and collectibles. If something catches your eye and you decide, once you're at home, that you want to purchase it, go to the checkout form at data.honoluluacademy.org or e-mail academyshop@honoluluacademy.org. The Academy Shop is open Tuesday through Saturday from 10 am to 4:30 pm and Sunday from 1 to 5 pm.

Saving $$ at the Academy: The Bank of Hawaii sponsors Bank of Hawaii Sundays every third Sunday of the month. On this day, the Academy has free admission and opens two hours earlier so you can enjoy the arts from 11 am until 5 pm Admission to the Academy is also free on the first Wednesday of the month. Mark your calendar!

AUTHOR'S CHOICE

★★★**Shangri La**. Tours are arranged through the Honolulu Academy of Arts. Your ticket to Shangri La also includes entrance to the Honolulu Academy of Arts. A visit to Shangri La is a once-in-a-lifetime opportunity to get an insight into the magnificent mind of a truly independent woman.

For tickets to Shangri La, call ☎ 1-866-DUKE-TIX Tuesday through Saturday between 8 am and 4:30 pm HST or visit www.shangrilahawaii.org or www.honoluluacademy.org. You can also e-mail the Honolulu Academy of Arts at shangrilatickets@honoluluacademy.org.

Like many people who live on the islands, Doris Duke visited Hawaii on vacation, became seduced by the lush scenery, exotic lifestyle and refreshing ocean views and decided to stay forever.

Her first trip to Honolulu was at the conclusion of a world-wide honeymoon in 1935, with husband James Cromwell, that included visits to the Middle East, India and south Asia. Once the couple made it to Honolulu, Duke turned what was supposed to be a two-week visit into a four-month stay and, eventually, an island home.

Doris Duke

She found herself enamored with the Islamic art and culture she viewed during her honeymoon travels as well as smitten with the island life. She combined the two cultures in 1937 when she started building Shangri La, her own personal paradise overlooking the Pacific Ocean and Diamond Head. Designed in collaboration with architect Marion Sims Wyeth, nearly every room in Shangri La contains a unique combination of media – wood, paper, enamel, stone, glass, ceramic, metal and fiber.

Doris Duke was able to travel extensively and collect such an impressive collection due to an inheritance from her wealthy father. By the time the future heiress was born in New York City on November 22, 1912, her father had already amassed two large fortunes, one from tobacco products and the other from hydroelectric power. When her father died in 1925, Duke, an only child, became the primary heir of his fortune.

Upon her death in 1993 at age 80, the Doris Duke Foundation for Islamic Art (DDFIA) was created in her will to promote the study, understanding and preservation of Islamic art and culture. In partnership with the Honolulu Academy of Arts, Shangri La was opened to the public in November of 2002 for private tours.

A visit to Shangri La is an amazing privilege. Located on five acres of oceanfront property, the property contains more than 3,500 objects from Duke's unfathomable collection of

Islamic art. Each room has a different theme with pieces collected from several visits to Iran, Morocco, Turkey, Spain, Syria, Egypt and India. This is a stunning task when you consider these pieces were collected and shipped in the 1930s and 40s. For instance, a visit to the Taj Majal inspired Duke to commission a marble bed and bathroom suite at Shangri La.

The main house is approximately 14,000 square feet and was built around a central patio open to the sky. Of the many homes that Duke had across the country, Shangri La is the only estate that she built from the ground up and filled from the inside out. She spent nearly 60 years collecting artifacts, which she transformed into massive painted ceilings, elaborately carved doorways, colorful textiles and ceramics. In fact, one-fifth of her collection is comprised of ceramics. Duke also favored decorative arts of the 17th through 19th centuries, including those made during the reigns of the Ottoman, Mughal, Safavid and Qajar dynasties.

The Playhouse with cascading pools

Although several of the rooms are closed to the public due to ongoing renovations, some of the most fascinating are the Turkish Room, the Damascus Room, with its ornate wood interior originally made in the 18th century for a wealthy mercantile home, the Mughal Garden and the "Playhouse." The Playhouse, across from the house and along the ocean shoreline, is a reduced-scale version of the 17th-century Chihul Sutan, a royal pavilion in Isfahan, Iran.

During the tour, guides highlight many of the estate's special features, such as a glass wall that can, with the hit of a switch, disappear into the ground using an Otis elevator mechanism. A similar wall on the other side of the house provides an open-air atmosphere when both walls disappear, allowing the trade winds and the sounds of the ocean to fill the home.

Doris Duke was an interesting character – she was friends with the legendary Kahanamoku surfing brothers and frequently entertained them at her home. But, she didn't build to impress;

few people were allowed in and she had a very loyal staff. She followed her father's advice to "trust no one."

Honolulu is very fortunate to have such a spectacular collection on display. A visit to this tranquil yet exotic locale is a wonderful addition to a visit to O`ahu and a great opportunity for locals to see the island in a different light.

Shangri La is open to the public for guided, small group tours from Wednesday through Saturday. The first tour begins at 8:30 am with the final tour starting at 1:30 pm. During busy seasons, you might want to reserve tickets in advance. Tours begin at the Honolulu Academy of Arts with a viewing of the "Arts of the Islamic World" exhibition and a short video introducing visitors to Shangri La. The tours then depart in minivans from the Honolulu Academy of Arts for the 15-minute drive to Shangri La (located in a quiet neighborhood). Tours last approximately 2½ hours, with 1½ hours on-site at the property. Admission is $25 and includes admission to the Honolulu Academy of Arts.

BUILT UP AN APPETITE?

The Pavilion Café, ☎ 808-532-8734, in the Honolulu Academy of Arts, is a convenient and pleasant spot to grab lunch before or after your tour of Shangri La. Open from 11:30 am to 1:30 pm Tuesday through Saturday, the Café overlooks lovely gardens and sculptures by Jan Kaneko and is shaded by a 70-year-old monkey pod tree. Chef Mike Nevin uses fresh island ingredients to create daily specials and the menu is comprised of sandwiches, salads, entrées and desserts. The Café also offers a generous selection of teas as well as beer and wine.

Honolulu Zoo, 151 Kapahulu Ave., ☎ 808-971-7171, www.honoluluzoo.org, is the only zoo in Hawaii and presents visitors with a unique look at some of the island's 1,300 animals, representing 300 species. In the middle of Kapi`olani Park, the zoo is home to an exciting variety of animal habitats, including the African Savanna, the Tropical Forest and Islands of the Pacific. This is the only US zoo originating from a King's grant of royal lands to the people. There is also a children's petting zoo and special seasonal programs. In the summer, a special summer concert, "Starbucks' Wildest Show in Town" takes place on Wednesday nights. The Honolulu Zoo is open 9 am to 4:30 pm Tuesday through Saturday. Admission is $8 for adults, $4 for kids six to 12 and $1 for children five and under.

**Kapi`olani Park**, 3840 Paki Ave., ☎ 808-971-2504, was named after the wife of King David Kalakaua, who reigned over Hawaii from 1874 to 1891. He made land grants available to the people of Hawaii in 1876 and in the same year a "Kapi`olani Park Association" was formed to manage the 108-acre park. The park was named Queen Kapi`olani Park in 1877. This is a fantastic place to spend the afternoon, have a picnic and just go for a brisk walk or jog.

North of Honolulu

The area north of Honolulu includes Nu`uanu Valley, Manoa, Tantalus and the Punchbowl Crater. A visit to these spots takes a couple of minutes and will instantly transfer you from a busy city to breathtaking scenery and gorgeous views of the Honolulu skyline with the Pacific Ocean in the background. O`ahu has three spectacular drives that go through tunnels built into the mountains. The H-3 freeway is one of the most scenic freeways in the world – it crosses the island by ascending through the rain forest and then tunneling for a mile through the near-vertical lush mountain cliffs, then descending on amazing mountainside bridges into Kane`ohe. The second scenic route is on the Likelike (Lee-kee lee-kee) Highway (Hwy 63), which also runs from Honolulu to Kane`ohe. The third route is the Pali Highway (Hwy 61), which goes past the amazing Nu`uanu Pali Lookout and takes you through two tunnels before ending in Kailua.

INTERSTATE HIGHWAY ON AN ISLAND?

H3 is Honolulu's newest highway and is an Interstate Highway also known as the John A. Burns Freeway. John A. Burns was the first governor of Hawaii and, in 1962, was elected to the first of three consecutive terms. Although the thoroughfare is called an "Interstate," this highway obviously doesn't go between states. Write it off to one of the idiosyncrasies of Hawaiian logic.

The H3 is also notorious for being one of the most expensive highways (1.3 billion federal tax dollars) in the country. Nonetheless, it's a beautiful drive full of lush foliage, quirky tunnels and fantastic views. The H3 begins in Halawa (not far from the Honolulu Airport) and can be accessed from H1, Route 78 and H201. The highway climbs the mountains dividing the island and bisects the Ko`olau mountain range. The last exit of the H3 is in Kailua on the Windward side of the island and will lead you to Kaneohe Marine Corps Base. Altogether, the H3 is 15.3 miles long and takes about 20 minutes to drive from start to finish.

Nu`uanu Avenue & the Pali Highway (Highway 61)

★★★**National Memorial Cemetery of the Pacific**, 2177 Puowaina Drive, ☎ 808-532-3720. Often referred to as the "Punchbowl," this breathtaking memorial lies in the middle of Puowaina Crater, an extinct volcano. Puowaina is roughly translated in Hawaiian to mean "Consecrated Hill" or "Hill of Sacrifice." People from all over the world come to visit this site as it is the final resting place for 33,259 victims of three wars – World War II, the Korean War and the Vietnam War.

The Punchbowl was officially dedicated on September 2, 1949, on the fourth anniversary of V-J Day. This massive and impressive cemetery is much more than just a place for memorials. The engraved names of 18,094 World War II heroes missing in action are honored in the 10 "Courts of the Missing" that flank the amazing staircase. The cemetery is one of Hawaii's top attractions and is a unique place for visitors to reflect on the meaning of war and pay homage to those who made the ultimate sacrifice for their country. At the center of the cemetery is a fascinating series of tile montages describing all of the attacks on the United States prior to the Vietnam era.

From the time you enter the memorial, you will be impressed by the well-manicured and very orderly condition of the cemetery, which lies on both sides of an impressive memorial. Parking is minimal but I've never had a problem. Once you park, walk up

View of Honolulu from the Punchbowl lookout

the white steps to view the fascinating images of wartime battles rendered in mosaics. Once you're done with this intriguing display, drive over to the Punchbowl lookout, which provides visitors with a can't-be-beat view of Honolulu skyscrapers with the Pacific Ocean in the background and Diamond Head to the left. One of my all-time favorite photos was taken from this lookout!

The National Memorial Cemetery of the Pacific is open daily from 8 am to 5:30 pm September 30 through March 1, 8 am to 6:30 pm March 2 through September 29 and 7 am to 7 pm on Memorial Day. The Administration Office is at the entrance to the cemetery. Visitors will find a goldmine of historical information and maybe even a chance to talk to one of the veterans who occasionally oversee the office. Admission is free.

Mind Your Manners: Visitors to the National Memorial Cemetery of the Pacific are requested to conduct themselves in keeping with the dignity and sacredness of the cemetery. Do not litter, cut, break or injure trees, shrubs or plants or use the cemetery as a picnic area.

Head northeast from downtown Honolulu up Nu`uanu Avenue towards the Nu`uanu Pali Lookout and you will find the 20-acre **Foster Botanical Garden**, ☎ 808-522-7066, at 50 N. Vineyard Blvd., between Liliha and Maunakea Streets.

The garden has been open to the public since 1931 and contains tropical plants collected from around the world over a 150-year period. The garden was started in 1853 when Queen Kalama leased a small area of land to William Hillebrand, a young German doctor and botanist. Hillebrand and his wife spent 20 years in Hawaii planting trees and plants before returning to Germany and publishing *Flora of the Hawaiian Islands* in 1888.

Orchid display at the botanical gardens

The property was later sold to Captain Thomas and Mary Foster who continued to develop the garden. When Mrs. Foster passed away in 1930, the 5½-acre site was bequeathed to the City and County of Honolulu as a public garden.

The garden has since expanded to 13½ acres and includes 26 specimens of designated exceptional trees, a large palm collection, a primitive cycad garden and a hybrid orchid collection. More than 75,000 visitors visit the garden annually and the site has been entered on the National Register of Historic Places. Guided tours are available and admission is $5 for adults and $1 for children six to 12.

For information about Honolulu Botanical Gardens, contact: Department of Parks and Recreation, 50 N. Vineyard Blvd., Honolulu, HI 96817, ☎ 808-522-7060, hbg@honolulu.gov, www.co.honolulu.hi.us/parks/hbg.

Royal Mausoleum State Monument, 2261 Nu`uanu Avenue, ☎ 808-587-0300. While in Nu`uanu, check out this fascinating chapel where Hawaii's Kamehameha and Kalakaua royal families were laid to rest before they were moved to private vaults. Located on 10 acres, the mausoleum now serves as a chapel and showcases a restored koa wood interior and altar. The mausoleum is open for viewing from 8 am to 4 pm Monday through Friday.

Queen Emma Summer Palace, 2913 Pali Highway, ☎ 808-595-3167 Museum, ☎ 808-595-3603 office/gift shop, www.daughtersofhawaii.org, doh1903@hawaii.rr.com.

Near the lush, green Nu`uana Valley, this secluded royal getaway was used by Queen Emma (1836-1885), King Kamehameha IV and their son, Prince Albert, as an escape from the summer heat in Honolulu. Born in 1836, Queen Emma represented the emerging cosmopolitan culture of the islands as she was descended from both Hawaiian chieftains and from John Young, an Englishman who became the friend and advisor of the great Kamehameha I.

DAUGHTERS OF HAWAII

The Daughters of Hawaii was founded in 1903 by seven daughters of American Protestant missionaries. They were all born in Hawaii and were citizens of the Hawaiian Kingdom before annexations and foresaw the inevitable loss of much of the Hawaiian culture. The women founded the organization "to perpetuate the memory and spirit of old Hawaii and of historic facts, and to preserve the nomenclature and correct pronunciation of the Hawaiian language." Nowadays, membership is open to any woman who is directly descended from a person who lived in Hawaii prior to 1880, with no restrictions on race. Membership at press time was about 1,400 women.

This beautiful and historic mountain palace is only a five-minute drive from Central Honolulu and is definitely worth a visit. Six 14-foot-tall Doric columns mark the entrance to the palace. Royal antiques and furnishings stand in their original places. The building, built in 1848, was slated to be demolished but was saved by the Daughters of Hawaii, who raised money to restore the Victorian-era home. The house was named Hanaiakamalama, after the ancestral home of John Young II, the son of the Englishman who was an advisor to Kamehameha. Queen Emma inherited the palace in 1857.

Nowadays the restored and furnished home offers a glimpse into the lifestyle of the Hawaiian Monarchy. The restored house has a fabulous collection of household furnishings and personal effects of Queen Emma and her family, Hawaiian artifacts and Hawaiian quilts. One of the highlights of the tour is a view of the Queen's Koa wood sleigh bed inlaid with brass and mother-of-pearl and a canoe-shaped cradle handcrafted from koa, kou, milo and kamani woods – an insightful reminder of Prince Albert who died in 1862 at the age of four.

In her later days, Queen Emma spent much of her time at the summer home caring for the garden. After her death, the property was sold to the Hawaiian government and was close to being demolished before the Daughters of Hawaii took over in 1915.

Laua`e fern

The gift shop in the back has some treasures you won't see anywhere else on the island. The palace, which sits in an unusual spot on the freeway but still in a neighborhood, has rental facilities and would be a beautiful setting for a wedding. There is a separate meeting room, which seats 100 people and has a stage and kitchen. The adjacent gardens, consisting of lokelani rose, kukui and laua`e and palapalai fern, with a picnic area, are an added bonus. The palace is maintained by the Daughters of Hawaii who have lovingly preserved this summer retreat in its charming Hawaiian-Victorian setting.

The home/museum is open daily from 9 am to 4 pm and is closed on major holidays. Admission is $6 for adults and $1 for children 17 and under. The senior discount is $4. If you have a group of 20 or more, reservations are recommended.

**★★★Nu`uanu Pali Lookout**. Commonly called the Pali Lookout, this is the site of King Kamehameha the Great's victory in battle over O`ahu chief Kalanikupule in 1795, forcing his opponents off the rocky precipice to their deaths below. Kamehameha's victory ignited the process of unifying all the Hawaiian Islands. Nu`uanu Pali Lookout (which translates to "Cool Height Cliff") overlooks the 985-foot cliffs of the Ko`olau Mountain Range. From the Lookout, you'll see majestic views of Windward O`ahu.

To get to the Pali Lookout, take HI east bound from Waikiki. Then take the Pali Highway (Route 61) via Nu`uanu Pali Drive. Follow the signs to the Lookout. There is lots of parking and admission is free. The Lookout is open from 9 am to 4 pm (weather permitting). And I'm warning you – it can get really windy up there. Hold on to your hats and small children!

The Manoa Area

Tea Stop: If you go to Manoa Valley, a stop at the **Waioli Tea Room & Bakery**, 2950 Manoa Road (corner of O`ahu Avenue and Manoa Road), ☎ 808-988-5800, www.thewaiolitearoom.net, is a wonderful and refreshing break during your drive around the island. Enjoy the refreshing afternoon tea service. Afternoon tea is served from 10:30 am to 3:30 pm by reservation only. Lunch is served from 10:30 am to 3:30 pm Monday through Friday. On Saturday and Sunday, breakfast is served from 8 am to noon and lunch from noon to 3:30 pm

Just north of Honolulu and on your way to the Contemporary Museum of Art, the Tantalus Rainforest in Makiki is a fresh change of scenery from the busy city. Located at 2,013 feet, the **Tantalus Rainforest and Mountain** offer visitors panoramic views of the Honolulu skyline while surrounded by an array of wildlife, flowers and exotic fruit trees.

Contemporary Museum of Art, Makiki, 2411 Makiki Heights Drive, ☎ 808-526-0232, www.tcmhi.org. This is my favorite museum on O`ahu – it's located away from the city on 3½ acres of terraced sculpture gardens with striking views of Honolulu. The museum is a peaceful place to spend the afternoon. The exhibits are always fascinating and the atmosphere is open and airy. The museum hosts exhibitions by some of the world's most renowned contemporary artists and one of the highlights is a permanent exhibit by David Hockney inspired by Maurice Ravel's opera *L`Enfant et les Sortilèges* (The Child and the Bewitched).

The Contemporary Museum of Art has an award-winning café that serves up some delectable dishes. The museum is open from Tuesday through Saturday 10 am to 4 pm and Sunday noon to

4 pm; closed Mondays and most holidays. Admission is $5 for adults and $3 for seniors and students. Children under 12 are admitted for free. Parking is free and plentiful.

AN EXTENSION OF THE MUSEUM

The First Hawaiian Bank at 999 Bishop Street in Honolulu has a special gallery highlighting Hawaiian artists sponsored by the Contemporary Museum of Art. The museum exhibits art created by resident artists, former residents of Hawaii and artists who have created a body of work in the islands. Admission is free and the museum can be viewed on Monday through Thursday from 8:30 am to 4 pm and Friday from 8:30 am to 6 pm.

Lyon Arboretum, 3860 Manoa Road, ☎ 808-988-0464, www.lyon-arboretum.com. This public garden, deep in the lush folds of Manoa Valley, is home to hundreds of tropical flower species, plants and trees. Set on 193 acres, this is a great spot to hike, bird watch and relax. To get to Lyon Arboretum, drive north on University Avenue, which turns into Oahu Avenue after you pass the University of Hawaii campus. Pass East Manoa Road and then turn right onto Manoa Road. Signs will direct you to Paradise Park and then to Lyon Arboretum.

Beaches

Ala Moana Beach Park. This expansive beach is a favorite among tourists and locals. Located just before Waikiki Beach, this stretch of land is a long wide strip of white powder and perfect for swimming as it is protected by an offshore reef. Adjacent to the beach is a 76-acre park with endless recreational activities.

Any spot at the park is a great place to watch a spectacular sunset, complete with a view of the harbor and the skyline. There are also shaded picnic facilities and vast grassy areas – great for taking a nap or having a get-together.

Underrated Beach Spot: Magic Island (`Ainamona) is a man-made cove just to the right of Ala Moana Beach Park. The tip of Magic Island has a sheltered cover, perfect for snorkeling and scuba diving. Beyond the breakwater point are caves, coral and lots of tropical fish. Early mornings are usually peaceful with few visitors.

Adventures on Land

Golf

Waikele Golf Club, 94-200 Paioa Place, Waipahu, ☎ 808-676-9000, www.golfwaikele.com. Ted Robinson designed this 18-hole par 72 golf course. It overlooks Pearl Harbor and has spectacular views of Diamond Head and the Ko`olau and Wai`anae mountain ranges.

Ala Wai Golf Course, 404 Kapahulu Avenue, ☎ 808-733-7387. This popular 18-hole municipal course is right next to Waikiki and is touted as the busiest golf course in the world, with over 180,000 rounds of golf played per year. This flat but sporty course sits along the Ala Wai Canal and offers great views of Diamond Head, the Ko`olau mountain range and the Waikiki skyline.

Hiking

**Pu`u `Ualaka`a State Wayside Park**, ☎ 808-587-0300, at Round Top Drive off of Makiki Street. This easy hike is family-friendly and begins at Pu`u `Ualaka`a State Wayside Park. Along the way, you'll see a fantastic 230-degree view of southern O`ahu from Diamond Head to Pearl Harbor. The park is in a 50-acre forest park on a cinder cone near downtown Honolulu.

In Hawaiian, **Maunawili Falls** translates as "Twisted Mountain. This easy 1½-mile (one-way) hike features a great view of the Ko`olau Mountains, small waterfalls and pools.

To get there from Waikiki, take HI westbound and exit at the Pali exit. Go through the mountains and turn right onto `Auloa Road. At the fork in the road, stay to the left on Maunawili Road. Follow the signs to Maunawili Falls.

A Visit to an Ancient Heiau (Traditional Hawaiian Temple)

Mauka Makai Excursions, 350 Ward Avenue, Suite 106, ☎ 808-225-2206 or 800-896-0596 (toll free), www.hawaiianecotours.net, leads visitors to O`ahu archaeological and cultural sites, including heiau. Depending on conditions, you might be able to visit Ulupo Heiau, a 1,000-year-old agricultural temple near the edge of Kawai Nui marsh or Pu`uomahuka Heiau, which stands on a ridge overlooking Waimea Valley on the island's North Shore. Company co-owner Dominic Kealoha Aki chants before entering any of these sacred places and presents a ho`okupu (offering) such as a wild pikake flower or a ginger blossom.

The company offers three excursions – the first is a full-day adventure where you will trek to half a dozen wahi pana (legendary/sacred) sites and visit a swimming hole and a sea cave with petroglyphs (rock carvings).

The second excursion takes you to the North Shore where you will visit many sacred sites throughout the area. This full-day activity is offered only on Saturdays.

The third excursion is a half-day visit to three or four sacred sites and gets you back in time for lunch. All of these hikes are medium intensity but make sure to bring lots of water.

The loosely marked trail to **Manoa Falls** leads to a natural enclave where you will discover a lovely waterfall that trickles down a sheer rock face into a lava-rock pool. The . 8-mile trail winds along the Waihi stream amid a forest of fruit trees, eucalyptus trees and giant ferns, ending at a viewing area set back from the base of the falls.

To get to the trailhead, go east on H1 and take the Punahou "Exit 23." Continue up Punahou toward the mountains. Punahou turns in Manoa road if you stay left at the fork in the road. When you come to a five-way intersection, stay on Manoa Road. Manoa Road then continues into the back of Manoa Valley and ends at Paradise Park. You can park in the Paradise Park parking lot for $5 or park in the lower neighborhood for free.

Pig hunting takes place on Wednesdays and Sundays from sunup to sundown on this trail. If you want to bring your dog along, you should consider another trail on these two days in order to avoid possible encounters with hunting dogs.

Running Clubs

NIKETOWN Honolulu, King Kalakaua Plaza, ☎ 808-943-6453, www.nikerunning.com/runningclub, has a club for runners and walkers of all levels. If you feel like getting a bit of a workout while you're in Honolulu, check out the **Nike Run Club**. The group meets every Wednesday evening at 6 pm and Saturday mornings at 9 am. Post-run refreshments are provided.

Architectural Tour of Downtown Honolulu

The American Institute of Architects (AIA), ☎ 808-545-4242, www.aiahonolulu.org, offers a downtown walking tour from an architectural perspective. The Architects group offers tours once a week by reservation only. The tour is offered from 9 am to 11:30 am on Saturdays for a minimal fee and some of the highlights include the restored Hawaii Theatre, State Capitol, `Iolani Palace, Kamehameha Statue and the Kamehameha V Post Office, among other sites. Bring comfortable walking shoes. Bottled water and a map are provided. Each tour is led by an AIA architect who relates history, cultural insights, anecdotes and much more. The tours begin at the AIA Honolulu office on the 4th floor of the Historic Stangenwald Building at 119 Merchant Street, Suite 402.

Adventures by Land & Water

The Honolulu Triathlon, ☎ 866-454-6561, www.honolulutriathlon.com, takes place in mid-May and consist of a 1½K swim, a 40K bike ride and a 10K run. A kid's triathlon is open to boys and girls age seven to14 with each young participant receiving an official race t-shirt and a finisher's medal. What a great way to get kids involved in sports!

Adventures on Water

Dinner Cruises

The Star of Honolulu, 1540 South King Street, ☎ 808-983-STAR, www.starofhonolulu.com, has a fantastic dinner cruise that departs from Pier 8, next to Aloha Tower. The tour starts with aloha, ends with aloha and is full of aloha! The tour begins at 4:30 pm and takes off with a friendly welcome from the crew and a tasty cocktail (try the obligatory Mai Tai) once onboard. I enjoyed the spectacular Three Star Sunset Dinner and Show. Dinner is served before sunset and squeezes in a five-course meal, including a help-yourself appetizer bar, a chicken shiitake mushroom pate over Nalo greens, and a whole Maine lobster and tenderloin steak dinner.

For More Elegance: Guests who book the Five Star Dinner Cruise can arrive at the Aloha Tower from Waikiki in a private limousine for $60 per person. The price also includes a ride back to your Waikiki hotel.

Visitors are encouraged to carouse around the ship during the sunset hour and after the almost-always-spectacular sunset, diners are treated to a fantastic show titled, "My Hawaii – Lei of Memories," which celebrates Hawaii's beauty and culture. The tour ends around 7:30 pm and leaves plenty of time for you to check out some of Honolulu's nightspots. The staff is very professional and this cruise feels authentically Hawaiian. There are three dinner packages to choose from – the Five Star, with Sunset Dining and Jazz for $169 per person, the Three Star, with a Sunset Dinner and Show for $119 per person, and the Star, with Dinner and a Show for $79 per person.

Saving $$$: Book a dinner cruise on the *Star of Honolulu* on their website and save 10%.

Navatek I

Atlantis Submarines, Pier 6, Aloha Tower Marketplace, ☎ 808-973-131, www.atlantisadventures.com, also has a sunset dinner cruise available aboard the 140-foot *Navatek I*. Atlantis provides a very professional, fun-loving evening with great food and superior entertainment. The enthusiastic staff encourages audience participation and the music ranges from contemporary hits to Hawaiian melodies. The tour offers two levels of dinner service – the Sunset Dinner Cruise Buffet (chicken, mahimahi, veggies, mashed potatoes) and the Royal Sunset Dinner Cruise (steak, lobster, taro rolls, salad, potatoes). The Royal Sunset also has a children's menu with chicken, fish, mashed potatoes and other kid-friendly entrées. The Sunset Dinner Cruise buffet is $75 for adults, $50 for children while the Royal Sunset cruise is $105 for adults and $67 for children. The *Navatek I* departs at 5:15 pm and returns at 7:15 pm.

Money-Saver: Atlantis offers many combination deals that can save you a bundle. For example, an Atlantis submarine tour and Sunset Buffet combination is $134 for adults and $82 for children. Guests can also combine the submarine tour with the Royal Sunset dinner cruise or a Heli USA helicopter tour combined with a Sunset Buffet combination. So, a little bit of planning can save you a lot of cash!

The Ali`i Kai Makahiki Dinner Cruise, ☎ 808-954-8652 or 866-898-2519 (toll free), is arranged by Roberts Hawaii, www.robertshawaii.com, and leaves from Pier 5 at Aloha Tour daily at 5:30 pm, returning at 7:30 pm. The dinner aboard the 170-by-50-foot catamaran, called *Ruler of the Sea*, is buffet-style, followed by a Polynesian dance show involving audience members. Discounts for the dinner can be found on the website.

Parasailing & Other Water Sports

X-treme Parasail, ☎ 808-737-3599, www.x-tremeparasail.com, has much more than parasailing – they also offer jet ski rentals, surfing lessons and combination packages. You can save $5 by booking online. X-treme Parasail offers side-by-side tandem parasailing, which is twice the fun and offers awesome views of Waikiki Diamond Head and much more! The fun starts at Kewalo Basin across from Ward Warehouse in slip A. Free transportation from nearly hotels is provided.

Diamond Head Parasail, ☎ 808-597-8646, also offers parasail trips. You can go up to 300 feet for $35 or 700 feet for $45. The company also has jet ski and 600-foot parasail combos for $85 or tandem jet ski rentals at $45 for 30 minutes.

Boat Rides

If you're not sure whether you're ready to sail above the ocean, you can always hop aboard the ***Honolulu Screamer***, ☎ 808-597-8669, a futuristic-looking boat with a 1,420-horsepower engine that provides thrill-seekers with an adrenaline rush.

Sailing

The Sailing Club Hawaii, ☎ 808-222-9768, www.HawaiiYachts.com, offers cruises out of Kewalo Basin, just west of Waikiki. Choose between a custom day cruise, sunset cruise or an interisland adventure.

Scuba Diving

Honolulu Scuba Company, ☎ 808-220-0577 or 808-225-6004, www.honoluluscubacompany.com, info@honoluluscubacompany.com. If you're a diving fanatic, this company is a dream come true. Besides regular daytime two-tank dives, they also specialize in night dives, wreck dives and beach dives, all of which start from their custom-built 37-foot dive boat. Some of the wreck dives include a visit to the *YO-257*, which lies about a mile offshore with Diamond Head crater in the background. This is an old 1943 World War II Navy ship, resting upright at about 95 feet high. Divers can access some of the interior cabins through holes that have been cut in the ship's exterior. About 50 yards away is the *San Pedro*, an old Korean fishing vessel that is home to white tip sharks and Hawaiian sea turtles.

Reef fish and coral (www.noaa.gov)

Hundreds of colorful reef fish, eels and sea turtles surround *The Sea Tiger*, which is one of Hawaii's newest wrecks and was made famous in the book, *The Hunt for the Sea Tiger* by Captain Mac. This Chinese merchant ship is 165-feet long. Just south of Waikiki is the Rainbow Reef, appropriately named for the hundreds of tropical reef fish that reside at the reef along with several large sea turtles. The Honolulu Scuba Company is the only operation that visits Moe's Reef, which is a turtle cleaning station – they come here to clean their shells with the help of the reef fish.

For an unusual dive, sign up for the Friday Fireworks night dive.

Honolulu Scuba company also offers introductory dive classes as well as private charters for larger parties. Transportation to and from your hotel is included and the boat has fresh water showers, roomy sun decks and the voyages include complimentary snacks and refreshments.

OTHER SCUBA SITES

Besides the *Yo-257* and the *San Pedro*, the Honolulu coast has several impressive scuba sites for beginners and intermediate divers. "Turtle Reef" is located off Kewalo Basin Park and divers might see turtles, lobsters, shrimp and various tropical fish. "Rainbow Reef," a 40-foot dive, can be accessed from Ala Moana Beach Park and is a great dive for beginners. "Magic Island" is at the cove on the end of Magic Island. It's popular due to its easy access to the ocean and because it is good for beginners and intermediate divers.

Surfing Lessons

There are dozens of surf instructors in Honolulu, ranging from organized companies to amateur surfers trying to make an extra buck. Most resorts have partnerships with activity companies that work off the property. These companies rent snorkeling, surfing and other water sports equipments, as well as provide lessons. Some of my favorites are listed below:

Girls Who Surf, ☎ 808-371-8917 or 808-561-3004 (nine locations throughout O`ahu), www.girlswhosurf.com, info@GirlsWhoSurf.com. This company is all about fun, adventure and surfing. It focuses on, but is not limited to girls. The instructors operate all over the island and provide free transportation from almost anywhere island-wide. Some of the most popular locales are Waikiki, Ko `Olina and the North Shore, depending on the weather and conditions. Call ahead for reservations and choose from basic, intensive or introductory lessons. All you need to bring is a towel and sunscreen – surfboards, rash guards and fins are provided by Girls Who Surf. The most popular lesson is the Basic Surf Option that gives you 1¾ hours of surf time plus about half an hour of travel time (all for $90). Check out their cool website for more information and a showcase of surf products and logo items.

Surf's Up: Outside of Waikiki, there are many surf spots along the Honolulu coast. Among the more interesting names are "Zeros," "Graveyards,"

"Suicides," "Browns," "Black Point," "Secrets," "Toes Reef" and "Fingers." How they got these names is a bit of a mystery.

Hawaiian Fire Surf School, 3318 Campbell Avenue, ☎ 808-737-3473 or 888-955-7873, www.hawaiianfire.com, surf@hawaiianfire.com. Where else in the world can you find Honolulu City Firefighters who teach surfing on the side – and love it! You can feel safe learning to surf with these guys as they're all trained in Open Water Rescue, EMT-B and CPR. All lessons leave from the Waikiki area and there are two daily tours – Tour 1 lasts from 7 to 11:30 am and includes a two-hour surf lesson; Tour 2 runs from 9:30 am to 2 pm with a two-hour surf lesson. The rest of the time is spent traveling to the surf spot and then a 45-minute safety lesson with beach instruction on basic surf moves. These tours are $99, while private one-on-one lessons are $169 for adults. Children under 12 are required to have a private lesson for $119. Lessons include everything you need – foam-covered surfboards, leash, reef shoes, rash guards and shade tents and chairs.

Questions About Surfing? Check out Surfline's Surfology at www.surfline.com for everything you need to know about surfing – photos, forums, a surf glossary, surf school, surf camps and lessons on how to watch the weather!

Hans Hedemann Surf School, ☎ 808-924-4778, www.hhsurf, is one of O`ahu's most well known surf schools and has a good reputation throughout the island. The company has branches at the Park Shore Waikiki right across from Waikiki Beach, at the Kahala Hotel and Resort on the Windward Coast and at Turtle Bay Resort on the North Shore. Hans Hedemann Surf School offers private lessons ($115/per hour, $150/two hours), semi-private lessons ($95/per hour, $125 per/two hours), group lessons ($50/per hour, $75/two hours), private lessons for kids ($115/per hour, $150/two hours), surf lessons with the master himself

(Hans Hedemann) ($250/hour), or lessons from their staff of professional surfers ($250/two hours).

If you're an experienced surfer who wants to forgo the lessons, **Ala Moana Beach** is considered the best surf spot on the southern shore of the island.

Snorkeling

Magic Island (Ainamoana) is the piece of land that juts out when you're in Ala Moana Park. This is one of the few snorkeling spots worth seeking out in the Honolulu area. Enter the ocean at the Magic Island Cove swimming area.

Whale Watching

Atlantis Adventures Pier 6, Aloha Tower Marketplace, ☎ 808-973-1311, www.atlantisadventures.com, offers whale watching tours during the wintertime whale season (mid-December through March). The 2½-hour tour begins at noon and includes a lunch buffet. An on-board naturalist shares whale watching tips and behavioral indicators. If you don't see any whales, you'll get a free cruise to try again. Atlantis provides free roundtrip transportation from select Waikiki locations. The cruise costs $58 for adults and $29 for kids two to 12.

Adventures by Air

Island Seaplane Service, 85 Lagoon Drive, ☎ 808-836-6273, www.islandseaplane.com, seaplaneservice@aol.com, will have you reliving the romance of Pan Am's famous "China Clipper" flying boats. This is one of the most exciting adventures available on O`ahu and there are several tours to choose from: The "Aloha Flight" last half an hour and includes a view of Honolulu Harbor, Waikiki Beach, Diamond Head

Crater, Hanauma Bay, Sea Life Park and the Pali pass, before ending with an exciting water landing; The "Islander Flight" is an hour-long tour that continues over Kaneohe Bay and along the Windward Coast of the island. This tour reaches all the way up to the North Shore, including world-famous surf spots like Sunset Beach and the Banzai Pipeline.

Larger parties might enjoy the "Pupu Party" (minimum 12 people) or the "Meal Deal" (minimum 20 people) where passengers are taken to a floating dock to enjoy Hawaiian music, Mai Tai punch and Hawaiian-style cuisine.

This is the only seaplane service available in all of Hawaii and the flights take off from Ke`ehi Lagoon in Honolulu. Complimentary van shuttle service is available from most Waikiki hotels.

You Look Familiar: Company founder Pat Magie has flown for many big screen movies and TV shows, including the Godzilla movie and the *New Fantasy Island* series in 1998. Magie has been so involved in the film industry that he is even a member of the Screen Actors Guild. Most recently, the company's seaplane base was seen in the cute O`ahu-based movie, *50 First Dates*, starring Drew Barrymore and Adam Sandler.

Heli USA, 99 Kaulele Place, ☎ 808-833-3306, www.heliusa.com, offers a spectacular tour of O`ahu that touches on all the highlights of the island such as Pearl Harbor, Battleship Row, Punchbowl National Cemetery and the Arizona Memorial. The tour also honors Hollywood as the pilot shows you the places made famous by movies and TV shows such as *Jurassic Park*, *Hawaii Five-O*, *Magnum P.I.*, *Pearl Harbor* and *Gilligan's Island*. During the tour, you'll be in the air for about 30 minutes, but plan on about two hours for the whole trip including transportation to and from your hotel. The cost at press time was $119 per person with an additional tax of $11 per person.

Heli USA also offers a "City Lights Helicopter Tour & Sunset Dinner Cruise" where guests enjoy a two-hour buffet dinner cruise before heading up in the helicopter for a post-sunset tour of Honolulu's night lights. This combination package is $159 per person with an additional tax of $5 per person.

Check the Heli USA website for on-line booking specials that can save you a substantial amount of money. Also, a free shuttle will pick up passengers staying at Waikiki hotels and take them back and forth to the Heli USA heliport.

Makani Kai Helicopters, 110 Kapalulu Place, ☎ 808-834-5813 or 877-255-8532, www.makanikai.com. Makani Kai Helicopters is different from the other companies as it only flies in O`ahu. There are several packages to choose from: The 15-minute "Holo Holo Tour" gives passengers a brief overview of Honolulu; a 30-minute "Pali Makani Tour" takes you through Honolulu and then along the southern shore of the island; a 45-minute "Hidden Oahu Tour" features Sacred Falls, a shear and splendid 1,000-foot cascade that can only be seen from the air; a 60-minute "Ali`i Sacred Falls Tour" that takes you by Sacred Falls and then onto the North Shore and the Dole Pineapple maze. The tours range from $89 to $225 per person and, unfortunately, they do not offer transportation to the Honolulu Airport where the helicopters take off.

Where to Eat in Honolulu

FOOD TOURS

Hawaii Food Tours, ☎ 808-926-3663 or 800-715-2468 (toll free), www.HawaiiFoodTours.com, FoodTours@HawaiiFoodTours.com, offers three tours: a daytime "Hole-in-the-Wall" Tour of Honolulu's best-kept culinary secrets, a three-course Luau-style Hawaiian Feast at sunset and a sophisticated Gourmet trilogy evening at three award-winning restaurants. The tours are led by Matthew Gray, whose résumé includes jobs as a former restaurant reviewer, food writer for *The Honolulu Advertiser* and as a Los Angeles-based chef who has cooked for many movie stars, celebrities and musicians.

The "Hole-in-the-Wall" Tour is offered daily from 10 am to 2 pm and will take you to four exotic restaurants with cuisines varying from Indian specialties to Portuguese doughnuts and Hawaiian plate lunches. The cost is $59 per person.

The "Hawaiian Feast in Paradise" is offered Monday and Thursday evenings from 6 to 9 pm. The dinner takes place at the world-famous Don Ho's Island Grill Restaurant in the Aloha Tower Marketplace and the three-course dinner tour costs $99 per person.

The crème de la crème is the "Gourmet Trilogy Tour for Food & Wine Lovers." The first stop is for champagne and appetizers before a second stop for the entrée course. The last stop is a restaurant for a rich and decadent dessert. All stops are served with an appropriate wine. The tour is offered on Tuesday and Wednesday evenings and lasts from 6 to 10 pm. The cost is $199 per person. Tip: Evening attire is required and gentlemen must wear slacks. Bon Appetit!

At Aloha Tower Marketplace

Bikini Cantina, ☎ 808-525-7288, www.bikinicantina.com, info@bikinicantini.com. Located on the second floor of the Aloha Tower Marketplace, this casual spot has great drink specials, spectacular sunset views and affordable cuisine – a Mexicale Burger with guacamole, salsa, lettuce, tomato and onions costs $9.95, "Surf's Up" taco salad is $10.95 and a Southwest Chicken Caesar Salad is $10.95. They also offer amusingly named entrées such as Ooh La-La Enchiladas, Thong Bikini Tacos, Beach Blanket Burritos and Sexy Mexy Chicken Wings. This is a great pau hana spot with nightly specials like Monday's margarita & mai tai madness; Thursday is College Night with "You Call It" $3.50 drinks. Happy Hour is daily from 3 to 7 pm and offers $2.50 Coors Light drafts and Bud Light drafts, $3.50 Kona Brewing Company Longboard drafts and $4 margarita and mai tais. $.

Practical Parking Tips: If you are going to dine at any of the restaurants at Aloha Tower Marketplace, park in the parking lot with the attendant directly across from the center. You can have your parking ticket validated at an Aloha Tower Marketplace restaurant or shop and save on parking costs.

Don Ho's Island Grill, ☎ 808-528-0807, www.donhos.net. Opened in December of 1998, this restaurant is named after the legendary crooner, most famous for the song "Tiny Bubbles." The restaurant offers lunch and dinner along with a Sunday brunch. For lunch, Don Ho's offers soup, salad, appetizers, and their trademark "surfboard pizzas," which are formed into the shape of the iconic emblem of Waikiki. Entrées include coconut shrimp, grilled island-style guava chicken, fish 'n chips, sandwiches, and loco moco, a famous Hawaiian plate that includes a burger patty with two eggs, steamed white rice and onion-mushroom gravy. For an only-in-Hawaii dessert, try the sweet potato haupia pie.

Valet parking is available for $2 with validation and is valid for up to three hours. Don Ho's is open on Sunday through Wednesday from 11 am until 11 pm with the Sunday brunch from 10 am to 2 pm. Thursday through Saturday the restaurant is open from 11 am to 2 am. Happy Hour specials are served daily from 3 to 6 pm. Lunch $$. Dinner $$.

Gordon Biersch, ☎ 808-599-4877, www.gordonbiersch.com. Although I don't usually promote chain restaurants, this one is a standout. Considered Hawaii's first brewpub, the spot has a great menu, spectacular view and fabulous ambiance. Open from 10 am to midnight Sunday through Thursday and 10 am to 1 am Friday and Saturday. Gordon Biersch beers include the Golden Export, Hefewiezen, Marzen, Dunkles, Blonde Bock and a seasonal special.

The Gordon Biersch Garlic Fries are legendary but the rest of the menu deserves a shot – sandwiches, pastas, stir-fries, pizzas and salads, like the Wedge Salad with crumbled bleu cheese and bacon with a marzen vinaigrette. The dinner menu includes more entrées such as salmon, steaks, ribs, chicken parmesan, as well as pastas, pizzas and sandwiches. Happy hour is held Monday through Wednesday from 4 to 6:30 pm and 10 pm to closing. The "Week Day Escape" happy hour has specials on beer, wine, martinis, margaritas, mojitos and some appetizers (including the garlic fries!). Lunch $$. Dinner $$-$$$.

Yes, there's even a **Hooters**, ☎ 808-524-4668, www.hooters.com, in paradise. On the street level with a view of the ocean, Hooters offers drinks, appetizers, and lots of chicken wing variations, burgers and sandwiches. Happy hour is from 3 to 6 pm and all day long on Tuesdays. Other specials included "Military Monday" where all active military members will receive 20% off food and merchandise. On Thursdays, kids under 12 eat off the kid's menu for free and then that night, "Trivia Night" starts at 8 pm. Lunch and dinner are available daily at Hooters and breakfast is served from 8 to 11 am on Saturdays and Sundays. Breakfast $. Lunch and Dinner $-$$.

Makino Chaya, ☎ 808-585-6360, is an all-you-can-eat Japanese buffet that is somewhat new to Aloha Tower. There are five different kitchens – a tempura kitchen, sushi kitchen (with 30 types of sushi), Makino's kitchen, Neptune Island (crab and lobster) and a Japanese teppan-yaki kitchen. This is the spot for seafood lovers! There's Alaskan king crab, half-shell oysters, snow crab legs, Dungeness crab, shrimp tempura, shrimp cocktail, sashimi and miso butterfish. A large lobster tank sits in the restaurant full of delicacies like fresh-caught uni (sea urchin). Makino Chaya is open for lunch from 11:30 am to 2 pm and dinner from 5:30 to 9 pm. Lunch is $10.98 and dinner $21.98 during the week. Prices go up a dollar on holidays and weekends. Mikino Chaya tends to get very crowded so prepare to wait or try to make a reservation. Lunch $. Dinner $$.

Hong Kong Harbor View Seafood Restaurant, ☎ 808-566-9989, www.shanghaibistrohawaii.com, offers authentic Cantonese cooking but also serves cuisine from several other regions of China. The restaurant has a great harbor view and one of its specialties is dim sum. Entrées include Peking Duck, fresh prawns stir-fried with dry garlic and coconut, tenderloin beef with black pepper sauce and mini chicken on Hong Kong-style cake noodles. The restaurant is open from 10 am to 10 pm and has a dim sum special from 10 am to 3 pm. Lunch $$. Dinner $$-$$$.

In the Ward Centers

The Ward Centers are made up of four buildings, with a fifth being planned for 2008. Ward Center and Ward Warehouse are located along Ala Moana Boulevard while the Ward Gateway Center and Ward Entertainment Center are inland along Auahi Street.

The family-popular **Big City Diner**, ☎ 808-591-8891, is in the Ward Entertainment Center. The diner offers breakfast, lunch, and dinner with a late night menu. Lick your fingers clean after the baby back pork ribs with a guava glaze or calamari tempura with wasabi aioli dipping sauce. Tuesday is "customer appreciation nite" offering 50% off pupus from 9 am to closing with a two-beverage purchase. The next day is "Wine Wednesday" offering 50% off all bottles and glasses of wine with lunch or dinner – all day long. Breakfast $. Lunch $$. Dinner $$

The Old Spaghetti Factory, 1050 Ala Moana Blvd., ☎ 808-591-2513, www.osf.com, is on the far western end of the Ward Warehouse section. This is one of my favorite chain restaurants and the Hawaii location has the traditional menu with some added Polynesian touches. Try the mango macadamia chicken salad or the Hawaiian-style spaghetti with Portuguese sausage. Lunch is served Monday through Friday from 11:30 am to 2 pm and dinner Monday through Thursday from 5 to 10 pm; Friday 5 to 10:30 pm, Saturday 11:30 am to 10:30 pm and Sunday 4 to 9:30 pm. Lunch $. Dinner $$.

Brew Moon Restaurant & Microbrewery, ☎ 808-593-0088, www.brewmoon.com, is on the second floor of the Ward Center. The Brew Moon menu is huge – and that's without even looking at the beers. There are dozens of pupus, lots of sandwiches, gourmet pizzas and salads. For a true splurge, try the Moon Feast – a full slab or ribs, BBQ chicken breasts, marinated shrimp, charbroiled skirt steak and grilled jalapenos for $58.

If you're not sure which beer to try, order the lunar sampler with six four-ounce samples of handcrafted beer. Beers include Moonlight (an American-style light lager), German-style North-Star Lager, MoonBerry Wheat, Big Band Pale Ale, Orian's Red Ale and Black Hole Lager. Lunch $$. Dinner $$$.

In the Ala Moana Shopping Center

California Pizza Kitchen, ☎ 808-941-7715 (on the 3rd level, between Macy's & Neiman Marcus), www.cpk.com. Open Sunday through Thursday 11 am to 10 pm, Friday and Saturday 11 am to 11 pm. This upscale pizza chain has a huge assortment of specialty pizzas (they're famous for their BBQ chicken pizza), chicken entrées, pastas, focaccia sandwiches and yummy desserts. The eatery also has a kid's menu for ages 10 and under, which includes salad, fruit, pasta, pizza and scaled-down desserts. $$.

Tsukiji Fish Market and Restaurant (on the fourth floor), ☎ 808-237-5444, is a newcomer to the Honolulu dining scene. Inspired by the original restaurant in Tokyo, this is a fish market/restaurant combination with lunch and dinner buffets. The restaurant is huge – it seats over 360 people and has three private conference rooms. In addition to the plentiful buffets (full of appetizers, sushi, sashimi, and traditional Japanese, Chinese and Korean dishes), Tsukiji also has sushi, Yakitori and Robatayaki bars which allow guests to experience authentic dishes prepared by Japanese chefs. For a different twist to Japanese dining, the chefs prepare live seafood on demand for guests.

The lunch buffet with the sushi bar is open daily from 11 am to 2 pm and the dinner buffet and sushi bar is open daily from 5 to 10 pm. The fish market is open daily from 11 am to 6 pm. Lunch $$. Dinner $$.

Genki Sushi (on the mall level), ☎ 808-942-9102, www.genkisushiusa.com. This is a bargain in the sushi department and has been repeatedly voted the best sushi in town. Diners who sit down to eat can watch the sushi swim by on a conveyor belt where you can choose whatever catches your fancy. The plates are priced by the color and are added up at the end of meal. You must try the spicy tuna roll! $.

Sam Choy's Breakfast, Lunch, Crab & Big Aloha Brewery, 580 N. Nimitz Highway, ☎ 808-545-7979, www.samchoy.com. How can you go wrong with a chef whose motto is "Never Trust a Skinny Chef"? Known for his fantastic palate and his jolly demeanor, Sam Choy is one of Hawaii's most innovative and famed chefs. The servings are hearty at this eatery. Breakfast entrées include various platters of breakfast favorites, omelets, loco moco variations and griddle favorites like banana macadamia nut pancakes. Lunch is big on seafood – try Sam's Bowl of Shellfish with steamed clams, mussels, shrimp, scallops and crab legs, an ahi salad or one of Sam's famous local plate lunches. Dinner includes much more seafood, such as ahi sashimi and Chef Sam's fried poke salad.

All of the "Big Aloha" beers are brewed on the premises. Try the Kakaako Cream Ale, the Ehu Ale, Kiawe Honey Porter or the James Cook Indian Pale Ale. You can sample 5 oz. servings of five brews for $6.95.

You'll see Sam Choy's Breakfast, Lunch, Crab & Big Aloha Brewery on your way from the airport toward Waikiki. Breakfast $$. Lunch $$$. Dinner $$$.

What a concept – two fantastic restaurants sharing one space. That's what you get when you visit **Hiroshi Eurasion Tapas/Vino**, 500 Ala Moana Blvd. at Restaurant Row. Hiroshi, ☎ 808-533-4476; Vino, ☎ 808-524-8466. Chef Hiroshi Fukui, wine expert Master Sommelier Chuck Furuya and successful chef and restaurateur D.K. Kodama came together to create the high-profile duo of eateries. At **Hiroshi Eurasion Tapas**, chef Hiroshi fuses Japanese and European ingredients to create tapas, like a sizzlin' Kona Kampachi Carpaccio, to larger plates like filet mignon and crab-stuffed mahimahi. **Vino** offers Italian-style tapas like seafood ravioli and crispy shrimp pasta. Sommelier Chuck Furuya pours more than 20 wines by the glass and can help with food and wine pairings. Hiroshi $$$. Vino $$.

Conveniently located next to the Honolulu Fish Auction building, **Nico's Pier 38**, 1133 N. Nimitz Highway, Pier 38, ☎ 808-540-1377, www.nicospier38.com, offers fabulous and affordable cuisine with a focus on fresh fish. Nico's is fine dining with French flair served on paper plates in a casual atmosphere! Breakfast is served from 6:30 to 9:30 am and offers local favorites like loco moco and fresh saimen or French toast and omelettes. Lunch is served after 10 am and includes classics like fish and chips with a ginger garlic cilantro dip and hamburgers, as well as local favorite chicken katsu and furikake (seasoned seaweed flakes) pan-seared ahi. Warning: A visit to chef Nico Chaize's stylish website may leave you with a severe yearning for Hawaii. The sound of crashing waves resonates on the home page and the daily specials are posted. You can also sign up for the mailing list and the specials will be e-mailed to you daily. Talk about daily appetite torture! Nico's Pier 38 is open from 6:30 am to 6 pm Monday through Friday and 6:30 am to 2:30 pm Saturday. $

Alan Wong's Restaurant, 1857 S. King Street (on the third floor), ☎ 808-949-2526, www.alanwongs.com. Alan Wong's has a fabulous reputation for using locally grown produce to create the best of Hawaiian Regional Cuisine. The menu offers a five-course menu and a seven-course menu tasting with a prix fixe (set

price). Otherwise, you can order from the menu that includes an exciting mix of pupus, entrées and dessert. Appetizers include a "New Wave" Opihi Shooter and Big Island abalone. Entrées include seafood, shrimp, Maui Cattle Company steaks and lamb chops. During lychee season, try Alan's lychee-ginger sorbet. Reservations are highly recommended. $$$.

Like every trendy and tourist-heavy destination in the world, Honolulu, too, has a **Hard Rock Café**, 1837 Kapi`olani Blvd., ☎ 808-955-7383, www.hardrock.com. Famous for its music memorabilia, this Hard Rock has on display one of Gwen Stefani's No Doubt onstage ensembles, a purple custom guitar from Prince and Paul McCartney's ivory Wings logo necklace which he wore during the group's 1976 tour.

And don't forget about the food and drinks! The restaurant offers comfortable American cuisine and lots of beer, wine and tropical drinks. Prices are reasonable and the atmosphere is fun, though it can get loud. The Hard Rock Café is open daily from 11 am to 11 pm for food and from 11 am to midnight for drinks. Lunch $$. Dinner $$.

Leonard's Bakery, 933 Kapahulu Ave., ☎ 808-737-5591, www.leonardshawaii.com, is famous among locals and tourists alike, mostly for their malasadas – a Portuguese doughnut hole made of potato flour and rolled in sugar. They also sell the Portuguese sweet bread known as pao doce. $.

Side Street Inn, 1225 Hopaka Street, ☎ 808-591-0253. This funky spot first opened as a bar 15 years ago but has transformed itself into a down-to-earth eatery with fantastic food and reasonable prices. Try the barbecued baby back ribs with a lilikoi sauce, flavorful steaks and fantastic fish dinners. Open Monday through Friday from 10:30 am to 1:30 pm and daily from 4 pm to 12:30 am. Plate Lunches $. Dinner $$.

Malasadas To Go: Check out www.leonardshawaii.com to find out where Leonard's Malasadamobile will be parked and serving delicious Portuguese treats.

Kincaid's Fish, Chop & Steak House, 1050 Ala Moana Boulevard, ☎ 808-591-2005, www.kincaids.com, offers a great variety of sandwiches and salads or combos of both for lunch. Dinner includes more seafood dinners as well as steaks, including their signature rock salt-roasted prime rib of beef. They also have oysters served any of three ways – with a Bloody Mary Granita, mushrooms and tarragon aioli or fresh off the half shell. Happy Hour is from 4 to 7 pm and then from 10 pm to closing. All draft beers are $3, as are house wines, margaritas, classic mojitos and house martinis.

Open from Sunday through Thursday from 11 am to midnight, Friday and Saturday 11 am to 1 am. Lunch $$. Dinner $$$.

In Kaimuku (just east of Honolulu & Waikiki)

12th Ave Grill, 1145 12th Avenue, ☎ 808-732-9469, www.12thavegrill.com. Opened in June 2004, the interior of this popular, award-winning neighborhood restaurant is lined with wooden booths and black-and-white images taken by local photographers. The menu offers salad, small plates like smoked ahi bruschetta, large plates like cinnamon braised short ribs, fish of the day or a grilled hanger steak with pommes frites. 12th Ave Grill is located on a side street between Koko Head Ave. and 12th Ave. Guests can park in the municipal parking lot behind the grill. $$.

Also in Kaimuki is **Jose's Mexican Café and Cantina**, 1134 Koko Head Avenue, ☎ 808-732-1833, www.joseshonolulu.com, which combines hearty Mexican entrées with yummy Hawaiian flavors. During Happy Hour (more appropriately "happy hours"), a pitcher of pineapple margaritas is only $9. Jose's is open for lunch every day at 11 am and the bar stays open late on Friday and Saturday nights. $$.

town, 3435 Wai`alae Ave., ☎ 808-735-5900, combines fresh ingredients with tasty presentation and has become one of the island's most-raved-about eateries. Although there are some standard dishes served all the time, the menu often changes to accommodate whatever is fresh and available that day. Owner and Chef Ed Kenney calls the cuisine "'contemporary American with an Italian sensibility." Salads and sandwiches are served at lunch, while dinner offers North Shore Cattle Company beefsteaks and half-chicken served with corn bread. Open 6:30 am to 9:30 pm Monday through Thursday and 6:30 am to 10 pm Friday and Saturday. The continental breakfast is offered from 6:30 to 11:30 am, lunch from 11:30 am to 2:30 pm, a limited "gap" menu from 2:30 to 5:30 pm and dinner from 5:30 to close. Lunch $$. Dinner $$.

Liliha Bakery & Coffee Shop, 515 N. Kuakini St, ☎ 808-531-1651, is open 24 hours a day except from 8 pm Sunday through 8 am Tuesday. This famous eatery serves Hawaiian-style breakfast and lunch and is famous for their fantastic "Cocoa Puff." The shop is small so you may have to wait since it is very popular. $.

In the W Honolulu Hotel

Diamond Head Grill, 2885 Kalakaua Avenue, ☎ 808-922-1700, www.starwoodhotels.com. The Diamond Head Grill is an upscale eatery that uses fresh ingredients to create an Asian, Euro-American and Polynesian cuisine. The grill is open daily from 7 to 10:30 am for breakfast and 6 pm to midnight for dinner. Breakfast $$. Dinner $$$.

On the Outskirts of Honolulu

Diamond Head Market & Grill, 3158 Monsarrat, ☎ 808-732-0077, www.diamondheadmarket.com, info@diamondhead-market.com. Opened in August 2002, this mostly take-out spot is very popular. Founder Kelvin Ro has been around the Honolulu food industry for quite a while. He works with local culinary schools for innovation and the food is reliable and of high quality. Ro also offers catering. The market is open from 7:30 am to 9 pm daily, with the grill open from 10:30 am to 9 pm. This eatery offers a huge selection of upscale plate lunches, which can also be made into a sandwich or a mini-plate lunch. Specialties include a Portobello burger plate and a chicken eggplant sandwich. Lunch and Dinner $.

The Dee-Lite Bakery, 1930 Dillingham Blvd., ☎ 808-847-5396, specializes in chiffon cakes with tropical flavors such as guava, coconut, passion fruit and lime. Herbert and Sue Matsuba first opened the café in 1959 on Mokauea. They've expanded quite a bit and Herbert Matsuba retired in 1990 and sold his bakery chain to Saint-Germain America.

Wahoo's Fish Taco, 940 Auahi Street, (cross-street is Ward Blvd.),☎ 808-591-1646, www.wahooshawaii.com, serves delicious and healthy fare with a combination of Mexican, Brazilian and Asian flavors. The restaurant is very clean, organized and fun to dine in with its tiki and surf themes. The concept is unique – you choose your style of entrée (taco, enchilada, several burrito options, salad) and then select your filling (blackened or flame-broiled fish or chicken, vegetar-

ian, shrimp, carnitas...). If that's too daunting, they have several combination plates to choose from. If you're in the mood for a pupu (appetizer), try the Baja rolls – flour tortillas spread with cream cheese and then stuffed with leaf spinach, chopped chicken and fresh salsa, then rolled, chilled and sliced. They also have soup, salads and sandwiches.

Wahoo's Fish Taco started in Costa Mesa, California where three brothers decided to create a small but healthy taco restaurant. The concept spread quickly and there are now 39 locations across California, Colorado, Texas and Hawaii. It is open Monday through Saturday from 10:30 am to 10 pm and Sunday from 10:30 am to 9 pm. $.

In Aiea

Bravo Restaurant, 98-115 Kaonohi Street (in the Pearlridge Uptown Center), ☎ 808-487-5544. Pasta is the star here at Bravo and the menu offers almost every Italian dish I can think of. Pasta is made fresh daily and one of the nice menu options is the mix-and-match with pastas and sauces. Otherwise, try one of their seafood specialties, among them seafood fettuccine or a combination platter where you can choose two pastas, such as the chicken parmigiana and the spinach & cheese ravioli. The dish is then served with spaghetti and marinara. If you're not in the mood for pasta, try one of their 10-inch pizzas or a sandwich, soup or salad. Open Sunday through Thursday 11 am to 10 pm; Friday and Saturday 11 am to 11 pm. $$.

Nightlife

Anna Bannana's, 2440 South Beretania Street, ☎ 808-946-5190. Entertainment can be found most weekends at this classic old-school pub (it's still rocking after 30 years!)

At the Ala Moana Center

Pearl, ☎ 808-944-8000 (Third Level). Pearl serves food and drinks from 4:30 pm to 2 am Monday through Thursday, 4:30 pm to 4 am Friday and 7 pm to 4 am Sunday. It is closed on Mondays.

The Mai Tai Bar, ☎ 808-947-2900 (Fourth Level). This open-air spot is great for a drink or pupu after a hard day shopping. Live music plays from 4 to 7 pm Monday through Friday, 1 to 4 pm on the weekends and then 9:30 pm to 12:30 am nightly. Happy Hour is from 8 to 11 pm.

EVER TRY KAVA?

If you feel like experimenting with something new, check out the **Kapahulu Kafe**, 766 Kapahulu Avenue, ☎ 808-732-7486, www.kapahulukafe.com, where you can try `awa (Hawaiian kava) in many forms. The menu (available for viewing on the website) offers the mud-like nutrient as a sluggish brown liquid or a lime-flavored Jell-o shot, among many other preparations. Café owner Daren Kimura also serves a Jell-o and cream soda `awa concoction which he claims is bringing in new customers. The café has free Wi-Fi and a food menu. Free validated parking is available in the rear of the building. The hours seem to be changing frequently so check the website for current information and a current calendar of events.

W Honolulu Bar, 2885 Kalakaua Avenue, ☎ 808-922-1700, is inside the W Honolulu Hotel and is a sophisticated place to have a drink. Try a "Mai Tai Martini" while listening to live music. The W Honolulu Bar offers live jazz on certain nights – call to find out who's playing. The Bar is open from 5:30 pm to midnight.

Where to Stay

CAMPING - STATE PARKS

☞ ☎ 808-587-0300 for more information.

**Kea`iwa Heiau State Recreation Area**. Located at the top of A`iea Heights Drive in A`iea, north of Honolulu. Campers can visit the remains of the Healing

Temple, Heiau Ho`olo. The park has forested camping, picnicking and hiking.

Sand Island State Recreation Area. Visitors can fish and camp at this park, located at the end of Sand Island Access Road near the entrance to the Honolulu Harbor.

Manoa Valley Inn, 2001 Vancouver Drive, ☎ 808-947-6019, www.manoavalleyinn.com, manoavalleyinn@aloha.net, is one of the few bed and breakfasts in the Honolulu area. The inn has seven suites and a country cottage for rent. I wasn't able to check it out, but reviews on the Internet slam it every which way. Check out the property before staying there. $$-$$$.

Diamond Head Bed and Breakfast, 3240 Noela Drive, ☎ 808-923-3360, www.diamondheadbnb.com, seems to have a much better reputation. Located in a quiet neighborhood on the slopes of Diamond Head, the property has three suites, all of which have a private bath, TV, mini refrigerator, phones and an outdoor lanai. Keep in mind that they don't accept credit cards! $$$.

For long-term rentals or for a less-expensive condominium stay, try the **Hawaiian King Condo-Hotel**, 417 Nohonani St, ☎ 831-239-3477, www.hawaiiankingcondo.com. Two condo units are available for rent in this complex. The condos have full kitchens, lanais and a swimming pool. Condos can be rented by the day, week or month. $$

Hawaiian King Condo-Hotel

The Ohana Honolulu Airport Hotel, 3401 N. Nimitz Highway, ☎ 808-836-0661 or 800-462-6262 (toll free), www.ohanahotels.com, is just a half-mile from the Honolulu International Airport. This property was recently renovated at the cost of $6 million and is designed for business and leisure travelers looking for accommodations close to the airport. I've stayed here between flights from Bali to Kaua`i when I had an early morning connection and another time when I had a cancelled flight and had to fly out early to San Francisco. It is very convenient and the 24-hour airport shuttle is reliable. The free wireless Internet access in the lobby can help tie up loose ends or finalize travel plans. The only disappointment was that the bar and restaurant, Willoughby's Restaurant, closes at 9 pm, which is just about the time I arrived at the hotel. $$-$$$.

W Honolulu Diamond Head, 2885 Kalakaua Avenue, ☎ 808-922-1700, www.starwoodhotels.com, is a smaller hotel with 49 rooms located at the foot of Diamond Head and Kapi`olani Park. Guests have access to a 24-hour fitness center and, when you check in, you're greeted with a cool, tropical beverage and a chilled face towel. $$$$.

Pearl Harbor
N
HUNTER PUBLISHING
East Loch
Middle Loch
FORD ISLAND BRIDGE
ARIZONA MEMORIAL DR
99
USS Missouri
Memorial Ticket Office
& Shuttle Pickup
USS Bowfin
PARKING
USS Arizona
Memorial Visitor Center
USS Arizona
Memorial
SARATOGA RD
WASP BLVD
FORD ISLAND BLVD
Pearl Harbor
Naval Base
FORD
ISLAND
Pearl Harbor
South Channel
USS Missouri
Pacific
Aviation
Museum
KAMEHAMEHA HWY
H1
Sub Base
Magazine Loch
¼ MILE
¼ KILOMETER
99
Southeast Loch

Pearl Harbor

At a Glance

On Sunday, December 7, 1941, shortly before 8 am, Japan attacked the US Armed Forces across the entire island of O`ahu. In less than two hours, Pearl Harbor and several other military installations were left smoldering, with devastating results. By the time the attack was over, shortly before 10 am, 21 vessels had been sunk or damaged and numerous aircraft stationed on Ford Island were heavily damaged. Six military sites on O`ahu were attacked, killing 2,390 Americans and destroying or damaging 21 vessels. This attack is considered the act that brought the United States into World War II. Japan officially declared war on the United States and Great Britain at 10:30 am. On December 8, 1941, President Franklin D. Roosevelt declared war on Japan. On December 11, 1941, Germany and Italy declared war on the United States, thus producing the World War.

IN THIS CHAPTER

Historical Fact: The famous term "Tora, Tora, Tora" was used by Japanese Commander Fuchida at 7:53 am to alert the Japanese fleet that their surprise attack had been successful.

The attack at Pearl Harbor was the epitome of what is known as a "sneak attack." Japanese forces arrived undetected just 230 miles north of the Hawaiian Islands. The attack, comprised of a torrent of bombs and torpedoes, included an aerial bomb attack on the USS *Arizona*. The bomb was so devastating that the ship sank to the bottom of the harbor in just nine minutes. The casualties on the USS *Arizona* totalled 1,177, with only 337 survivors. The ship continued to burn for over two days.

Painful Memories: During the attack, the hospital ship *Solace* was moored on the northern edge of Ford Island. From the ship, Army doctor Eric Haakensen captured the bombing and sinking of the USS *Arizona* on 16mm film. His footage of the tragedy is shown in the USS *Arizona* Memorial theater presentation.

Pearl Harbor is now one of the most recognizable war memorials in the world and contains several impressive sites that will leave you with a new sense of pride and a painful reminder of the devastating affect that war can have on the world.

Did You Know? The majority of the US Pacific Fleet was moved to Pearl Harbor in 1940 as peace negotiations began to falter with Japan.

In this chapter, I will describe the four main Pearl Harbor attractions that no visitor to O`ahu should miss: USS *Arizona* Memorial, USS *Bowfin* Submarine Park & Museum, the Battleship *Missouri* Memorial and the new Pacific Aviation Museum. You can tour the inside of each vessel, although the USS *Arizona* was the only vessel in Pearl Harbor during the attack. The others were relocated to Pearl Harbor.

Sightseeing

Polynesian Adventure Tours, ☎ 808-833-3000 or 800-622-3011 (toll free), offers a variety of Pearl Harbor tours. If you're staying at a hotel, the concierge should have various options to choose from.

The USS Arizona Memorial

The USS *Arizona* Memorial, 1 Arizona Memorial Place, ☎ 808-422-0561 (recorded message) or 808-422-2771 (National Park

Service Representative), www.nps.gov/usar, www.arizona-memorial.org or www.pearl-harbor.com, commemorates the site where World War II began, with the attack on Pearl Harbor of December 7, 1941. A tour of the memorial enables guests to experience history through the Park's many interpretive exhibits including a historical museum and a tour of the ship. The tour, sponsored by the National Park Service, is 75 minutes and includes a 23-minute documentary film, a shuttle boat ride and a visit to the memorial.

The Memorial welcomes about 1.5 million visitors annually.

This site is the final resting place for many of the 1,177 service members who lost their lives on that fateful day. The attack created the greatest loss of life on any US warship in American history. The 184-foot-long memorial, which was officially dedicated on Memorial Day 1962, spans the mid-portion of the sunken battleship. It stands as a reminder of this "Day of Infamy" – the worst naval disaster in American history. It is important to remember that the memorial was built to honor not only the fallen crewmembers of the sunken battleship, but also all members of the US Armed Forces who died as a result of the Pearl Harbor attack. The site was designated a National Historic Landmark in 1989. The National Park Service took over operations in 1980 and has worked hard to ensure the preservation and interpretation of the tangible historical resources associated with attack, including the rich memories of its survivors. The memorial is only accessible by a short boat ride, which departs from the visitor center. Open daily from 7:30 am to 5 pm. Closed Thanksgiving Day, Christmas Day and New Year's Day. Entrance is free although donations to sustain the Memorial and its related programs are appreciated.

The accessible portion of the Memorial is the above-water mid-section of the sunken battleship. Narrated audio tours are available in seven languages for a small fee at the visitor center front desk. Informational brochures are printed in 35 languages.

How to Get There

The USS *Arizona* Memorial Visitor Center is located adjacent to Kamehameha Highway, near the Aloha Stadium, between Ford Island Bridge and Pearl Harbor's Makalapa Gate. To get to the Memorial from Waikiki, take the H-1 Freeway to the Airport Viaduct and follow the signs to the Memorial Exit 15A. As one of Oahu's most popular sites, Pearl Harbor is clearly marked along the H-1 and is very easy to find. If you're going by The Bus, route numbers 20 and 42 will bring you to Pearl Harbor.

Security Precautions

Security is very strict on all of the Pearl Harbor attractions. Prohibited items include handbags, fanny packs, backpacks, camera bags, diaper bags, luggage and anything else that could contain something. Storage containers are available in the visitor center parking lot from 7:30 am to 5:30 pm. There is a small fee for the lockers and they are not sufficient for luggage and suitcases. What you **can** bring with you is a camera and video-recorder. Cell phones are discouraged and must be turned off once the program begins in the theater, on the Navy shuttle boat and the Memorial. There is a dress code – shirts and shoes are required and no bathing suits are allowed. Members of the Military should were their Dress Whites or better.

The USS *Arizona* Memorial is comprised of the memorial itself, the USS *Arizona* Memorial Museum and the USS *Arizona* Memorial Visitor Center.

The USS Arizona Memorial Visitor Center

The first stop for most visitors to Pearl Harbor is the Memorial Visitor Center, which was built in 1980 by the US Navy. Located inside the center are two theaters, a museum, a bookstore, restroom, a small snack bar, pay telephones and shoreline exhibits outlining the Pearl Harbor attack. This is also the spot where you will pick up your free tickets for entrance into the USS *Arizona* Memorial program tour. There are no restroom facilities at the Memorial so make sure your party takes care of business before the boat ride!

Obtaining Tickets to the Memorial

With an average of 4,500 visitors a day, a visit to the USS *Arizona* Memorial can be a test of wills. Your best bet is to get there early (the Memorial opens at 7:30 am and the first program begins at 7:45 am in the summer and 8 am in the winter). Tickets are free, on a first-come, first-served basis. When you enter the visitor center, you will be asked to line up for a numbered program ticket, which is your free admission to the memorial tour. When your program number is called, you will be assembled at the theater entrance in preparation for the program tour, which includes a 23-minute documentary film depicting the attack on Pearl Harbor, a short boat trip and a self-guided tour of the USS *Arizona* Memorial. If you would like a narrated tour of the memorial and the story of December 7, 1941, an audio tour is one hour long and takes visitors to 23 destinations. The tour is narrated by Academy Award winner and US Navy veteran Ernest Borgnine. The audio is available in seven languages: English, French, Japanese, Korean, Mandarin, German and Spanish.

Survivor Tales: Although 2,390 lives were lost on December 7, 1941, thousands of service members survived. Pearl Harbor survivors regularly come to the USS *Arizona* Memorial Visitor Center to tell their stories and provide visitors with a first-hand look at what happened that fateful day.

A Face Lift for the Memorial

A fund has been set up to build a new USS *Arizona* Memorial Visitor Center, www.pearlharbormemorial.com. The cost of the new facility is estimated at $52 million and the new center will increase the current exhibit capacity and showcase Pearl Harbor survivors' memorabilia and other artifacts. The current facility was built more than 27 years ago on filled land that is slowly sinking. Construction is scheduled to begin at the end of 2007 and, if everything goes as planned, the new and improved visitor center will open on Dec. 7, 2009, the 68th anniversary of the

Pearl Harbor attack. To donate, contact the Pearl Harbor Memorial Fund, c/o Arizona Memorial Museum Association ☎ 808-487-DEC7 or 866-DEC-1941 (toll free), or visit the website.

The USS Arizona Memorial Museum

The USS *Arizona* Memorial Museum, inside the visitor center, is home to several artifacts of the ship and her crew, other US Pacific Fleet ships and the US Armed Forces from the December 7, 1941 attack through the Battle of Midway. The collection includes a model of the Japanese aircraft carrier IMS *Akagi*, the flagship of the deadly attack force. Another model presents a view of the USS *Arizona* before the attack. One of the more unusual items in the museum is the twisted remains of a Japanese torpedo that was headed toward Pearl Harbor's Battleship Row before the weapon got lodged in the harbor floor, perhaps saving hundreds of sailors' lives in the process. As you peruse the museum, you will also view the oversized photographic murals depicting the raging fires that burned for days after the attack.

The visitor center contains a bookstore filled with books, videos, DVDs, posters and other mementoes of the USS *Arizona*, the Pearl Harbor attack and the War in the Pacific. You can also purchase bookstore items on-line at www.pearlharbormemorial.com.

Special Day: A Pearl Harbor Day Ceremony is held every December 7.

The Memorial

Once you arrive at the Memorial itself, you will discover three distinct areas. The Entry Room holds flags of the nine states for which the eight great battleships and the USS *Utah* were named. Today, the USS *Utah* still rests in Pearl Harbor. The Assembly Room is an open area where ceremonies are held and visitors can closely examine the shadowy remains of the USS *Arizona* below. The Shrine Room displays the names of the 1,177 service members who perished on that fateful day on the USS *Arizona*. It also honors the survivors who have been interred on the ship in recent years.

The Memorial was designed by renowned architect Alfred Preis and the unique bridge-like white structure is a must-see in O`ahu. The Memorial straddles, but does not touch, the USS *Arizona* and is 184 feet long, 36 feet wide and 21 feet high at the ends, tapering to 27 feet wide and 14 feet high at the center.

According to the creators of the memorial, it symbolized America's initial defeat and ultimate victory in World War II. Don't miss the "Tree of Life" feature, which was purposely, designed into the structure and also graces the entryway of the visitor center.

Did You Know? The USS *Arizona* was carrying 1.4 million gallons of fuel when she sank. More than 60 years later, approximately two quarts of fuel a day still surface from the ship. Pearl Harbor Survivors refer to the oil droplets as "black tears."

Battleship Missouri Memorial, ☎ 808-973-2494 or 877-MIGHTYMO, www.pearlharbormemorial.com. Called the "Mighty Mo," this memorial commemorates the site of the surrender ending World War II. The "Mighty Mo" is the last battleship ever built by the US. It is three football fields long and over 20 stories tall. The "Mighty Mo" survived kamikaze attacks and was the site for the Japanese surrender of World War II. It is now in Battleship Row at Pearl Harbor.

Visitors to the Memorial can relive America's conflicts and glories as well as take to the skies and visit the new Combat Flight Simulator that allows visitors to re-fight the pivotal Battle of Midway. And now you can enjoy a variety of dining options at the Truman Line Mess Deck, which is the same kitchen that served thousands of American soldiers as well as President Harry S. Truman.

The Mighty Mo is open daily from 9 am to 5 pm and the ticket office is open from 9 am to 4 pm. The battleship is next to the USS *Arizona* Memorial Visitor Center. Entrance costs $16 for adults or $8 for children four to 12 years old.

Security Note: No bags are allowed on board. If you have any questions, call the Memorial's office for answers.

USS Bowfin submarine
(www.hnsa.org)

USS *Bowfin* Submarine Park & Museum, 11 Arizona Memorial Drive, ☎ 808-423-1341, www.bowfin.org. An important part of Pearl Harbor history, the USS *Bowfin* was launched on December 7, 1942 and was nicknamed the "Pearl Harbor Avenger." She sank 44 enemy ships during the course of her nine extraordinary war patrols. The museum also has a waterfront memorial that was erected to remember the 52 American submarines and the more than 3,500 submarines lost during World War II.

The park is operated by the non-profit Pacific Fleet Submarine Memorial Association. The site is funded by proceeds from admissions and the gift shop, which are used to continue the preservation and restoration of the USS *Bowfin*. The park is open daily from 8 am to 5 pm. The last tour begins at 4:30 pm. Due to safety concerns, no children under the age of four are allowed on the submarine although they are allowed to visit the museum and mini-theatre at no charge. Entrance for the Submarine & Museum adult tour is $10 or $4 for children ages four to 12. For admission to the museum only, adults are charged $5 and children ages four to 12 are charged $3.

Money Saving Tip: Combination tickets for Pearl Harbor attractions are available at Bowfin

Park. For example, an adult can pay $20 for an unguided tour of the USS *Bowfin* and the USS *Missouri*. For more information, visit www.bowfin.org.

The newest attraction at Pearl Harbor is the **Pacific Aviation Museum**, Hangar 37, Ford Island, 319 Lexington Blvd., www.pacificaviationmuseum.org, reservations@pacificaviationmuseum.org, ☎ 808-441-1000 or US7-DEC-1941 (toll free). This museum occupies World War II hangars in Pearl Harbor that still bear the scars as our nation's first aviation battlefield. The museum is dedicated to showing the patriotism and valor of the American aviators in the Pacific. Exhibits include a 1942 Japanese Zero aircraft and its opponent, the Wildcat, in full diorama exhibits. The facility also includes the tropical 1940s-themed Blue Heaven Café, a gift shop, flight simulators and souvenir photography. Tickets are available from travel desks throughout Honolulu and at the USS *Bowfin* ticket office. The museum is open daily (except for Christmas Day, Thanksgiving Day and New Year's Day) from 9:30 am to 4:30 pm. General admission is $14 for adults, $7 for children ages four-12 and $7 for an aviator's guided tour.

To get to the museum, obtain a ticket through an approved travel desk or at the USS *Bowfin* ticket office. The *Bowfin* is located next to the USS *Arizona* Memorial. You will then board the Ford Island Trolley at the Trolley stop in front of the USS *Bowfin* Memorial for your trip to the Pacific Aviation Museum.

Organizers suggest allowing two hours for a visit to the museum and, as the museum is on an active Military Base, diligent security procedures are in effect. No bags are allowed on the Trolley.

Adventures on Land

Tours

Home of the Brave and Top Gun Tours, ☎ 808-396-8112, www.pearlharborhq.com, offers two fabulous and informative tours. The company has special relationships with the US Army, Air Force, Navy, Park Service and the DOD WWII Commemoration Committee allowing access to historic points of interest on O`ahu.

The "Pearl Harbor Hawaii Victory Tour" takes you on a one-of-a-kind journey that goes back to the 1940s. The tour is held from 6 am to 2 pm and your first stop is the Pearl Harbor Visitor Center and the Arizona Memorial. Stop #2 is Wheeler Army Airfield, which was the site of several major historic aviation events prior to December 7, 1941. The tour then moves on to the Schofield Army Barracks, the largest Army base outside the Continental United States, which as an interesting museum dedicated to the history of the 25th Infantry "Tropic Lightning," where you will enjoy World War II pictures, tanks and weapons. The next stop on the tour is Fort Shafter, the oldest US Military base on O`ahu, which was completed in 1907. The tour takes you around beautiful Palm Circle and visits Lt. General Walter T. Short's famous residence – Quarter 5. A buffet lunch is served at the Fort Shafter Military Club, which overlooks the club's golf course.

After lunch, you head to the Punchbowl National Cemetery, the beautifully landscaped resting place for more than 30,000 American sailors, soldiers and airmen.

The tour then takes you to downtown Honolulu and the Home of the Brave Museum, where you can browse the gift shop for special reminders of your tour.

The company's second tour was just about to open at press time and is called "Honolulu's Wartime Walk." It lasts from 4 to 9 pm and includes dinner at the famous Murphy's Restaurant, where citizens and sailors have hoisted glasses for over 150 years. The tour starts at Aloha Tower and, after dinner, guests will visit historic sites and the Home of the Brave Museum.

Leeward O`ahu

At a Glance

The leeward side of the island is the west side and is typically drier than the other sides of the island. Located on the coastal side of the Wai`anae Mountains, this area was created between 2.7 and 3.4 million years ago. The Wai`anae mountain range is the older yet smaller of the two ranges that make up O`ahu. The highest point of this range is Mount Ka`ala, which rises 4,017 feet above the ocean.

IN THIS CHAPTER

One of the most prominent landmarks on the leeward side is the 640-acre Ko Olina Resort & Marina, which includes the luxurious JW Marriott Ihilani Resort & Spa at Ko Olina, Ko Olina Golf Club and Ko Olina Marina.

Weather

In the winter, temperatures range from a high of 80°F to a low of 65°. In the summer, temperature range from 86° to 71°.

History

In ancient times, walking into Wai`anae required either climbing over the rugged Waianae Range at Kolekole Pass or crossing dry and challenging terrain to the north or south. The area was iso-

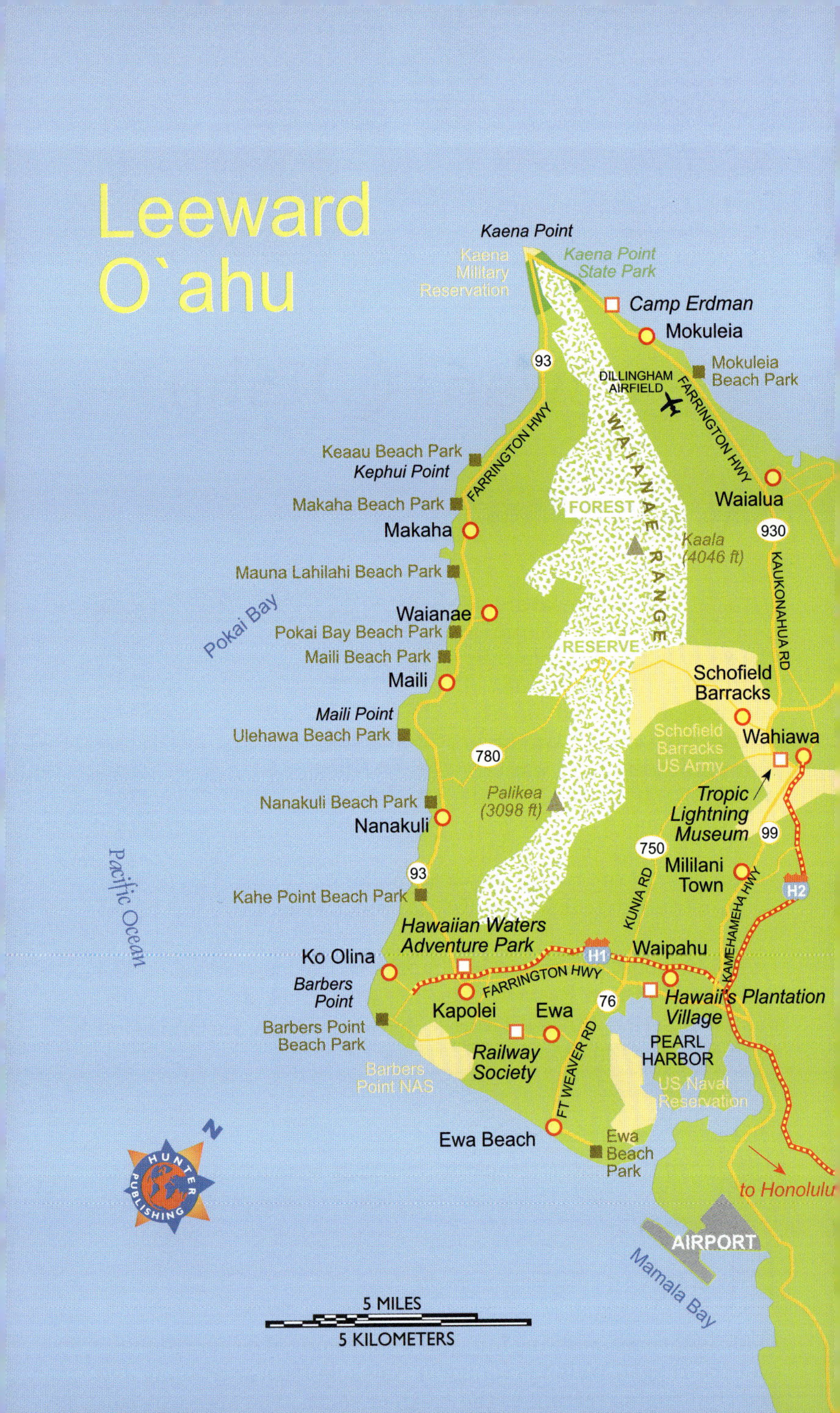

Leeward O`ahu
Kaena Point
Kaena Military Reservation
Kaena Point State Park
Camp Erdman
Mokuleia
Mokuleia Beach Park
93
DILLINGHAM AIRFIELD
FARRINGTON HWY
WAIANAE RANGE
FOREST
RESERVE
Keaau Beach Park
Kephui Point
Makaha Beach Park
Makaha
Waialua
Kaala (4046 ft)
930
KAUKONAHUA RD
Mauna Lahilahi Beach Park
Pokai Bay
Waianae
Pokai Bay Beach Park
Maili Beach Park
Maili
Schofield Barracks
Maili Point
Ulehawa Beach Park
Schofield Barracks US Army
Wahiawa
780
Tropic Lightning Museum
Palikea (3098 ft)
Nanakuli Beach Park
Nanakuli
99
750
Mililani Town
KUNIA RD
KAMEHAMEHA HWY
H2
Pacific Ocean
Kahe Point Beach Park
Hawaiian Waters Adventure Park
Waipahu
H1
Ko Olina
Barbers Point
FARRINGTON HWY
Kapolei
Ewa
76
Hawaii's Plantation Village
Barbers Point Beach Park
PEARL HARBOR
Railway Society
FT WEAVER RD
Barbers Point NAS
US Naval Reservation
Ewa Beach
Ewa Beach Park
to Honolulu
HUNTER PUBLISHING
N
AIRPORT
Mamala Bay
5 MILES
5 KILOMETERS

lated and, when Kamehameha the Great conquered O`ahu in 1795 and Christianity was first introduced to the island, the Waianae district kept itself separate from the rest of the island.

The separation was a mixed blessing for Wai`anae. Governor Boki and his wife Liliha were traditionalists who offered an alternative to rapidly embracing the Christian religion.

Residents are conscious of the value of water and in 1878, Herman Wedemeyer created the Waianae Sugar Company. Water from the freshwater springs in the Waianae Range was used to create the sugar. In 1879, brothers John, James and Lincoln McCandless dug the first successful artesian well in Nanakuli, Hawaii to provide 2,400 gallons of water an hour

`Ewa

At a Glance

With its sugar mill history, `Ewa is an interesting throwback to the days when sugar ruled the islands. A ride on the Hawaiian Railway can help you understand the importance of sugar in Hawaii's history.

Adventures on Land

Golf

Coral Creek Golf Course, 91-111 Geiger Road, Ewa Beach, ☎ 808-441-4653, www.coral-creekgolfhawaii.com, is an 18-hole championship, par-72, 6,808-yard course. One of the highlights (and challenges) is the 636-yard, par-5 11th hole – the longest hole in all of Hawaii.

Hawaiian Railway

The Hawaiian Railway, ☎ 808-681-5461, www.hawaiianrailway.com, is the only active railroad on O`ahu. The train runs down Hawaii's historic railroad tracks year-round, with two

departures – one at 1 pm and another at 3 pm. Tickets for the 90-minute ride are $10 for adults and $7 for children ages two to 12 and seniors over age 62. Bring cash because credit cards are not accepted.

The second Sunday of the month is reserved for the luxurious Parlor Car that was built in 1900. Tickets for this ride are $20 and reservations are required. The trains run at about 15 miles per hour and a narrator explains the history of the train and tells stories about how sugar trains were used on the plantations. The train yard also has an inviting picnic area and a gift shop.

Where to Stay

Vacation Rentals

Hawaiianvacation.com has a special section for `Ewa Beach vacation rentals. Check out www.hawaiian-vacation.com/regions/Ewa-Beach-Hawaii.html.

www.vrbo.com has vacation rentals listed by the owners.

Kapolei

At a Glance

Kapolei is a small area west of Pearl Harbor, best known being home to the Hawaiian Waters Adventure Park. Kapolei is often referred to as "O`ahu's Second City" and is about 24 miles from Waikiki.

Adventures on Water

Hawaiian Waters Adventure Park

Hawaiian Waters Adventure Park, 400 Farrington Hwy., ☎ 808-674-WAVE, www.hawaiianwaters.com. The hours of this family fun park vary greatly so your best bet is to call the information line. During the slower seasons (when the kids are in school) they are closed on Tuesdays and Wednesdays. This is the only water park in Hawaii (with 25 acres of fun, sun and water) and is open all year, although the hours tend to vary depending on the weather from September to May. Call for park hours during that season. Although it's a family resort, the park (which is about 30 minutes west of Waikiki) has an adults-only area called Cutter's Island, with a pool, hot tub and adult beverages. Kids of all ages can cruise in tubes down the 800-foot-long continuous river called "Kapolei Kooler." Some of the more exciting rides include "The Cliffhanger," which is a free fall down six stories, and the "Volcano Express," a 5½-story slide where five rides can race to the finish line. New to the park is "Da Flowrider" – the ultimate ride, which costs an additional fee. You can go headfirst or try standing up if you have what it takes. The park also has the Windjammer Food Court, changing rooms, showers, restrooms, lockers, life vests and bodyboards for rent. Many bus packages are available from most major Waikiki Hotels. Also – you can't bring food, drinks or glass into the park.

Admission is $35.99 for adults, $25.99 for children ages three to 11, $14.99 for senior citizens and children age two or under can get in for free. To get to Hawaiian Waters from Waikiki, take Exit 1 off H-1 West. Parking is free. Woo-hoo!

HAWAIIAN WATERS PARK DIRECTORY

Call ☎ 674-9283 for information, with the following extensions:

Park Hours and Directions	Ext. 115
Special Events & Da Flowrider	Ext. 102
Company Picnics	Ext. 104
Youth/Non-Profit Groups	Ext. 206
Tour Packages	Ext. 107
Birthday Party Packages	Ext. 111

Also, the information message will let you know if there are any promotions going on. For example, when I last called they said there was a promotion with Times supermarket in Oahu where you could pick up a coupon for $7 off adult admission.

Adventures on Land

Golf

The Kapolei Golf Course, 97-701 Farrington Highway, ☎ 808-674-2227, www.kapoleigolfcourse.com. Ted Robinson created this 18-hole championship golf course. Opened in 1995, the Kapolei Golf Course occupies 191 acres of former sugar cane lands and is up-to-date with GPS-equipped golf carts.

Ko Olina

At a Glance

Ko Olina is made up of the secluded 640-acre oceanfront property that use to serve as a playground for Hawaiian royalty. Today it includes the fabulous JW Marriott Ihilani Resort & Spa at Ko Olina and also has a golf club, a marina and tennis facilities.

Beaches

Kahe Point Beach Park

This park is known for its great shore and spear fishing. It is also a fabulous place to snorkel, as the water is usually clear and there is a huge fish population. The beach is just north of the massive Ko Olina Resorts.

Hawaiian Electric Beach Park

Also known as "Tracks," this beach is adjacent to Kahe Point Beach Park directly across from the highway and the looming Hawaiian Electric Company Power Plant. The power plant makes this spot a popular scuba diving spot because of the underwater pipes that feed warm water into the area and attract a variety of fish. Snorkeling should be reserved for intermediate or advanced swimmers as a moderate swim is needed to reach the best viewing. Also, there are no lifeguards, so be aware of your surroundings. Scuba divers will enjoy this beach as it has a gentle slope and sand bottom, which makes it an easy entry for shore dives. Keep your eyes open for Hawaiian green sea turtles and spinner dolphins – both species tend to hang out in the waters off Electric Beach.

Nanakuli Beach Park

Nanakuli Beach Park, 82-269 Farrington Highway, translates in Hawaiian as "To Look At The Knee." Since this beach is on the dry side of the island, be sure to bring plenty of water and sunscreen. A hat and sunglasses don't hurt either.

Adventures on Land

Tennis

The Ihilani Resort & Spa has a tennis garden where the courts are open from 7 am to 8 pm. Private and semi-private lessons are available as well as clinics for adults and kids.

JUST FOR KIDS

The Ihilani Resort & Spa has a hands-on, interactive ocean adventure program called the Kahihimanu I Ke Kai, which is just for kids. Youngsters will be able to participate in a feeding and interpretation session with reef sharks, stingrays, starfish, sea urchins and sea cucumbers in the resort's saltwater ponds. The programs is offered at 9 am and 11 am for children ages 10 and older and at 1 pm for kids ages four through 10. The informative and fun program is held on Monday, Tuesday, Wednesday, Friday and Sunday. Reservations (☎ 808-679-0079 or 800-626-4446 toll free) are recommended and the cost is $29. 50 for children staying at the resort; $34 otherwise.

Golf

Ko Olina Golf Club, 92-1480 Aliinui Drive, ☎ 808-676-5300, www.koolinagolf.com, offers a challenging 18-hole championship course with water features, multi-tiered greens and no parallel fairways. This is one of the premier golf courses in Hawaii. They also have a golf shop and an academy.

Adventures on Water

Boating

Ko Olina Marina, 92-100 Waipahe Place, ☎ 808-679-1050, info@koolinamarina.com, has a variety of activities for visitors.

Visitors can charter a private yacht, the *Kai `Oli`Oli* (☎ 808-677-1277 or 888-677-1277, www.OceanJoyCruises.com) that will take them up the entire Wai`anae Coast from Ko Olina Marina to the northern tip of the island, the sacred Ka`ena Point. Snorkeling is available to those who feel like exploring the waters and the company offers a delicious lunch buffet including mai tais, refreshing beers and soft drinks.

Snorkeling Tours

Visitors to Ko Olina Marina are also able to take a snorkeling excursion aboard a 53-foot catamaran with ***Hawaii Nautical***, ☎ 808-234-SAIL. The company offers morning, afternoon and sunset cruises.

Whale Watching

A two-hour whale-watching tour (during the winter months) on *Hawaii Nautical* costs $50 for adults and $45 for children. If you don't see any whales, you're invited to come back aboard and take another another tour for free. The tours leave from Ko Olina Marina.

Sailing

**The Sailing Club Hawai`i**, ☎ 808-222-9768 or 800-908-5250, www.HawaiiYachts.com, offers tours on its luxury yacht and has several sailing options to choose from. Prospective sailors can take a two-hour sailing lesson and honeymooners can enjoy a romantic dinner aboard the yacht. The Sailing Club Hawai`i also offers overnight sails as well as interisland adventures.

Where to Stay

Resorts

JW Marriott Ihilani Resort & Spa at Ko Olina, 92-1001 Olani Street, ☎ 808-679-0079 or 800-626-4446 (toll free), www.ihilani.com. This glorious resort is just far enough away from the Waikiki for comfort and is a paradise on its own, with white sand beaches and luxurious rooms. AAA has awarded the resort its four-diamond rating. The 17-story resort has 387 rooms, 36 suites, four restaurants and three bars. There are also four man-made lagoons for swimming, a pool and a top-notch spa. For a special treat, reserve one of the west-facing ocean-view or deluxe ocean-view rooms for fabulous views of the Wai`anae Mountains.

The 640-acre Ko Olina property has four coves along a turquoise lagoon where you may see dolphins spinning near the golden beaches.

SPA ALERT

The **Ihilani Spa** is a full-service destination spa with several Hawaiian and Polynesian treatments. This place is huge – 35,000 feet – and includes an outdoor lap pool and fitness center. The spa also has saunas, roman pools, steam rooms and relaxation lounges. Among the many fitness programs available, the new "Hip on Hula" class is a fun way to get into shape. This hour-long session teaches guests basic hula moves that provide an intensive workout for the hips and legs. Take advantage of one of the 19 treatment rooms for an only-in-Hawaii spa experience. Indulge!

Hawaiian Translations: Ihilani translates to "Heavenly Splendor" in the Hawaiian language while Ko Olina means "Place of Joy."

To get to the JW Marriott from the Honolulu Airport (it's about 18 miles west), take the H-1 Freeway, going west to Waianae. Stay on the freeway for approximately 25 minutes and exit at the Ko`Olina exit. Continue on this street, pass the resort security gate and turn right on Olani Street. Self-parking is $18 a day versus valet parking for $18 a day. As I always say "Always Valet!" $$$$$

HAWAIIAN LEGEND

The *Naupaka Blossom* is the symbol of the Ihilani Resort and Spa and it has an interesting historic tale behind it. In old Hawaii, it was customary for the son of a chief (*Ali`i*) to marry only the daughter of a chief. To marry any other was *kapu* (against the law).

One *Ali`inui* (junior chief and son of an *Ali`i*) named Kaipo lived near the shoreline where he enjoyed fishing. One day, his father told him that he was to marry Leilani, the daughter of an *Ali`i*. Kaipo was not happy with the arrangement so he took off to the mountains to start a new life.

One day, as he was wandering through the mountains, Kaipo met a beautiful young woman with a flower in her hair. Her name was Pua (which means "flower"). The couple soon fell in love.

Pua taught Kaipo how to hunt and survive in the mountains and, although he was happy to be with her, he yearned for his days back by the ocean where he could fish. Kaipo wanted to show Pua what a good fisherman he was. The couple soon left the mountains as Kaipo thought that, if his father saw how happy he was with Pua, he would allow Kaipo to marry her.

Although Kaipo's father was happy to see his son, he was not happy to learn of the proposed marriage to Pua, a commoner. The *Ali`i* sent for his guards and ordered them to take Pua back to the mountains. As they escorted Pua away, she stopped and took the flower from her hair. With tears in her eyes, she told Kaipo, "Take this flower and always remember me." Kaipo took the flower and tore it in half. Then he said, "This flower will never be complete until we are together again."

According to legend, the two lovers will be reunited only when the *Naupaka-Kahakai* (the beach flower) and *Naupaka-Kuahiwi* (the mountain flower) are once again brought together.

Where to Eat

Restaurants at JW Marriott Ihilani Resort & Spa (☎ 808-679-0079)

Naupaka Terrace serves breakfast, lunch and dinner in a casual atmosphere with open-air views of the pool and lagoon. The cuisine is contemporary Pacific Rim and, in addition to the regular menu, Naupaka Terrace offers a daily breakfast buffet and a Saturday night seafood buffet. Naupaka Terrace is open Monday through Thursday from 6:30 am to 2 pm and 5:30 pm to 10 pm. The restaurant is open from 6:30 am to 10 pm on Friday, Saturday and Sunday. Breakfast $$. Lunch $$. Dinner $$$.

For dinner, **Azul** serves international fare using fresh herbs, vegetables and fresh fish caught daily off the coast. This elegant

restaurant has received the esteemed AAA four-diamond award and has been noted for "Best Wine List" by *Wine Spectator.* Try to get a table on the terrace for a romantic dining experience. Azul also has a champagne brunch on Sundays from 9:30 am to 2 pm. Dinner is served daily from 5 to 10 pm. Dinner $$$. Brunch $$$.

Ushio-Tei (which means "the subtle tides of Hawaii") is open for dinner and offers Kaiseki dining at the sushi bar or authentic Japanese cuisine in one of the private tatami rooms. Ushio-Tei also offers Tabehodai, an all-you-can-eat buffet. They are open Thursday through Monday from 5:30 to 9 pm. $$$.

The Poolside Grill is open for lunch, offering snacks and lighter fare. The grill overlooks the ocean and pool. It's a great place to relax and have a drink and a snack. $$.

Hokule`a Bar is located on the lobby level and offers a great place for sipping cocktails while enjoying a pre-dinner or after-dinner snack. The bar is open nightly from 5 pm to midnight and live entertainment is scheduled for Saturday nights from 8 to 10 pm. $$.

Wai`anae

At a Glance

Located on O`ahu's southwest corner, Wai`anae is home to many Hawaiian homesteads and farmlands that line Farrington Highway. From this highway, there are stunning views of the Waianae Range. The Wai`anae Boat Harbor offers fishing and diving charters for locals and tourists.

Beaches

Ma`ili Beach Park

Before you reach Ma`ili Beach Park, you'll see a distinctive round hill at the northwest end of the park called Pu`u Mailiili, which

was formally known in Hawaiian as Kalaeokakao (Goat Point). In 1778 Captain Cook brought goats to the island. In the 1800s, large numbers of wild goats grazed in this area and were protected under the *kapu* (forbidden) law.

The Ma`ili Beach Park, 87-021 Farrington Highway, is named for the numerous pebbles (ili`ili) found nearby. This is a nice swimming beach in the summer months but it disappears in the winter due to the large swells. Swimmers beware of a sudden drop-off from the coral reef into deep water. The beach park has restrooms, showers, barbecue grills, picnic tables and lifeguards.

Poka`i Bay Beach Park

Poka`i Bay Beach Park, 85-037 Waianae Valley Road, translates in Hawaiian to "Night of the Supreme One" and is named after the legendary Hawaiian chief, Poka`i, who is believed to brought the first coconut palm tree to Hawaii. Poka`i Bay is well protected, even in the wild winter months, and is great for swimming year-round. Lifeguards patrol the beach and the park also has picnic tables, barbecue grills, restrooms and showers.

Surf's Up: The Leeward side of O`ahu has dozens of surf spots, many with interesting names like "Bathtubs," "Green Lantern" and "Free Hawaii."

Adventures on Water

Scuba

Electric Beach by Kahe Point and **Tech Reef** by the Ko Olina Resort are nice beginner/intermediate scuba spots that can be entered from the shore. Watch out for the 15-foot tiger shark that is known to frequent the area!

Makaha

At a Glance

Makaha is north of Wai`anae and is home to some awesome surf spots (for experts only). The area is a little quieter and more remote than the rest of O`ahu and you might forget which island you're on!

Sightseeing

Makaha Beach

Makaha Beach, 84-369 Farrington, is one of Hawaii's most famous surfing spots and is the site of an international surf competition every year. The winter waves prove to challenging to boogie boarders and surfers alike, while in summer, Makaha has the widest strand of sand on the leeward side of O`ahu. During high surf periods, Makaha Beach can be dangerous and even deadly. Always check with lifeguards before entering the ocean. Amenities include picnic tables, showers and restrooms.

Kaneaki Heiau

Kaneaki Heiau is believed to be named after Ku, a god associated with agriculture. Others believe that the heiau first served Lono, the god of agriculture and peace. Construction of the heiau began in the 15th century and, after five more phases, the heiau doubled its size by AD 1650. You must have permission (☎ 808-695-8174) to visit the prayer towers, grass huts and altar.

Makua Cave

Makua Cave is a lava cavern 450 feet in length and large enough to explore. It's on the mountain side of the road right before Ka`ena Point State Park. This cave is also known as Kaneana Cave and is believed to be home of a legendary shark goddess who held power in the waters off the coast of Ka`ena Point. In legend, the goddess would emerge from the cave in the form of a woman and lure unsuspecting victims into the cave.

Yokohama Bay

Yokohama Bay is the last stretch of sandy beach on the leeward coast. Experienced divers and shell collectors alike will enjoy this beach for its abundance of shells, due to the rocky bottom and aggressive ocean.

Adventures on Water

Tours

Wild Side Specialty Tours, ☎ 808-306-7273, Wai`anae Boat Harbor Slip A5, www.sailhawaii.com. This company provides a huge variety of adventurous tours, including a morning wildlife sail, afternoon whale watch and sunset tours. See the website for all of the amazing combinations and some great reviews of the tours available.

Adventures on Land

Golf

Makaha Resort & Golf Club, ☎ 808-695-9544, www.makaharesort.net/golf.asp, is a naturally beautiful and challenging course. You'll share the lush course with birds and peacocks, against a background of sheer volcanic cliffs that tower 1,500 above the course.

Where to Stay

Resort

Makaha Resort & Golf Club, 84-626-Makaha Valley Road, ☎ 808-695-9544 or 866-576-6447 (toll free), www.makaharesort.net. Located along the rugged cliffs of the Wai`anae Mountains, this is one of O`ahu's best-kept secrets. Its location offers a serene yet scenic atmosphere. A bonus is the 18-hole championship golf course at the resort. The resort also has a restaurant and lounge, wireless Internet access in the lobby and poolside, spa services and a laundry facility.

The Makaha Resort has 173 guest rooms, including 20 suites. The rooms are pleasantly decorated with a Polynesian feel. Standard rooms offer garden and mountain views. Deluxe and one-bedroom suites have vaulted ceilings with views of the gardens and mountains or the ocean and golf course. Standard Room $$-$$$. Suites $$$-$$$$.

Luaus

Germaine's Luau, ☎ 808-949-6626 or 800-367-5655 (toll free), www.germainesluau.com, is considered the best on O`ahu. The dinner includes an American/Hawaiian buffet with traditional island and continental fare. Fruit punch and soft drinks are served as well as Germaine's special Mai Tai's and Blue Hawaii's. The buffet includes Kalua pig, island fish, teriyaki beef, fried chicken, green salad, poi (taro potato), lomilomi salmon, pineapple coleslaw, three bean salad, rolls and, for dessert, haupia (coconut pudding), fresh pineapple, vanilla coconut cake and chocolate cake.

Germaine's is west of Honolulu, about a 45-minute to one-hour drive from Waikiki. Take the H-1 Freeway West and follow the signs to Wai`anae. Leave the freeway at Exit #1 (Campbell Industrial Park) that loops over the freeway and proceeds toward the ocean on Kalaeloa Blvd. to the very end. The luau is at Olai Street on Barbers Point. It is offered daily from 6 pm (gates open at 5:30 pm). The show begins with a shell lei greeting, a cocktail hour with live Hawaiian music and then an Imu ceremony and a Royal Court Presentation.

Dinner begins at 7 pm and includes a fantastic Samoan fire-knife dancer.

The cost is $65 for adults, $55 for juniors ages 14-20, $45 for children ages six to 13 and children under five are free.

Free round-trip transportation from Waikiki is available from Germaine's. Pick-up time is between 4 and 4:30 pm. If you want to drive yourself, good news! – parking is free.

Web Booking Special: If you book your tickets to Germaine's Luau on their website, you'll receive a free gift bag (which they value at $35) for each paid adult at regular price.

Just north of Germaine's Luau is the **Paradise Cove Luau**, ☎ 808-842-5911 or 800-775-2683 (toll free), www.paradisecovehawaii.com, reservations@paradisecove.com. Paradise Cove has several luau packages to choose from: the Hawaiian Luau Buffet, Royal Ali`i Service and the Deluxe Luau Package. Paradise Cove is more of a whole experience with the dinner just being a small part of the evening.

North Shore
5 MILES
5 KILOMETERS
Pacific Ocean
Pacific Ocean
Turtle Bay
Kahuku Point
Kawela
Waialee
Paumalu
Sunset Beach
Pupukea Beach Park
Haleiwa Beach Park
Waimea
Haleiwa Beach Park
Mokuleia Beach Park
Mokuleia
Camp Erdman
Kaena Military Reservation
Kaena Point
Kaena Point State Park
DILLINGHAM AIRFIELD
FARRINGTON HWY
Waialua
Walalua Bay
Haleiwa
83
KAMEHAMEHA HWY
930
99
KAUKONAHUA RD
FOREST RESERVE
WAIANAE RANGE
Kaala (4046 ft)
93
Makua Point
Schofield Barracks
780
80
Wahiawa
to Pearl Harbor
Wahiawa Botanical Gardens
Dole Plantation
Puu O Mahuca Heiau State Monument
Waimea Falls Park
Waimea Valley Audubon Ctr
Hale O Lono Heiau
KAMEHAMEHA HWY
Kahuku
Makahoa Point
Malaekahana State Recreation Area
Laie
Laniloa Peninsula
83
Hauula Beach Park
Hanuula
Aukai Beach Park
Sacred Falls State Park
Punaluu
Punaluu Beach Park
Kahana Bay Beach Park
Swanzy Beach Park
Kahana
Kaaawa
Kalae-oio Beach Park
Kahana Valley State Park
KOOLAU RANGE
FOREST RESERVE
Puu Kaaumakua (2681 ft)
Kualoa Point
Waikane
N
HUNTER PUBLISHING

North Shore

At A Glance

Considered the surfing capital of the world, the North Shore of O`ahu is where you'll find those famous surf spots that you've heard of – Sunset Beach, the Banzai Pipeline and Waimea Bay. It's also the most laidback part of the island, with only one major resort and a vast scattering of more low-key vacation rentals and beach bungalows. The North Shore area spans from La`ie on the northwestern side of the island to Kaena Point on the eastern edge. Although only about 40 miles from busy Waikiki, the mellow North Shore seems a world away.

IN THIS CHAPTER

SURF LESSONS

If you're interested in learning to surf, O`ahu is the place to start. Besides being great exercise, you're guaranteed to come back with some great "Hang Ten" stories to tell your jealous buddies at home!

Most of the year, you'll be able to find kind enough waves to accommodate beginners. If you're interested in learning to surf, heading to the professionals is suggested as they will give you helpful hints to getting up on your board, ocean safety tips and provide you with the proper equipment.

Here are a couple of surf schools that serve the entire island:

Hans Hedemann Surf School, ☎ 808-924-4778, www.hhsurf.com, is one of O`ahu's best-known surf schools and has a good reputation throughout the island. Hans Hedemann Surf School has been around for more than 17 years and has a roster of high-profile clients like Adam Sandler, Cameron Diaz and Justin Timberlake. The company has branches at the Park Shore Waikiki right across from Waikiki Beach, at the Kahala Hotel and Resort on the Windward Coast and at Turtle Bay Resort on the North Shore. They offer private lessons ($115/per hour, $150/two hours), semi-private lessons ($95/per hour, $125/two hours), group lessons ($50/per hour, $75/two hours), private lessons for kids ($115/per hour, $150/two hours), surf lessons with the master himself, Hans Hedemann ($250/hour), or lessons from their staff of professional surfers ($250/two hours).

Girls Who Surf, ☎ 808-371-8917 or 808-561-3004, (nine locations throughout O`ahu), www.girlswhosurf.com, info@GirlsWhoSurf.com. This company is all about fun, adventure and surfing, focusing on but not limited to girls. The instructors operate all over the island and provide free transportation from almost anywhere island-wide. Some of the most popular locales are Waikiki, Ko `Olina and the North Shore, depending on the weather and conditions. Call ahead of time for reservations and choose from basic, intensive, introductory or a package of lessons. All you need to bring is a towel and sunscreen – surfboards, rash guards and fins are provided by Girls Who Surf. The most popular lesson is the Basic Surf Option that gives you an hour and 45 minutes of surf time plus about half an hour of travel time (all for $90). Check out their cool website for more information, plus a showcase of surf products and logo items.

Surf Culture

The winter months, from October through March, bring huge waves to the North Shore of O`ahu and the area is a Mecca for "Big Wave" surfing. The enormous ocean wave swells are generated by seasonal storms 2,000-3,000 miles north of Hawaii. Winds help push the waves toward the islands and the swells slowly build on top of one another to create mas-

sive waves reaching heights of 25 feet and more. Waimea Bay is one of the world's most famous surf spots and is reserved for only the most experienced surfers. For the rest of us, watching the pros is the closest we'll ever get to "hanging ten." The stretch of coast between Waimea Bay and Sunset Beach is excellent for roadside viewing of the big wave surfers. And when the waves are really BIG, you may see tow-in surfers, who are taken out to the huge waves by jet skis so they can drop down the sheer faces of the 25- to 50-foot waves.

TRIPLE CROWN OF SURFING

In 1983, world champion surfer and Hawaii state senator Fred Hemmings started the Triple Crown of Surfing competition. The concept behind the Triple Crown was to have a champion emerge after surfing the three major surf spots on O`ahu's North Shore – Hale`iwa Ali`i Beach Park, Sunset Beach and the Banzai Pipeline (for the men). Women started competing in 1997 and they compete at three sites – Hale`iwa Ali`i Beach Park, Sunset Beach and Honolua Bay (in Maui). The event is held over a period of 12 days, with the actual competition taking place on the days with the biggest surf.

For the rest of us, this is a spectator sport and the roadways are clogged with cars and surf fans watching the amazing talent. For more information, contact www.triplecrownofsurfing.com, www.aspworldtour.com or www.surfline.com. Information can also be found by calling the Surf News Network at ☎ 808-596-SURF (7873).

Lifeguards are on full alert during the wild winter surf season but you should still use caution and common sense when deciding whether or not to enter the ocean. When it becomes too dangerous, officials will close the beach and post warning signs along the shoreline.

EDDIE WOULD GO

When cruising around the Hawaiian Islands, it is almost guaranteed that you'll see a bumper sticker or T-shirt with the slogan "EDDIE WOULD GO." The saying was inspired by legendary Hawaiian lifeguard and surfer, Eddie Aikau, who died tragically while attempting to help others.

Born May 4, 1946 on the island of Maui, Aikau first learned how to surf at Kahului Harbor. He moved to O`ahu in 1959 with his family and, at age 16, he left school to start working at the Dole pineapple cannery. The young Hawaiian bought his first surfboard with his earnings and, in 1968, Aikau became the first lifeguard hired by the City and County of Honolulu to work on the dangerous North Shore. Not one life was lost while he served as a lifeguard at Waimea Bay, where he frequently had to brave surf 20 feet high. Besides saving many lives, Aikau also surfed the huge North Shore waves and won several awards, including the 1977 Duke Kahanamoku Invitational Surfing Championship.

In 1978, the Polynesian Voyaging Society was seeking volunteers for a 30-day, 2,500-mile journey that would follow the ancient route of the Polynesian migration between the Hawaiian and Tahitian island chains.

Aikau, who was 31, joined the venture as a crewmember. The *Hokule`a* left the Hawaiian Islands on March 16, 1978. About 12 miles south of Moloka`i, the double-hulled canoe developed a leak in one of the hulls and later capsized. Aikau grabbed his surfboard and started paddling toward Lana`i in an attempt to get help. Although the rest of the crew was rescued by the US Coast Guard, Aikau was never seen again.

The Quiksilver Big Wave Invitational in memory of Eddie Aikau is held at Waimea Bay. The interesting part of this competition is that it is only held when open-oceans swells reach at least 20 feet (or wave face height of over 30 feet). When this occurs, 24 big-wave riders are invited to participate in two rounds of competitions. In the true spirit of Eddie Aikau, no jet skis are allowed for tow-ins and all surfers must paddle themselves into the waves. Surfers all over the world watch the surf reports and, when it is believed that the waves might be big enough to hold the competition, they all head to O`ahu for a chance to compete in the event.

In the 22-year history of the event, the competition has been held only seven times. It was last held in December 2004 when Bruce Irons of Kaua`i won the competition.

"Eddie Would Go" refers to the brave Hawaiian's legendary life and his daring reputation to save someone – "Eddie Would Go, When No One Else Would or Could. Only Eddie Dared."

For more information about the competition, log on to www.surf.quiksilver.com and, for more information about Eddie Aikau, visit www.eddiewouldgo.com, where Stuart Holmes Coleman's book about the Hawaiian hero can be seen and/or ordered.

La`ie

La`ie is home to the Mormon Temple, Brigham Young University and the Polynesian Cultural Center, which is Hawaii's most popular paid attraction. The area also contains some of the quieter beaches on the island that are great for swimming and other water activities.

La`ie Hawaii Temple

Shopping

A Foodland grocery store is located in the La`ie Shopping Center that also contains a movie theatre, video rental shop and the post office. At Foodland, ask for a Maika`i card, a free discount card that saves you money on many items.

Sightseeing

Polynesian Cultural Center, ☎ 808-293-3333 or 800-367-7060, www.polynesia.com. Named one of the most popular visitor attractions in Hawaii, this 42-acre park promotes all of the Polynesian communities including Fiji,

Hawaii, Aotearoa (New Zealand), Marquesas, Samoa, Tahiti and Tonga. The center opened in 1963 as a non-profit dedicated to help preserve the cultural heritage of Polynesia. It employs about 1,300 people, including 750 students from 70 countries and from nearly every state.

The center brings to life the traditions, history and hospitality of seven Pacific cultures. Visitors can mingle with natives of each culture as they demonstrate exotic hip-swaying dances, spear-throwing, climbing coconut trees barefoot, tribal tattooing and making jewelry. Two IMAX theatres are also on the property, as well as authentic Polynesian games and a tropical canoe ride.

The Center's Gateway Restaurant comfortably seats about 1,000 diners and is considered the largest restaurant in the South Pacific. Its décor includes 40-foot representations of Easter Island stone sculptures and 60-foot images of Maori manaia birdman figures.

Just for Kids: A "Passport to Polynesia" is available at the ticket booth for all children, offering activities and opportunities to collect stamps of every culture. It also contains some brain-picking questions for kids as well as coupons for meal deals at nearby restaurants.

The Polynesian Cultural Center is open Monday through Saturday from 12:30 to 9 pm. The Center is closed on Sundays. General admission packages start at $40 for adults and $36 for kids. Children under age three are free. Upgrades to other Polynesian Cultural Center packages, including the Ali`i Lu`au and the Horizons night show, are available for purchase.

If one day isn't enough for you and your family to explore the Polynesian Cultural Center there are special promotions for people who order some of the higher-end package deals, allowing visitors to return at no charge over the next three days.

Luau Alert! The Polynesian Cultural Center has one of the most extravagant dinner shows. Called "Horizons," more than 100 native performers show such talents as fire walking and fire knife dancing. An authentic Polynesian arts and crafts marketplace is also open during the show. But this is a *dry* luau, meaning there is no alcohol served. Remember, the Church of Jesus Christ of Latter-day Saints runs the center.

**La`ie Point**, which juts out into the ocean right from the middle of town, is one of Oahu's most popular spots to take photos. It is home to two natural wonders – the arched isle known as Kukuiho`olua and the rocky point with intense, crashing waves. To get to La`ie Point, pass the Polynesian Cultural Center on Kamehameha Highway (Hwy 83) and turn onto Anemoku. Make a left on Naupaka and take it to the end at the parking area.

Also known as Moku`auia, **Goat Island** can be seen offshore when visiting the Malaekahana Bay State Recreation Area, which is about .4 miles past the Polynesian Cultural Center. The island is about 600 feet offshore and is a bird sanctuary with over 10 species of seabirds.

Goat Island has three beaches, which are accessible by foot at low tide by wading over the reef that extends from Cooke's Point to the point of Goat Island that extends closest to shore. You can find out when low tide occurs by looking in the newspaper. You can also get to the island by paddling over on a surfboard, raft or kayak if the water conditions are calm. Wear reef shoes or old tennis shoes to protect your feet.

Hawaiian History: La`ie, which means "Leaf of the `ie`ie vine," is named for the legendary princess La`ieikawai, who was hidden away in a nearby freshwater pool to protect her from mortal men.

Beaches

**La`ie Beach Park** is located south of the town of La`ie. It's a quiet beach with a large coral reef, which makes it nice for swimming as the reef protects swimmers from the surf. Beginning and intermediate surfers and boogie boarders also enjoy La`ie Beach Park. Watch the ocean conditions closely as there are no lifeguards or facilities.

Hukilau Beach Park is on La`ie Bay, just north of the town of La`ie. In the Hawaiian language, "huki" translates to pull and "lau" means net. In the mid-1900s, the community would gather to pull the fishing nets into the shore and would then celebrate their catch with a festival. The Hukilau festivals were held at this beach from the 1940s through the 1970s. This nice sandy beach is a great place to have a picnic or just enjoy the sun. Be careful as there are no lifeguards or facilities.

Malaekahana State Recreation Area, just north of La`ie, is good for swimming, bodysurfing, beach-related activities and shore fishing. Don't be surprised if you see some of the endangered Hawaiian green sea turtles – they have made Malaekahana Bay their home.

Adventures on Water

Surfing

There are several spots around La`ie that are not well known and are hard to find. That means they're less crowded than the others, which is a great quality on a busy surf island.

Goat Island is about 600 feet offshore from Malaekahana Bay State Park north of La`ie town. This is a great spot for shortboard and longboard surfing as well as bodyboarding. Goat Island is good for surfing year-round, but especially during the winter.

PCC is across from the Polynesian Cultural Center (PCC, get it?). Park along the highway and grab your shortboard for year-round actions. Bodyboarders will also enjoy PCC.

Scuba Diving

Goat Island is also a great beginner/intermediate scuba spot as well as a fun place for snorkeling. Scuba divers can enter from the beach for this shallow dive. You'll see lots of reef fish, lobsters, crabs and octopuses.

Body Surfing/Boogie Boarding

Pounders is at La`ie Beach Park and is good for body surfing and boogie boarding.

Where to Eat

Hukilau Café, 55-662 Wahinepe`e Street, ☎ 808-293-1253. Located off the Kamehameha Highway, this hide-away serves breakfast and lunch and has a fabulous word-of-mouth reputation. Breakfast is served from 7 to 11 am and the famous beef stew omelette is legendary. The delicious French toast is made with Hawaiian sweet bread and pancakes can be made with bananas, coconut or blueberries. Lunch is served from 10 am to 2 pm and guests rave about the teriyaki beef plate. The mahimahi tempura and shrimp tempura plate lunches are also worth a mention. $.

> *Tiki-Style Mickey D's:* Next to the Laie Inn this is the only tiki-style McDonalds I've ever seen. Its unique A-frame architecture and Hawaiian décor make it worth checking out! It also has a local specialty – chili-rice and eggs with Spam, and saimin.

L & L Drive Inn, 55-510 Kamehameha Highway (in the La`ie Shopping Center), ☎ 808-293-8887, www.hawaiianbarbecue.com, calls its cuisine Hawaiian Barbecue. It's fast food and there are several locations throughout O`ahu, the other Hawaiian Islands, and states like California, New York, Colorado, Texas and Utah. Plate lunches are popular and include a main entrée such as kalua pork served with two scoops of rice and one scoop of macaroni salad. $.

Where to Stay

Laie Inn, 55-109 Laniloa Street, ☎ 808-293-9282 or 800-526-4562, www.laieinn.com, laieinn@hawaii.rr.com. The best thing this inn has going for it is the location. Right next to the Polynesian Cultural Center, the 49-room, two-story Laie Inn is a bit old but it does have free parking. The only reason to stay here would be if you were going to visit the Polynesian Cultural Center and wanted to avoid a late-night drive back to Waikiki or Windward O`ahu. Rooms range from doubles to queen and king sizes. The inn charges $10 per extra adult. Free wireless high speed Internet access is available. $$.

Vacation Rentals

For vacation rentals in La`ie and the surrounding area, check out www.vrbo.com, which stands for "Vacation Rentals By Owner."

Vacation Rentals.com also has listings for houses and cottages in the La`ie area. Visit them at www.vacationrentals.com.

Camping

Malaekahana State Recreation Area, north of La`ie, has a wooded beach park with camping facilities in the Kahuku Section. Camping permits for tent spaces are $5. The site has picnic tables, fire pits, toilets and hot outdoor showers. For more information about camping in State Parks in O`ahu, call ☎ 808-587-0300.

Large, spacious tent cabins have been built by the **Friends of Malaekahana**, ☎ 808-293-1736, PO Box 305, La`ie, HI 96762, and are an inexpensive way to camp in a beautiful beach park. Some cabins are $35 per night, accommodating up to six people;

there are also beach houses that sleep 10 for $60 a night. Contact the Friends of Malaekahana for a brochure. And plan ahead as there is often a waiting list for these popular spots.

Kahuku

This small village is mostly known for its yummy, locally raised shrimp that are usually sold from side-of-the-road shrimp trucks. And if you see a roadside truck or stand offering Kahuku sweet corn, pick some up!

THE FAMOUS KAHUKU SHRIMP TRUCKS

Just north of La`ie sits the small community of Kahuku, which is famous for its roadside shrimp trucks full of locally-raised, jumbo prawns seasoned in a myriad of combinations. Some of my favorites include garlic shrimp scampi, hot and spicy shrimp and sweet and spicy shrimp. The plate lunches run between $10 and $12 and are usually served with two scoops of rice, macaroni salad, a green salad or pineapple slices. Keep in mind that the shrimp can be very messy as they are unpeeled, so make sure you have lots of napkins.

Here's a listing of some of Kahuku's most famous shrimp trucks:

Giovanni's graffiti-covered shrimp is one of the oldest and best known of the shrimp truck. Alert garlic lovers: Giovanni's has a delicious garlic shrimp with huge chunks of garlic in the sauce. It's fun to check out the

North Shore

graffiti penned by customers from around the world on the truck while waiting for your order!

You can also find some of the colorful trucks on either side of Kahuku from Kualoa to Hale`iwa. Most of the trucks have picnic tables nearby and refreshments are available.

Some of the other reputable and popular shrimp trucks include **Blue Water Shrimp**, which offers more than just shrimp, **Famous Kahuku Shrimp Truck**, **Fumi's Kahuku Shrimp and Seafood**, **Macky's Kahuku Sweet Shrimp**, **Romy's Kahuku Prawns and Shrimp Hut** and the **Shrimp Shack**.

The shrimp trucks are so popular that in 2005 the Turtle Bay Resort held a "Battle of the North Shore Shrimp Trucks" in which Macky's Kahuku Sweet Shrimp won the competition. Boy, would I have loved to be one of the judges!

Did You Know? This tiny town has been home to some major talent. Popular musician Jack Johnson graduated from Kahuku High School, as did famous Chef Sam Choy and award-winning surfer Pancho Sullivan.

Adventures on Land

Golf

Kahuku Municipal Golf Course, 56-501 Kamehameha Highway, ☎ 808-293-5842. This par-35 course is open every day except Christmas Day and New Years Day from 7 am to 5 pm. Green fees are very inexpensive – $20 for non-residents and $3 for seniors. The course also has golf club rentals, a driving range and golf lessons.

Adventures on Water

Surf Spot

Right off the 7th hole of the Kahuku Golf Course is a surf spot named **Seventh Hole**. This isolated place is best in winter and shortboarders will like the big lefts and short rights.

Turtle Bay

Much of the activity in the Turtle Bay area revolves around the recently renovated Turtle Bay Resort, which is in the midst of gorgeous white-sand beaches, ironwood forests and a tropical countryside. From December through April, whales can be seen frolicking in the ocean during their annual migration from Alaska.

Sightseeing

Beaches

Crescent-shaped **Kawela Bay** lies west of Turtle Bay and is a nice swimming spot. The bay offers calm turquoise water and is great for snorkeling and diving. It's also famous – the beach is featured in the movie, *Joe vs. The Volcano* and the *Magnum P.I.* television series.

Adventures on Land

Horseback Rides

Horseback Rides are available at **Turtle Bay Resort**, ☎ 808-293-6000. Guests can enjoy a 45-minute trek throughout the 880-acre resort.

Golf

Turtle Bay Golf Course, ☎ 808-293-8574, www.turtlebayresort.com, features 36 holes of championship golf on two courses – The Arnold Palmer Course and the Fazio Course.

NEED TIPS FOR TEEING OFF?

The Turtle Bay Golf Academy, ☎ 808-293-8574, www.turtlebayresort.com, offers private instruction, golf schools and clinics. Instructors are highly trained and all lessons begin with the student telling the instructor what his or her objectives are. Choose from an hour lesson, a series of four one-hour lessons, a one-hour video instruction, a golf fitness lesson or a two-hour playing lesson. Golf schools are offered on a full-day (8 am to 2:30 pm) or half-day (8 am to noon) basis. The student teacher ratio is 3:1 and the rates go down if you have more than one person in your group.

If you're just looking for a quick refresher, you can have a golf professional spend 10 minutes with you going over the basics. This is a complimentary service offered by Turtle Bay. The practice range is open from 7 am to 4:30 pm.

Adventures in Air

Helicopter Rides

Paradise Helicopters, ☎ 808-969-7392, www.paradisecopters.com, info@paradisecopters.com. The company runs its helicopters right off of a helipad at the Turtle Bay Resort. There are several tours available, from the 60-minute O`ahu Experience, the 40-minute Best of O`ahu, the 20-minute North Shore & Waterfall Adventure and – for the fearless – the 45-minute O`ahu X-TREME, which hovers over the island in a helicopter with NO DOORS! E-mail the company for a brochure if you would like more information.

Saving $$$: Booking with Paradise Helicopters over the Internet can save up to $66 per couple.

Adventures in Water

Snorkeling

Kuilima Cove, on the eastern side of the Turtle Bay Resort, is a sheltered and serene snorkeling spot perfect for beginning snorkelers. The cove is enclosed by a natural rock barrier, which protects the area and its visitors from waves. The water clarity is excellent and the average depth is roughly neck-deep. The bottom is primarily coral flats scattered with large rocks that make a happy home for fish. If you're lucky, you may even see a humuhumunukunukuapua`a, the famous former Hawaii state fish. You can park on the grounds of Turtle Bay – just drive through the main gates and head toward the resort. The Kuilima cove parking lot is on the right-hand side near the tennis courts.

Where to Eat & Stay

At Turtle Bay Resort

21 Degrees North, ☎ 800-203-3650 or 808-293-8811, www.turtlebayresort.com. Open Tuesday through Saturday 6 to 10 pm. Even the entrance to this fabulous restaurant is exotic. It looks as if you're entering a tiki bar as you walk over a small dark bridge with birds chirping and surrounded by tropical plants.

Inside, the décor is wall-to-wall windows overlooking Turtle Bay. Local ingredients are used whenever possible and all produce is 100% organic. I would describe the menu as upscale Pacific Rim cuisine with a Hawaiian twist. Appetizers include blackened ahi, Kahuku shrimp with avocado and hearts of palm and the North Shore Waialua tomato salad with spicy crab. Entrées include Kona lobster, opakapaka, crab crusted Hawaiian sea bass, rosemary-crusted Colorado lamb rack and filet mignon. The highlight of my meal was the 21 Degrees Signature Chocolate Soufflé with a crème Anglaise sauce – yummy! $$$$.

Lei Lei's Bar & Grill, ☎ 808-293-2662, serves breakfast (7 am to 10:30 am), lunch (10:30 am to 4:30 pm) and dinner (5 pm to 10 pm). Breakfast is limited, with choices such as a croissant sandwich or Hawaiian sweet bread French toast. Lunch choices include appetizers, chicken and fish plates, sandwiches and burgers and salads (including a mouth-watering seared ahi sashimi caesar). Dinner is a bit more upscale, with appetizers like oyster shots, escargot, ahi poke and a crab dip. Seafood, pasta entrées, prime rib, herb-crusted chicken and baby back ribs make up the dinner menu. Breakfast $. Lunch $$. Dinner $$$.

Lei Lei's
(Courtesy of Limtiaco Co.)

The Palm Terrace caters to the buffet crowd. The breakfast buffet ($21.95 for adults, $11 for kids four-11) is held daily from 6:30 to 10:30 am and has every breakfast item you can think of. They also serve a regular menu with pancakes, waffles, eggs Benedict, omelets and steak and eggs.

The Palm Terrace Lunch Buffet is served from 11:30 am to 2:30 pm and costs $23.95 for adults and $12 for children four-11. If you order off the menu, try the black and blue ahi sashimi, stone-fired pizza, shredded Kalua pork BBQ sandwich, fish sandwiches, and fish and chips.

The dinner buffets at the Palm Terrace change nightly – Friday night ($29.95) is prime rib and Hawaiian lomi salmon; Saturday night ($32.95) is prime rib & seafood with Alaskan king crab legs and peel-and-eat shrimp; Sunday night ($29.95) is an Italian buffet with a pasta action station, where you can mix and match unlimited plates of pastas and sauces; and Monday night ($29. 95) is a Mexican buffet and fajita action station. Breakfast $. Lunch $$. Dinner $$$ (not including buffets).

Luau Alert: The Turtle Bay Resort ha,s its own special "Legends of the North Shore Luau" which is held every Friday at 6 pm in a beautiful setting overlooking Kuilima Bay. Enjoy the variety of Polynesian dancing – a fast hip-dance from Tuamotu Island, the Samoan Slap Dance and a fire-dance performed to Tahitian music. The luau costs $85 for adults and $55 for children ages four to 11.

Hang Ten Bar & Grill. This is the casual spot at Turtle Bay, with an open-air atmosphere and casual grub like buffalo wings, chicken Caesar salad and a basket of fries. They also have a lot of fish entrées such as a grilled ahi sandwich and rolled fish tacos with blackened mahi mahi. The Hang Ten Bar & Grill is open for lunch and cocktails. $$.

Bay Club is geared toward sports fans with a 52-inch plasma television, billiards, darts, foosball and shuffleboard. There's also late night entertainment with dancing and cocktails.

Hang Ten Bar & Grill
(Courtesy of Limtiaco Co.)

Where to Stay

Resort

Turtle Bay Resort, ☎ 800-203-3650, www.turtlebayresort.com, has specials, including seven nights for the price of six, along with breakfast and a dinner luau for two. Ensconced on 880 acres, the Turtle Bay Resort is only about an hour's drive from central Waikiki. The Resort has 443 hotel rooms, as well as beachfront cottages and villas. The resort is situated so that every room has a view of the Pacific Ocean.

Lobby of Turtle Bay Resort
(Courtesy of Limtiaco Co.)

This is not the Turtle Bay Resort you may have visited years ago. The entire property has been renovated and the rooms are refreshingly comfortable. Rooms range from the basic ocean view guest room to a 2,000-square-foot Ali`i Presidential Suite or a 2,391-square-foot four-bedroom villa. $$$$.

Condominiums

The Estates at Turtle Bay have several individually owned condominiums available for rent. Call ☎ 888-200-4202 or 808-293-0600 or visit www.turtlebay-rentals.com, 56-565 Kamehameha Hwy. The Estates have five pools and four tennis courts. Most condos have a full-size kitchen, washer/dryer, telephone and cable TV. $$$-$$$$.

Sunset Beach

Sunset Beach is a two-mile stretch that, in the summer, is great for swimming and snorkeling and, in the winter, is one of the best surfing beaches in the world.

> *Surf's Up:* All along the northwestern shore of O`ahu lie dozens of surf spots with amusing names that I'm sure have legendary stories behind them. Don't be surprised to hear local surfers talk about "Phantoms," "Freddyland," "Backyards," "Gas Chambers," "Log Cabins," "Left Overs," "Avalanche" or "Hammerheads" (so named because it sits near a hammerhead shark breeding area).

Beaches

Located at 59-104 Kamehameha Highway, **Sunset Beach** is the king daddy of all surfing beaches. It has long stretches of beige sand and stunning views of the ridges of the Wai`anae Mountains. Lifeguards are usually present and the beach has picnic areas. Warning: From June through September, there have been incidents of stinging limu (seaweed)!

Surfing

There are dozens of surf spots along the North Shore between Sunset Beach and Hale`iwa. For a better description of all the spots and to get a more detailed view of the surfing locales, one of the best resources is **Franko's O`ahu Surfing Map**. This compact map is printed on durable, rip-proof and waterproof paper and can be found at bookstores and surf shops. Franko's also has maps for scuba divers. For more information, visit www.frankosmaps.com.

Surfing The Web About Surfing: During the winter months, the big waves come to the North Shore. Check out www.surfline.com for pictures of the extra-large waves! You can also call ☎ 808-596-SURF for surf information or log onto www.surfnewsnetwork.com.

Waimea

Giant waves are welcomed by hundreds of surfers during the winter months and the Waimea area becomes a tourist attraction of its own. During summer, the waters are calm and welcoming.

Shopping

Foodland in Waimea is the main grocery store on the North Shore. Be sure to ask for a Maika`i card, which is the Hawaii-based chain's version of a discount card.

Beaches

Located down the road at 61-031 Kamehameha Highway, **Waimea Bay Beach Park** is a nice place to swim in the summer but the wintertime is a different story. This is the home of some of

Waimea Bay Beach

the largest, most dangerous and spectacular surf in the world. Lifeguards are on duty and the beach has restrooms, showers, pay phones and picnic areas.

`Ehukai Beach is home to the **Banzai Pipeline**, a tubed surf break that got its nickname when famous surf cinematographer Bruce Brown shouted out, "Banzai," while narrating the film *Surf Safari*. During the winter surf months, the beach is busy with spectators. In the calmer summer months, swimming for us mere mortals is possible. `Ehukai, which translates as "Reddish Tinged Water," has restrooms available as well as picnic areas, showers, phones and lifeguards.

**Kewa`ena Beach** is a relatively undeveloped beach between Waimea Bay and `Ehukai Beach. At Kewa`ena Beach, you can look north and view the famous surf site called "Off-the-Wall" or "Kodak Reef" or look to the south to see the dangerous surf spot called "Log Cabins."

Jump Rock: Also called "da Big Rock." this huge, jagged rock is a hub of activity as brave souls jump into the ocean from its many sides. The jump can only be done in the summer months when there are no waves and the waters are calm. For a birds-eye view of what the jump looks like, you can check out homemade videos on YouTube.

Adventures on Land

Hiking

Waimea Valley Audubon Center contains an 1,800-acre valley which was home to the high priest of O`ahu for more than 600 years. Visitors to the park can still see the remains of temples, shrines, agricultural terraces and village walls.

The center is home to 36 garden collections with more than 200 plant families and more than 1,000 genera. Four of the gardens feature Hawaiian plants including three that focus on native, or endemic, plants.

One of the most popular activities in the valley is a visit to Waimea Falls. It's a three-quarter-mile walk to the falls and, if weather permits, you can take a dip in the cool pool below the falls. This is one of the few waterfalls in O`ahu that you can swim in.

To get to the Waimea Valley Audubon Valley, take H-1 westbound to H-2 heading to the North Shore. Take the Wahiawa Exit and then get on Kamehameha Highway. Turn right into the park just after passing the Waimea Bay Beach Park. For more information about Waimea Valley Audubon Center, 59-864 Kamehameha Highway, call ☎ 808-638-9199, or visit www.audubon.org. Admission is $8 for adults and $5 for children ages four to 12. Parking is free.

Adventures on Water

Snorkeling

Shark's Cove is so-named because it is home to white tipped reef sharks. This species of shark is generally non-aggressive but that does not give you permission to approach or provoke them! This cove is a great snorkeling area in the summer time when the waves are calm. Shark's Cove is nearly non-existent during the winter when the waves crash over it.

White tip reef shark

During the calm months of March through October, make sure you wear shoes at all times (either reef shoes or old tennis shoes) as there are sharp coral and rock formations.

Shark's Cove is part of Pupukea Beach Park and is accessible through the beach park. Parking is free in front of the cove and you can follow a short footpath from the beach park to the reef. Restrooms and showers are available at the beach park.

In the calm months, the area has several tidepools that smaller children can safely wade through.

Hale`iwa

Hale`iwa calls itself the "Surfing Capital of the World," and, once you cross over the old double-arched white-washed Hale`iwa Bridge, you'll realize you're in a different and fascinating world. The bridge crosses over Anahulu Stream and is itself a landmark. Once over the bridge, you'll find several shopping centers and places to eat.

Author's Note: This section on Hale`iwa includes Hale`iwa town as well as the rest of the North Shore located to the west, all the way to Kaena.

Shopping

In Hale`iwa, you'll find the **Haleiwa Shopping Plaza**, 66-149 & 66-187 Kamehameha Highway, ☎ 808-637-5095, and the **North Shore Market Place**, 66-250 Kamehameha Highway, ☎ 808-637-4413. Most shops in both centers are open daily.

The North Shore Market Place is home to the **North Shore Boardriders Club**, ☎ 808-637-5026, which has everything you need to surf as well as the latest surf fashions. **Barnfield's Raging Isle Surf & Cycle Shop** has a huge selection of off-road bicycling gear as well as surf gear, including surfboards designed by North Shore legend Bill Barnfield.

The **North Shore Community Chamber of Commerce**, ☎ 808-637-4558, www.gonorthshore.org, is also located in the North Shore Market Place and can provide you with visitor information, community events and maps of the area.

Other stores in the North Shore Market Place include **North Shore Glass Blowers**, ☎ 808-637-4853, **Great Pacific Patagonia**, ☎ 808-637-1245, **Polynesian & Global Handicrafts**, ☎ 808-637-1288, **Silver Moon Emporium boutique**, ☎ 808-637-7710, and the **Strong Current Surf Shop**, ☎ 808-637-3406.

Sightseeing

North Shore Surf and Cultural Museum (in the North Shore Market Place), ☎ 808-637-8888. This small and informal museum is open most afternoons and anyone interested in surfing will enjoy the visit. The museum has a large collection of old and antique surfboards as well as a variety of other North Shore novelties. Admission is free.

Haleiwa Beach Park is also known as "Ali`i" beach park, or "King's" or "Royal" Beach and is right at the entrance of Haleiwa town. Swimming is best in the small-protected bay on the south side of the beach.

Haleiwa Beach Park

Mokule`ia Beach Park, 68-919 Kaena Point Road, is next to Kaena Point on the Western side of the North Shore past Dillingham Airfield. The long, white sand beach is somewhat desolate due to its far-out location but those who do visit will find great windsurfing and a beautiful beach. As always, be careful as there are no lifeguards assigned to this beach. There are restrooms available and fresh water.

Adventures in Water

Surfing

Surfing is everything here! If you're interested in learning more about the area, visit any of the local surf shops and they can answer your questions about lessons, tides, currents and surf spots.

Hale`iwa is a great spot to learn surfing when the waves are small. On other days, leave this to the experts. Longboarders, shortboarders and bodyboarders will all have an awesome time here when the waves are right.

Scuba Diving

Just east of Hale`iwa town is **Kaiaka Bay Beach Park**, which is home to several great dive spots. **Turtle Street** is a boat dive a half-mile off Kaiaka Bay. This is good for beginners and intermediate divers and you're almost guaranteed to encounter sea turtles. **Hale`iwa Trench** is a more advanced dive spot accessible from the beach at Hale`iwa Boat Harbor.

Shark Encounters

AUTHOR'S CHOICE

There are two companies that offer these popular and exciting shark tours that consist of up to six people being put into a metal cage in a location about three miles offshore where the sharks are roaming. This is a fantastic way to get over your fear of sharks!

Hawaii Shark Encounters, Hale`iwa Boat Harbor, ☎ 808-351-9373, www.hawaiisharkencounters.com, departs four times daily, depending on the weather, and costs $105 for adults and $70 for children. The website has videos showing underwater views of the sharks you may see on the tour!

These tours are VERY popular and I suggest you make reservations before you leave the Mainland.

North Shore Shark Adventures, Hale`iwa Boat Harbor, ☎ 808-228-5900, www.sharktourshawaii.com, leave from slip #35 and visitors will travel on one of two boats – the *Kailolo I* and the *Kailolo II*. Masks and snorkels are provided and passengers have an opportunity to take photos. Two-hour tours cost $120 per person or $60 if you just want to observe. Call and ask about available discounts. If you want transportation from your hotel, the company charges an additional $45.

Adventures in Air

Glider Rides

Mr. Bill's Original Glider Rides, ☎ 808-637-0207, www.honolulusoaring.com, start out at Dillingham Airfield on the Farrington Highway (Hwy 930). The bubble-topped sailplanes can carry one or two passengers high above Oahu's North Shore where the visibility averages 30-40 miles. Also called Honolulu Soaring, the company has been soaring the North Shore skies since 1970. A 20-minute flight can attain altitudes of 3,000 feet or more and longer flights are available. The brave and fearless can add seven to ten minutes of aerial aerobatics to their ride and you can determine the extent of the excitement – mild or wild!

A 30-minute scenic ride runs about $129 for one person or $238 for two people. Prices go up and down depending on length and extras (like loop-d-loops). Mr. Bill's is open seven days a week from 10 am to 5:30 pm, including all holidays. To get to the glider-port entrance, pass Dillingham Airfield entrance #1 for 1½ miles to entrance #2.

Internet Special: Mr. Bill's offers a free tee shirt per ride when you book online – just present your online booking receipt when you arrive at the glider-port.

Where to Eat

Haleiwa Joe's Seafood Grill, 66-011 Kamehameha Highway, ☎ 808-637-8005, www.haleiwajoes.com. This is one of my favorite restaurants on the North Shore. If the weather's nice, try to get a seat on the outdoor deck. I have a photo of myself with friends having a drink at Haleiwa Joe's and when I later saw the movie, *The Big Bounce*, there's a scene where Morgan Freeman and Owen Wilson are sitting at the same table!

The pupus are amazing – try the Paradise Pupu Platter with sticky ribs, sushi, Thai-style calamari and poke. Larger plates include noodle bowls, fresh fish, coconut shrimp, prime rib and lobster. Haleiwa Joe's is open daily for lunch and dinner and they have live entertainment on Fridays. Lunch $$. Dinner $$$.

Pizza Bob's (in the Haleiwa Shopping Center), ☎ 808-637-5095, serves pizza, salads, sandwiches and burgers in a pleasant indoor/outdoor setting. $.

Paradise Found Café, 66-443 Kamehameha Highway, ☎ 808-637-4540. For innovative vegan and vegetarian dishes, try out this funky little café tucked in the back of the Celestial Natural Foods store, next to the Haleiwa Post Office. $.

Matsumoto Shave Ice, 66-087 Kamehameha Highway, ☎ 808-637-4827, is an authentic Hawaiian shave ice stand. Choose from several flavors and, if you're brave, add adzuki beans to your treat.

Jameson's By The Sea, 62-540 Kamehameha Highway, ☎ 808-637-6272, www.jamesonshawaii.com. Jameson's is the most upscale restaurant in this very casual beach town. The lunch menu includes pupus such as salmon pâté and crab-stuffed mushrooms, grilled crab and shrimp melt sandwiches, salads and shrimp or chicken stir-fry entrées. For dinner, try the large Caesar salad with Cajun ahi, one of the various fresh fish dinners ,or sweet Australian lobster tail. The restaurant also has a children's menu with tuna fish sandwiches, hamburgers, fried shrimp and more. Jameson's is on the water in Haleiwa and is very popular for sunset viewing, so come early or late, or be prepared to wait. If you do have to wait, they have a full bar with wine, beer and tropical drinks.

On Monday through Friday, lunch is served from 11 am to 5 pm and dinner is from 5 to 9:30 pm On Saturdays and Sundays, brunch is from 9 am to noon, lunch from noon to 5 pm and dinner from 5 to 9:30 pm. Lunch $$. Dinner $$$.

Cholo's Homestyle Mexican Restaurant & Margarita Bar (in the North Shore Market Place), ☎ 808-637-3059, www.cholosmexican.com. Cholo's is THE Mexican food place in Haleiwa. The portions are huge and the combinations are innumerable. Cholo's fish tacos with fresh ahi are amazing and there are several vegetarian dishes such as veggie taco salad or nachos. The heapings are huge and the prices affordable. And it gets busy here so be prepared to wait. Cholo's is open daily from 10 am to 9:30 pm for lunch and dinner and until 11 pm for drinks. $.

**Kua `Aina Sandwich Shop**, 66-160 Kamehameha Highway #C, ☎ 808-637-6067. This roadside café has large and reasonably priced sandwiches, hamburgers and salads. They are famous for their burgers, which come in big and bigger sizes. Bonus: the fries are homemade. Kua `Aina is open daily from 11 am to 8 pm. Don't forget your cash because they don't take credit cards. $.

Café Haleiwa, 66-460 Kamehameha Highway, ☎ 808-637-5516. Renowned for its fabulous breakfasts, Café Haleiwa is a mainstay in this surf town. The satisfying omelets have names like the "Off the Wall" and "Off the Lip," with eggs, sausage, bacon and rice. The walls are decorated with surf memorabilia and signed photos from famous surfers like Kelly Slater. Open daily from 7 am to 2 pm. $.

Waialua Bakery, 66-200 Kamehameha Highway, ☎ 808-637-9079, has awesome sandwiches with homemade bread, vegetarian specials, yummy smoothies and, to top it off, homemade ice cream. $.

Where to Stay

Accommodation Tips: Hale`iwa and the surrounding area is not known for its abundance of places to stay. Most visitors stay at The Turtle Bay Resort or book a vacation rental. There are two hostel-type accommodations but they are not recommended!

Vacation Rentals

Hawaiian Beach Rentals, ☎ 800-853-0787, www.hawaiianbeachrental.com, has an extensive listing of vacation homes and condos on the North Shore.

Check out **www.vrbo.com** for a list of privately owned vacation rentals.

Sunset Homes, ☎ 808-637-2400, www.sunsethomes.net, rents beach cottages on the North Shore.

Beach Bungalows

Ke Iki Beach Bungalows, 59-579 Ke Iki Road, ☎ 808-638-8829 or 866-638-8229 (toll free), www.keikibeach.com, info@keikibeach.com. Feel like living the life of a high-priced beach bum? Welcome to Ke Iki Beach Bungalows, a cute beachside compound with 11 bungalows – five oceanfront and six with garden views. The bungalows are named after Hawaiian fruits and flowers – "Lilikoi," "Bird of Paradise," "Plumeria," and "Hibiscus." They are simple and pleasant, decorated in a Bali-meets-Hawaii theme. The setting is peaceful and there are many calming places to relax on the property, plus it's only about 30 seconds from the beach. Rates for the one- and two-bedroom bungalows range from $195 to $230 per night, with a ridiculous cleaning fee of $50 to $100. (I don't usually mind paying a cleaning fee but my bungalow had a dirty toilet, used soap in the shower, food crumbs in the kitchen and no batteries – not even dead ones – in the remote control!) And there's no maid service. Quiet hours are from 10 pm to 8 am.

Amenities include Wi-Fi Internet service, a washer and dryer, cable TV and ample parking. I also admire the fact that ocean safety is highly emphasized. There are no lifeguard stations in front of the bungalows but lifeguards on ATVs regularly patrol the beaches. Check with them is you are unsure whether it's safe for swimming. Manager Greg Gerstenberger is one laidback guy, but very helpful and attentive.

KE IKI HISTORY

In 1953, Mr. and Mrs. Talbott walked down the gangway of the ship that brought them to Honolulu from San Francisco. Upon hearing Hawaiian music and viewing hula dancers on the dock, Mr. Talbott turned to his wife and said, "We are not going back." Days later, Mr. Talbot asked the owner of a soda fountain where would be a good place on the island to buy land. A man at the end of the counter mentioned that he had some land on the north shore of the island where he was going to build his dream home. He then said he worked for Dole Pineapple and was being transferred to Maui. The man said he had an acre and a half out there where he had planted a bunch of coconut palms and he would sell the property for the right price. The Talbotts eventually bought the property for around $11,000 (keep reading if that amount didn't make you pass out!).

About the same time, the old Haleiwa Hotel (where Haleiwa Joe's restaurant now sits) was being torn down due to old age (it was built in the 1800s) and termite damage. On the property there were a few small bungalows built by the military in 1937. Mr. Talbot bought the bungalows and then moved them to his property. Meanwhile, he had built a small studio while the beachfront bungalows were being finished.

Years later, Mr. Talbott succumbed to illness and Mrs. Talbot hired someone to take care of what they had named "Ke Iki Hale," when she moved to Honolulu to spend the rest of her days. The street-side buildings were added around 1963. Ke Iki Hale had many visitors over the years, with Alice Tracey being the property manager for 26 years. In 2000, a renovation and a change in management was completed and the name was changed to Ke Iki bungalows.

Windward O`Ahu

At a Glance

To get to Windward O`ahu from Honolulu, continue past Waikiki and Diamond Head and head to Kalaniana`ole Highway (Highway 72) for a scenic trek that takes you out of busy Honolulu and into a natural paradise. Along the way, you'll pass one world-class resort, several natural attractions and several smaller and charming towns surrounded by some of the world's favorite beaches.

IN THIS CHAPTER

You can also get to Windward O`ahu by following Kalakaua Avenue out of Waikiki, heading toward Diamond Head. The road changes into Diamond Head Road and, instead of heading up to the peak, keep going right on Kahala Avenue. You'll pass gorgeous Kahala Beach and Wai`alae Beach Park before the road ends at The Kahala Hotel & Resort.

If you want to check out the glorious Kahala Hotel & Resort, take a break. If not, head back up Kealaolu Avenue and get onto Kalaniana`ole Highway (Highway 72) headed east. You'll follow along the south shore of the island, passing many beach parks (which I will detail below), passing through Hawaii Kai (this is where one Costco is located) and toward the Koko Head area. This drive is where you'll be happy you rented that convertible! Next up is Hanauma Bay State Park and the Halona Blow Hole.

Gossip Alert: Next to the Halona Blow Hole is Halona Cove where the steamy beach scene between Deborah Kerr and Burt Lancaster reportedly took place in *From Here to Eternity*. Keep in mind that I've heard of three beaches throughout the islands that claim to be the beach in the movie!

Chinaman's Hat

As you head up the west side of the island, you'll see Makapu`u Head (home to the Makapu`u Lighthouse) and then past Sea Life Park. Next up is Waimanalo Bay, home to O`ahu's longest sandy beach, and then the busy town of Kailua, which has shopping, great dining and lots of water activities. If you bypass Kailua, make sure you get onto Highway 83 headed north, which will keep you going up the Windward Coast. To get to Kailua, turn onto Kailua Road and head toward the ocean. To get back, follow the signs to Highway 83 and get on the northbound lanes.

Next up is Kane`ohe Bay, where, on the western end of the bay, you'll see famous and hard-to-miss Mokoli`i Island, better known as "Chinaman's Hat." This is also where you'll find 4,000-acre Kualoa Ranch, which offers many outdoor adventures. Highway 83 then continues up the coast, passing beach after beach, until you get to the town of La`ie, which is where the North Shore (another chapter!) begins.

DAY TRIP

If you only have one day to check out the windward side of O`ahu, there is a 35-mile loop that will present you with fabulous views, breathtaking cliffs and seascapes and honest, down-to-earth communities. Head east on Kalaniana`ole Highway (Highway 72) to get out of town and then return along the Pali Highway (Highway 62) on your way back. If you take this route in the opposite direction, you'll miss all the fantastic views!

Windward O`ahu
Walalua Bay
Sunset Beach
Paumalu
Waialee
Kawela
Kahuku Point
Waimea
KAMEHAMEHA HWY
83
Haleiwa
to Kaena Point
KAMEHAMEHA HWY
99
80
Wahiawa
H2
Kahuku
Makahoa Point
Malaekahana State Recreation Area
Laie
Laniloa Peninsula
Hauula Beach Park
Hanuula
Aukai Beach Park
Sacred Falls State Park
KOOLAU RANGE
Punaluu
Punaluu Beach Park
Kahana
Kahana Bay Beach Park
Swanzy Beach Park
Kaaawa
Kaaawa Beach Park
Kalae-oio Beach Park
FOREST
Kahana Valley State Park
Puu Kaaumakua (2681 ft)
RESERVE
Waikane
Kualoa Point
Waiahole Beach Park
Waiahole
Kaneohe Bay
Pacific Ocean
Pearl City
Elead (4265 ft)
Senator Fong's Gardens
Laenani Beach Park
Puu Kawipo (2450 ft)
Kahaluu
Aiea
Heeia
99
H3
836
Kaneohe MCAS
MOKU MANU ISLANDS
H201
Kaneohe
H1
to Pearl Harbor
Kaneohe Beach Park
65
Kokokahi
LIKELIKE HWY
63
83
Kalaheo
H3
Kailua Bay
Sand Island State Park
61
Kailua
PALI HWY
61
Kailua Beach Park
HONOLULU
Puu Konahuanui (3105 ft)
WAIKIKI
Military Reservation
KALANIANAOLE HWY
Wailea Point
5 MILES
5 KILOMETERS
Waimanalo Bay
H1
Lyon Arboretum
Waimanalo Bay State Recreation Area
Diamond Head Beach Park & Lighthouse
Kuliouou
Waimanalo Beach
Hawaii Kai
Sea Life Park
Koko Head Park
Makapuu Point
72
Halona Blow Hole
Waialea Beach Park
Wailupe Beach Park
Manalua Bay
Kuliouou Beach Park
Koko Head
Hanauma Bay Nature Preserve
HUNTER PUBLISHING
N

First, you pass Hawaii Kai and the Koko Marina Center on your left. Keep driving until you see the sign for "Hanauma Bay" and, after that, you're officially out of the city. You'll then pass 642-foot-high Koko Head that is then dwarfed by 1,208-foot Koko Crater.
Kailua Beach and famous Lanikai beach are the next stops on your tour (don't forget the sunscreen!) and then its time to head back to Honolulu along the Pali Highway. Your last hurrah will be the Nu`uanu Pali Lookout on the right-hand side right after the two Pali tunnels. Make sure to signal when you turn or you may get "stink-eye" from other drivers. You can view the entire windward coast from the vista point. Hopefully, you'll be able to head back into Honolulu at sunset and get a view of the skyline during that magic time. If you're headed to Waikiki, take H-1 east once you get into town and follow the signs to Waikiki.

Now that you know your way around Windward O`ahu, I'll give you more details about the fantastic towns and quirky sites that make up this side of the island.

Kahala

At A Glance

When people think of Kahala, most people associate it with the fabulous Kahala Hotel and Resort. There's a little more to the area – a shopping center, quiet neighborhoods and great beaches.

Shopping

$ The main shopping area is the Kahala Mall, www.kahalamallcenter.com, located right off the H1, inland from The Kahala Resort & Spa. The anchor stores at the mall are Macy's and Longs Drugs. The center also has a Barnes & Noble Bookseller (in case you forgot your beach read!), several clothing stores, surf shops, jewelry and an 8-plex movie theater.

COMING SOON

Whole Foods Market, www.wholefoodsmarket.com. This ultra-trendy natural food store is slated to open in the spring of 2008. The store will occupy the 26,000 square-foot space vacated by Star Market in 2007. Whole Food Market was founded in 1980 in Austin, Texas, employing about 39,000 people in total and with nearly 200 locations in North America and the UK. The health-conscious **Aloha Salads**, www.aloha-salads.com, restaurant recently opened a branch in Kailua. This eatery has a "Design Your Own Salad" made up of dozens of ingredients. They also have subs, signature salads and soup. $$.

Adventures on Water

Dolphin Encounter

The **Kahala Hotel & Resort** offers a hands-on Dolphin Encounter where professional trainers from the Dolphin Quest organization help guests understand these wonderful animals. The six dolphins – Hoku ("Star" in Hawaiian), Niele ("Nosey"), Liho ("Rare and Precious"), Nainoa ("The Wanderer"), Kolohi ("Rascal"), and Kainalu ("Ocean Wave") – provide an educational and fun experience that is available only in O`ahu. Visitors and guests to the Kahala can enjoy an unforgettable experience as they come face-to-face with these friendly creatures. Carefully supervised sessions include shallow water interaction and underwater views of these amazing mammals.

Children enjoying the Dolphin Encounter

A two-hour children's program is available for small groups of kids aged five to 12, including interactions with tropical fish, stingrays and turtles. If you're interested in staying at The Kahala Resort Hotel & Resort and want to get in the water with the dolphins, look on the website for the Kahala Dolphin Encounter package deal, which combines a special room rate with one adult Dolphin Encounter for two people. The package requires a four-night minimum, which, considering the opulence and privacy of this property, won't be hard to tolerate! The resort's 26,000-square-foot natural lagoon is home to six Atlantic bottlenose dolphins, sea turtles and tropical fish. For more information, ☎ 808-739-8918 or 800-248-3315, or visit www.kahalaresort.com/activities/dolphin-quest-encounter.cfm or www.dolphinquest.org.

Surfing

Hans Hedemann Surf School, ☎ 808-924-4778, www.hhsurf.com, is one of O`ahu's best-known surf schools and has a good reputation throughout the island. The company has branches at the Park Shore Waikiki right across from Waikiki Beach, at the Kahala Hotel & Resort on the Windward Coast and at Turtle Bay Resort on the North Shore. The Surf School offers private lessons ($115 per hour, $150/two hours), semi-private lessons ($95 per hour, $125/two hours), group lessons ($50 per hour, $75/two hours), private lessons for kids ($115 per hour, $150/two hours), surf lessons with the master himself, Hans Hedemann ($250/hour), or lessons from their staff of professional surfers ($250/two hours).

Water Toys, Diving & Snorkeling Equipment

The Kahala offers a variety of water sport rentals, including kayaks, rafts, sailboats, skin diving and snorkeling equipment. Inquire at the hotel's concierge or check at the beachfront kiosks.

Where to Eat

In the Kahala Hotel & Resort, ☎ 808-739-8888

Hoku's, ☎ 808-739-8780, is the Kahala's signature restaurant and offers sophisticated yet contemporary cuisine, combining Hawaiian, Asian and European flavors. This is one of my favorite upscale places to eat in O`ahu. Every table in the multi-level dining room has a view of the Pacific Ocean. Hoku's is open Monday through Sunday 5:30 to 10 pm with a Sunday brunch from 10:30 am to 2 pm. The restaurant has a pleasant ocean setting and the open kitchen offers hot woks, a kiawe wood grill and wood-burning ovens. Dinner $$$$. Brunch $$$$.

Plumeria Beach House, ☎ 808-739-8760, is open daily from 6:30 am to 10 pm with a Sunday brunch held from 11 am to 2:30 pm. It offers upscale versions of lunch favorites like salads, sandwiches, seafood and pastas. A breakfast buffet is offered daily and themed dinner buffets are offered on Thursday, Friday and Saturday nights. Entertainment is provided nightly at sunset. Breakfast Buffet $$. Breakfast $$. Lunch $$. Dinner $$$. Dinner Buffet $$$$.

Plumeria Beach House

The Veranda, ☎ 808-739-8895, designed to bring visitors back to the romance of old Hawaii, is open daily from 2 to 10:30 pm for snacks and 2 to 5 pm for afternoon tea. The tea service offers a selection of 13 hand-blended teas, along with homemade scones, pastries and other delectable treats. The tea sandwiches include smoked salmon and cucumber, watercress and tomato, prosciutto and Maui onions or roasted Peking duck with hoisin sauce. The restaurant has indoor and outdoor seating and is also open from 2 pm to midnight for cocktails. Live jazz music and an intimate dance floor complete your evening at the Kahala Hotel & Resort

TOP-OF-THE-LINE TEAS

Afternoon Tea at the Veranda is an elegant and stylish way to spend the day. The Kahala Hotel & Resort uses fine teas made by French tea maker Mariage Fréres, famous for making some of the incredibly diverse, elegant and beautiful teas in the world. Guests can order a single pot of loose leaf Mariage Frères tea, or a Simple Tea Service with scones, pastries and cookies. The Classic Tea Service includes scones, clotted creams, tea sandwiches and your choice of tea. All of this comes in the Royal Tea Service but it also includes a glass of Champagne with a strawberry. The services range from $8 to $42.

Tokyo-Tokyo, ☎ 808-739-8901, offers authentic and elegant Japanese cuisine nightly from 5:30 to 10 pm The restaurateurs combed Asia to find furnishings, artwork, porcelain, pottery, crystal, silverware and linens for the restaurant. Only the highest-grade ingredients are used, including "Koshihikari" rice produced in Uonuma, Japan, natural unprocessed salt from Izu Oshima, organic soy sauce aged to perfection in special Japanese cedar barrels from Izu Oshima and Wagyu beef directly imported from Kogoshima prefecture – the highest grade beef (A-5 grade) that Japan has to offer. This delectable beef is only available in Hawaii at Tokyo Tokyo where five ounces will cost you $150! (24-hour advance reservations are need to enjoy this special dining experience). $$$$.

Seaside Grill, ☎ 808-739-8770, is a casual spot with a direct view of the Pacific Ocean, open from 11 am to 5:30 pm for lunch and 10:30 am to 6 pm for cocktails. They put a special twist on traditional "paper plate" fare such as French fries with bacon, white cheddar cheese, onion rings and a macadamia nut pesto ranch dressing. $-$$.

At the Kahala Mall

California Pizza Kitchen, ☎ 808-737-9446 (next to Macys), www.cpk.com. Open Sunday through Thursday 11 am to 10 pm; Saturday and Sunday 11 am to 11 pm. This popular upscale pizza chain focuses on over 25 specialty pizzas (such as the famous Original BBQ Chicken pizza) but they also have chicken entrées, pastas, focaccia sandwiches and a large dessert selection. They also offer a children's menu for ages 10 and under, including salad, fruit, pasta, pizza and scaled-down desserts. $$.

L&L Drive-Inn, ☎ 808-732-4042, has fast food Hawaiian barbecue cuisine with many combinations of pork, fish, chicken and beef. L&L also has burgers, sandwiches, saimin and musubi (a block of rice with your choice of meat in the middle and then wrapped in flavored, dry seaweed). $.

Chili's, ☎ 808-738-5773, www.chilis.com. This American favorite has a little bit of everything – soups, salads, steaks, burgers, chicken, Mexican entrées and a great kid's menu. $$.

Where to Stay

Resorts

The Kahala Hotel & Resort, 5000 Kahala Avenue, ☎ 808-739-8888 or 800-367-2525, www.kahalaresort.com, is considered by many to be the most fabulous resort on O`ahu and is a favorite among the rich and famous (and me!). Located on the outskirts of Honolulu, the resort has 343 rooms and suites, six restaurants and lounges, private cabanas on an amazing beach and excellent service all around. Only 11 miles from Honolulu, it's a whole different world. There are no rows of fancy hotels or highrises. Located on 6.5 acres in a posh neighborhood, the 10-story Kahala sits on a gorgeous 800-foot-long crescent-shaped beach and overlooks both Diamond Head and Koko Head Craters. Opened by Conrad Hilton in January 1964, the hotel became independent in March of 2006. The resort also has an efficient shuttle service, which will take you to the Kahala Mall, Waikiki and the Ala Moana Shopping Center.

FASCINATING FACTS ABOUT THE KAHALA

- The groundbreaking of the Kahala was in 1962. The resort opened in 1964.
- The resort cost $12 million to build.
- More than 100 coconut palms were planted and 18,000 yards of fine sand were barged in from Moloka`i to pad the 1,800-foot stretch of beach.

- Room rates at the newly opened Kahala Hilton were $26 per night for a standard room and $150 per night for the Presidential Suite! 44 years later, in 2008, a standard room starts at $295 per night and the daily rate of the Presidential Suite is $ 4,325.
- The Kahala was the first major resort to have air-conditioning in all the rooms.
- There are 28,000 multi-colored pieces of lava glass in the chandeliers.
- Baseball legend Joe DiMaggio was one of the first guests who dined at the Maile Restaurant on opening day.
- A beach bar was opened and used as the location for "Rick's Bar" in the TV series *Magnum PI*. The bar is now a popular wedding venue and has been renamed Kahala O Ke Kai.

The 312 standard guest rooms are a spacious 550 square feet with a plantation style décor. Courtyard, Garden View and Mountain View Rooms $$$$. Mountain Lanai, Dolphin Lanai, Ocean View, Beach Front $$$$$.

Big Time Splurge

For VIPs or those who want to feel like VIPs, the Kahala Hotel & Resort has a new suite program that offers VIP services. An advance concierge questionnaire will help the staff customize your visit, detailing everything from your airport transportation and car rental to dining reservations and spa and Dolphin Quest reservations. Guests are picked up in a complimentary limousine and in-room seasonal appetizers and refreshing cocktails are offered. A housekeeper is available to help unpack your bags and do your laundry. At the end of the day, fresh-baked cookies are sent to the room. One-bedroom suites are $1,600 a night and two-bedrooms are $4,700.

HOLLYWOOD LOVES THE KAHALA

Conrad Hilton fashioned the Kahala Hotel & Resort as a secluded retreat away from the hustle and bustle of Waikiki and it was instantly embraced by the Hollywood crowd. Back in those days you could find John Wayne, Frank Sinatra, Lucille Ball, Tony Bennett, Eva Gabor and Jack Lemmon lounging around the pool. More recently, Elton John, Burt Reynolds, Janet Jackson, Whitney Houston, Nicolas Cage, Cameron Diaz, Billy Joel, Alec Baldwin, Sean Penn, Adam Sandler, Drew Barrymore and Michelle Pfeiffer have visited this lovely resort. The Kahala is also a favorite among royalty with Queen Elizabeth II, Prince Philip, Emperor Hirohito, Prince Rainier, Princess Grace, Indira Gandhi, the Dalai Lama, Prince Charles, Princess Diana and every United States President since Lyndon Johnson having visited the property. When I asked one of the bartenders who his favorite celebrity guest and not-so-favorite celebrities were, his answer was easy: Cameron Diaz and Adam Sandler are the coolest and singer Bobby Brown his least favorite.

Kahala Hall Of Fame: Don't miss the "Hall of Fame" where pictures of the Kahala's famous guests line the walls. It's fun to linger and browse the photos.

The resort also has five gorgeous Spa Suites, each 550 square feet with a personal relaxation area, changing room, private shower and a signature infinity-edged soaking bath. Thre is a state-of-the-art CHI Fitness Center at the Kahala as well, with a steam room, sauna and Jacuzzi. $$$$$.

Vacation Rentals

Mele Manuku is a three-bedroom, three-bath property that sleeps six. This island-style house fronts Kahala Beach and is great for families. The house is air-conditioned, with a pool, gourmet kitchen and free parking. If you're interested, check out www.triphomes.com and look for Property 41568. The price is $1,000 a night with a minimum one-week rental.

VRBO (Vacation Rentals by Owner), www.vrbo.com has many vacation rentals throughout the islands. Check out #45464 (Hale Koa Falls) for a four-bedroom, four-bath vacation home in Kahala that sleeps eight. The house has a lava rock spa and steam bath, a rooftop putting green and a 600-foot glass atrium. The rate for this home is $900 per night. ☎ 808-371-4881 or inquire through the website.

Shortly after leaving Kahala, you'll cross over the Hawaii Kai Marina Bridge.

Hawaii Kai

At a Glance

The largely residential area was developed by Henry J. Kaiser around the Maunalua fishpond and wetlands area known as Kuapa (meaning "fishpond wall"). The Hawaii Kai or Koko Marina was dredged from Kuapa Pond starting around 1959.

In 1961 Kaiser-Aetna entered into a lease agreement with landowner Bernice Pauahi Bishop Estate to develop the 521-acre fishpond into residential tracts with a marina. Now, many of the homes in Hawaii Kai sit along the water with glorious views all around.

Shopping

$ **The Hawaii Kai Towne Center**, 6700 Kalaniana`ole Highway (at Keahole Street), ☎ 808-396-0766, www.hawaiikaitownecenter, is the main attraction in this mostly residential area. This is where you'll find Costco, a City Mill Home Improvement Center, Ross Dress for Less, over 20 specialty stores and many waterfront restaurants.

In case you're having a Starbucks withdrawal, you'll find one here. There is also a Jamba Juice, Outback Steakhouse and the

Studio Café, which is a casual coffee shop that serves breakfast and lunch.

Costco, 525 Alakawa Street, ☎ 808-526-6103, in Hawaii Kai, is a fabulous place to pick up some Hawaiian treats, souvenirs and trip essentials like beach towels, boogie boards and water toys. They also have beautiful tropical flower bouquets and, if you're in need of a quick snack, all Costco members know about the quick and cheap pizza and hot dogs available at the warehouse giant. Located north of Honolulu in the Iwilei section of Honolulu, Costco is open from 11 am to 8:30 pm Monday through Friday, 9:30 am to 6 pm Saturday and 10 am to 6 pm Sunday.

Koko Marina Center, 7192 Kalaniana`ole Highway, ☎ 808-395-4737, www.kokomarinacenter.com, has over 60 waterfront shops and restaurants and a Grand Eight-Theatre Cineplex.

Snack Break: Stop at the **Koko Marina Center** to pick up water, sunscreen, food or gas. And if you're a die-hard, this is the last Starbucks for another 15 miles.

Activities: There are several shops at Koko Marina Center that provide all of the activity information you will need – they can tell you about the snorkeling, surfing, parasail and other water activities you may be interested in.

Adventures on Land

Golf

Hawaii Kai Golf Course, 8902 Kalaniana`ole Highway, ☎ 808-395-2358, www.hawaiikaigolf.com. Hawaii Kai has two courses – the "Championship Course" and the "Executive Course." The Executive Course was designed by Robert Trent Jones and is 2,323 yards, par 3 layout. The Championship Course was designed by William Bell and opened in 1973. It measures 6,614 yards from the championship tee and has wide fairways and large greens. Check the website for course layouts.

Hiking

Kuli`ou`ou Ridge: This hike takes about three hours round-trip (a 1,700-foot-climb that is 3.4 miles round-trip) for the experienced hiker and takes you to the Ko'olau summit and back. The trail begins at the back of Kuli`ou`ou Valley on the town-side of Hawaii Kai. The trail has many switchbacks with fantastic views of the Waimanalo coast and of the coastline from Hawaii Kai to Diamond Head.

Adventures on Water

BOBs (Breathing Observation Bubbles)

BOB's Hawaii Adventure, ☎ 808-396-1331, is open from 8 am to 4 pm and offers a new way to experience the ocean – with high-tech breathing observation bubbles (BOB). BOBs are easy to use and operate, environmentally friendly, underwater scooters that have nearly 365-degree visibility. With the BOB, you scoot across the ocean floor with what looks like an old-fashioned diver's mask – but it's bright yellow. No swimming experience is needed and this adventure is available for people ages 12 and up.

Other Water Sports

Information on Jet skis, bumper tubes, scuba, snuba, powerboats, water rockets and parasailing can all be found at **Hawaii Water Sports Center**, ☎ 808-395-3773, www.hawaiiwatersportscenter.com, in the Koko Marina Center. They are open daily from 8:30 am to 5:30 pm and offer a variety of combination deals such as a three-ride special for $79 (think a bumper tube, banana boat and water rockets).

Parasailing

Hawaii Water Sports Center can also arrange for you to parasail 300 feet over the crystal blue waters of Maunalua Bay and see the staggering coastline of

O`ahu from Diamond Head to Koko Head. The cost is $59 per person.

Waverunners

The Hawaii Water Sports Center can also provide you with two-seater waverunners that will have you riding the tropical waves of Manunalua Bay. The price is $49 per person based on two people riding.

Bumper Tube

Want a bit of a thrill? Try the bumper tubes at Hawaii Water Sports Center. A US Coast Guard captain will take you and your friends out to the marina and give you the ride of your life. Hold on tight to the handles of the bumper tube and fly over the wake – over and over. This thrill costs $29 per person and they have tubes that hold two or three people.

Banana Boat

Six people can ride on this thrilling water toy provided by Hawaii Water Sports Center. Shaped like a banana, the captain will take passengers through the marina, riding fast enough for people to randomly fall off as they lose their grip. First one off is a rotten egg! The thrill will cost you $29 per brave rider.

Wakeboarding

Wakeboarding is like surfing and waterskiing – you ride a boogie-board-sized wakeboard behind a boat and, after a couple of lessons, you may be catching air. The boat ride, instruction and wakeboard are all provided for $49 through Hawaii Water Sports Center.

Scuba Diving

Hawaii Water Sports can arrange for you to head out to the clear waters of Maunalua Bay and check out the abundant marine life, including colorful reef fish and sea turtles. A scuba shuttle takes you to the dive boat, which is about a mile off shore. The cost is $59 and they welcome beginners and experienced divers.

Island Divers Hawaii, ☎ 808-423-8222 or 888-844-3483 (toll free), 377 Keahole Street, Hawaii Kai Shopping Center. Hawaii Kai and Maunalua Bay boast the largest numbers of dive sites and Island Divers Hawaii can guide you to the best dives or provide lessons. There are many wrecks to be explored underwater, such as the *Corsair*, a sunken World War II-era plane.

Waterskiing

Waterski through the warm waters of the Koko Marina behind one of Hawaii Water Sport's top-of-the-line boats. If you're an experienced skier, try the challenge of skiing through a six-ball course in the upper marina. This activity is $49 per person, per ride.

Surfing

Hawaiian Water Sports Center also offers surfing lessons in a secluded bay. This is a bargain at $79 for two hours, including transportation to the surf spot.

> *Surf's Up:* Windward O`ahu has some surf spots with interesting names, so don't be surprised to hear surfers talking about "Suicides," "Generals," "Middles," "Pipe Littles," "Full Point," and "Half Point."

Where to Eat

At the Koko Marina Center

In addition to the chains like Papa John's Pizza, Taco Bell and Subway, there are some memorable restaurants in the Koko Marina Center.

Assaggio's Ristorante Italiano, ☎ 808-396-0756, is located in the heart of Koko Marina Center and has won many awards for its authentic Italian food. Lunch is served Monday through Friday 11 am to 2:30 pm, dinner Sunday through Thursday 5 pm to 9:30 pm and Friday and Saturday nights from 5 pm to 10 pm. Lunch $$. Dinner $$$.

Kona Brewing Company, ☎ 808-394-KONA, www.konabrewingco.com. You'll get a kick out of the website! This Big Island brewery has come a long way! If you like to try local brews while you travel, this is the spot for you. Their Fire Rock Pale Ale is famous throughout the islands, although they also have a

Black Sand Porter, Castaway IPA, Da Grind Buzz Kona Coffee Stout, Hula Hefeweizen and Old Blowhole Barley Wine. You can get a sample of four six-ounce glasses for $8. For grinds, they serve hand-tossed gourmet pizzas, pupus, sandwiches, salads and desserts. The 7,000-square-foot restaurant is set on the docks of Koko Marina and offers seating for 275 guests. The interior design is unique, with koa wood furnishings and brewing equipment such as an old brew kettle used for exterior signage. Retractable full-panel windows offer a refreshing breeze. Kona Brewing Company is open Sunday through Thursday from 11 am to 11 pm (kitchen closes at 9 pm) and Friday and Saturday 11 am to 11 pm (kitchen closes at 10 pm). $$.

Zippy's Restaurant, ☎ 808-396-6977, www.zippys.com, is an institution in Hawaii. Besides being open 24 hours a day, they have affordable local-style food as well as treats from famous Napoleon's Bakery Favorites. Zippy's is known throughout the islands for its chili. The restaurant, which has been in Hawaii Kai for 14 years, has a full-service dining room and a take-out counter. In-house diners will be able to look out at nearby Kuapa Pond. If you want to eat like a local, eat at Zippy's. $.

Once you leave Hawaii Kai, the highway climbs up a steep grade. Halfway up is a scenic point on your left. Although there is ample parking, be careful, since you have to cross traffic to get to the lookout. The lookout offers fantastic views of Maunalua Bay and nearly 10 miles of coastline, from Koko Head to Diamond Head.

Koko Head

At a Glance

Koko Head is a massive 642-foot-high ancient tuff cone in the headland that defines the southeastern side of O`ahu. The neighboring 1,208-foot-high Koko Crater overshadows Koko Head.

Sightseeing

There are many spectacular natural attractions around Koko Head and you could easily spend an afternoon exploring these amazing sites.

Halona Blow Hole

Halona Blow Hole lies off of Kalaniana`ole Highway. Named after the Hawaiian word for "peering place," this geyser is a natural and unpredictable wonder. When breaking surf inside the Kaiwi Channel is forced through an L-shaped lava tube, it produces a tremendous pressure that periodically creates a spectacular explosion of water. Do not get near the blowhole itself – there are barriers set up to prevent this but some people are persistent. The barriers were reinforced after a young man went beyond the barriers and looked down into the blowhole, which immediately blew up and threw the young man into the air and then down the chute. They found his body in the ocean.

Koko Crater Botanical Garden

Koko Crater Botanical Garden, ☎ 808-522-7060 (for guided tours), www.honolulu.gov/parks/hbg/kcbg.htm. This 60-acre botanical garden is set within Koko Crater and is home to thousands of flowering plants, many of which prosper in the crater's desert-like surround-

Plumeria
(K.W. Bridges)

ings. The garden is located past Sandy Beach Park. At the traffic light on Kalaniana`ole Highway, take a left on Kealahou Street and follow that street until you get to Kokonani Street. Turn left and that will take you to the entrance of the garden. Admission is free. Allow yourself an hour and a half to walk through the two-mile loop around the garden. Wear comfortable shoes as you view a variety of dry land plant collections from Hawaii and around the world.

Beaches

Sandy Beach Park

Sandy Beach Park, 8800 Kalaniana`ole Highway. When the waves are calm, this is a dreamy swim spot. When the waves are big, this is a very dangerous park! When the surf's up, the beach has a treacherous shorebreak and strong rip currents. If swimming doesn't look good, combing the beach for shells is always fun. Experienced shorebreak bodysurfers make this sport look fun and easy, but remember – they are experienced. Sandy Beach is as famous for its beautiful sandy shoreline as it is for the number of broken necks, backs and other injuries that frequently occur here. Talk to a lifeguard if you have any questions. The beach park has picnic areas, phones, showers and restrooms.

Makapu`u Beach Park

Makapu`u Beach Park, 41-095 Kalaniana`ole, translates in Hawaiian to "Bulging Eyes." The beach is below Makapu`u Point, considered to be Hawaii's easternmost tip. From the beach, you can see Manana (Rabbit) Island, which is a popular scuba destination since the water is shallow. This picturesque beach can be a little iffy for swimming but is popular for body-surfing. It's just a great place to hang out – there are picnic areas, barbecue grills, restrooms, showers, phones and lifeguards.

Adventures in Water

★★★Hanauma Bay Nature Preserve

Hanauma Bay Nature Preserve, ☎ 808-396-4229, is about 10 miles east of Waikiki, just off Kalaniana`ole Highway. There are many road signs that will point you in the right direction.

Need Equipment? **Snorkfin Rentals** at Hanauma Bay, ☎ 808-203-4137, is the only authorized snorkel rental shop at Hanauma Bay. They provide snorkel gear at an affordable price.

This half-mile crescent of sand facing the reef-filled waters of a volcanic cinder cone is one the most popular snorkeling beaches in all of Hawaii. Thanks to recent efforts to save the reef, the reserve is beginning to look alive. The parking lot fills up early in the morning so try to get there by midday. The admission fee is $5 and the park also has a visitor center as well as some compulsory rules on how to approach the reef. No alcoholic beverages or pets are allowed at Hanauma Bay.

Don't Feel Like Driving? **Rabi Trans**, ☎ 808-371-3335, www.rabitrans, offers an air-conditioned ride from Waikiki to Hanauma Bay. They'll even throw in a mask, snorkel and fins. The cost is $15 per snorkeler round-trip from Waikiki, which doesn't include the $5 admission fee. You can make reservations and pay for the tour through their website.

Summer hours: Open daily from 6 am until 7 pm except on Tuesdays. The preserve is closed all day on Tuesdays. On the second and fourth Saturdays of each month, it is open until 10 pm.

Winter hours: Open daily from 6 am until 6 pm except on Tuesdays. The preserve is closed all day on Tuesdays. On the second Saturday of each month, Hanauma Bay remains open until 10 pm.

Author's Tip: Keep in mind that the Hanauma Bay Nature Preserve is closed on Tuesdays all year-round. It would be a bummer to get all your snorkeling gear and family ready to go, only to find the park closed.

Waimanalo Bay

At a Glance

Welcome to O`ahu's longest sandy white beach. There are several beach parks along the bay and snorkelers will be pleased with the conditions and the variety of tropical fish in this shallow, reef-protected bay. This area also has some interesting shopping and not-to-miss sites.

Shopping

$ **Patrick Ching's Naturally Hawaiian Gallery**, 41-1025 Kalaniana`ole Highway, ☎ 808-259-5354, www.PatrickChingArt.com. This roadside gallery has been attracting visitors for years. Ching can often be found at the gallery. His art is much admired throughout the Hawaiian community as well as with tourists, many of whom make return trips to the gallery. He teaches painting workshops internationally and at his Naturally Hawaiian Gallery. In his spare time Ching is a horseman and a well-known rodeo clown. He is also the author of several best-selling books, including *Sea Turtles of Hawaii* and *The Tale of Rabbit Island.*

Sightseeing

Makapu`u Lighthouse

The Makapu`u Lighthouse, built in 1909 and automated in 1974, is one of Hawaii's most familiar landmarks. A two-mile paved trail to the lighthouse provides visitors with a fantastic view of the entire Windward coastline and even the island of Moloka`i in the distance. Manana (Rabbit) Island and Kaohikaipu Island can also be seen from this vista point. If you're fortunate enough to visit during the whale season (December to April) you may see the amazing humpback whales traveling through the Moloka`i Channel.

To get to the lighthouse, follow Kalakaua Avenue past the Honolulu Zoo and Kapi`olani Park. Turn right onto Diamond Head Road and follow the signs going east (to your left) to Kalaniana`ole Highway (Route 72). Pass Hanauma Bay and Sandy Beach Park and the Hawaii Kai Golf Course. About half a mile past the golf course on the right is a gate blocking the trail entrance. Parking is available along the street – no cars are allowed on the trail. Don't forget water and sunscreen, as there is no shade along the trail. There are also no restroom facilities so take care of business before you leave. Although the trail is considered a moderate hike, there are some steep spots, so be prepared.

JUST FOR FOODIES

The legendary **Nalo Farms**, 41-574 Makakalo Street, ☎ 808-259-7698, www.nalo-farms.com, is in Waimanalo and is renowned throughout the islands for growing world-class greens in a small yet famous farm. Owner Dean Okimoto has been called a "celebrity farmer" and his Nalo Greens can be seen on menus throughout the island. The warm days and moderate nights of Waimanalo create the perfect climate for his greens – arugula, mizuna, tatsoi, red mustard, red Russian kale, pepper cress, tango, red and green oak leaf lettuce, red and green romaine and beet greens. They are grown in composted volcanic soil with few, if any, pesticides. Fate stepped in when up-and-coming chef Roy Yamaguchi told Okimoto that if he'd grow greens, Yamaguchi would take them all and pay cash. Tours of the farm are available from Monday through Friday from 10 am to 2 pm Each tour requires a minimum of 10 people and admission $8 per person. Plan ahead as there is a one to two-month waiting list for reservation.

Sea Life Park

Sea Life Park, ☎ 808-259-7933, www.sealifepark-hawaii.com, is about 15 miles from Waikiki on Oahu's lovely Makapu`u Point. The world-class marine attraction has a perfect location, perched between the beautiful Ko`olau Mountain Range and breathtaking Makapu`u Beach. Some of the more popular programs at Sea Life Park include the Dolphin Adventure, in which participants can touch the dolphins and even pose for a kiss from the friendly animals. A trainer is always nearby to educate visitors about these amazing creatures. If you're more of a spectator than a participant, you may want to check out the Hawaiian Dolphin Show where sea lions dance, penguins parade around and dolphins do their tricks.

Aerial view of Sea Life Park
(Kathleen Walling Fry)

One of the rare inhabitants of the park is a "wolphin" named Kekaimalu, which means "the peaceful sea." The wolphin is a hybrid between a false killer whale and an Atlantic bottlenose dolphin. Kekaimalu was born on May 15, 1985 and now weighs about 690 pounds. She eats 45 pounds of fish a day. Although hybrid animals are generally sterile, Kekaimalu gave birth to a baby girl on December 23, 2004.

Frigate bird

The Sea Life Park is also home to a Seabird Rehabilitation Facility that takes in 200 to 400 birds a year. The facility's goal is to release as many of these birds as possible after caring rehabilitation. Some will never be able to be on their own so they are permanent residents of the facility. These birds looked very happy in their environment when I visited.

Food and beverages are available at the Sea Lion Café, which offers usual park fare such as nachos, hot dogs, etc.

The park is open daily from 9:30 am to 5 pm and, at press time, admission was $29 for adults and $19 for juniors. The Dolphin Royal Swim costs $199, while the regular Dolphin Swim Adventure will run you $149. These prices include admission to the park.

> *Luau Alert:* The Sea Life Park also has a luau every Monday, Wednesday, Thursday, Friday and Sunday at 6 pm. The luau costs $80 for adults or $50 for children and lasts three hours. It includes an all-you-can-eat Hawaiian buffet and a spectacular fire dance show presented by Tihati!

Manana (Rabbit) Island and Kaohikaipu Island

You can see these two islands offshore right after passing the Sea Life Park. Today the islands are seabird sanctuaries and a breeding area for many bird species.

Beaches

Kaiona Beach Park

Kaiona Beach Park is a popular spot for launching canoes or kayaks and snorkeling can be good at times. There's no sign labeling the beach but if you see a sign for the Waimano Canoe Club, you're in the right place. The park has showers and restrooms available.

Waimanalo Bay Recreation Area

This 75-acre state park at 41-1055 Kalaniana`ole Highway is also referred to as Sherwood Forest due to the heavily wooded ironwood forest just inland from the beach. This is a great spot for a lightweight hike or long beach walk.

Waimanalo Beach Park

Waimanalo Beach Park is in the center of the Waimanalo Bay Recreation area and provides visitors and locals with a mostly calm swimming area. Lifeguards, restrooms, showers, pay phones are accessible at the park. Waimanalo Beach Park is off Aloiloi Street and is popular for swimming, bodyboarding and surfing.

Sunrise at Waimanalo Beach

Bellows Field Beach Park

Bellows Field Beach Park, 41-043 Kalaniana`ole Highway, is great for swimming, especially in the summer months when kids come to swim, boogie board and body surf. Watch out for signs warning about the Portuguese men-of-war that are known to frequent beaches on the Windward side of the island. Amenities include picnic areas, showers, restrooms and lifeguards (in the summer and on weekends).

Adventures in Water

Scuba Diving

Manana (Rabbit) Island is a superb dive spot for advanced divers. It is just off Makapu`u Beach Park on the southwest point of O`ahu. Although the water is shallow, the best diving is done off a boat, either on the seaward side of Manana Island or along the ridge at a 40-foot depth that runs between Manana Island and the O`ahu shore. Be on the lookout for lobster, triton trumpets, helmet shells, whitetip reef sharks and tiger sharks.

Island Divers Hawaii, ☎ 808-423-8222 or 888-844-3843, www.oahuscubadiving.com, offers dive charters, scuba training, introductory dives, and wreck diving (only available on O`ahu!).

*Moloka`i Express Warning:* Be careful of getting trapped in the "Moloka`i Express," a swift-moving current that whips around Makapu`u Point, bringing in clean waters and, occasionally, an unsuspecting diver. The large population of fish located here is also attractive to sharks, especially the very territorial tiger shark. Do not ignore a tiger shark sighting. Vacate the area as soon as possible!

Where to Stay

Camping

Waimanalo Beach Park, Waimanalo Bay Beach Park and Bellows Field Beach Park are all county parks that allow camping as long as you have a permit. For more information about camping in county parks, call ☎ 808-523-4525 or visit www.co.honolulu.hi.us/parks/permits.htm.

Vacation Rental

If a beach house sounds more fun than a resort or camping, check out the **Waimanalo Beach House**, ☎ 808-531-1411, www.hawaiian-sunrise.com, broder@hawaii.rr.com. On six-mile-long Waimanalo Beach, this spacious house has room for nine people. The main house has three bedrooms and two bathrooms (including a Jacuzzi tub), a large living area and a dining room with koa wood flooring. An unattached studio guest room can serve as a fourth bedroom. At press time, the beach house went for $700 per night.

Kailua

At a Glance

Kailua is a laid-back beach town with some fabulous beaches. The community has a great shopping center, access to beaches and relaxing eateries. The town is cute and is a great place to stop when you're traveling around. In fact, in Kailua, a local decree states that no building may rise higher than the tallest palm tree in town. Be wary though – this side of the island can get as much as 80 inches of rainfall a year.

Kailua is actually the shopping center to go to on the Windward Coast – it has grocery stores, surf shops, activity centers, restaurants and tons of little shops. Take the time to stroll through the town center before hitting the beaches.

Shopping

Farmers' Market: The Kailua Thursday Night Farmers' Market is held every Thursday from 5 to 7:30 pm at the Kailua Parking Garage (behind Longs Drugs). Check the www.hfbf.org/FarmersMarketKailua.html to see the day's specials as well as a list of vendors and their location at the market. A local-style dinner is usually offered by one of the vendors for a small price.

Alii Antiques of Kailua I & II, 9-A Maluniu Avenue, ☎ 808-261-1705, has wooden bowls and trays, etched-glass platters and cocktail shakers from the thirties. This is the spot to get vintage Hawaiiana like Koa lamps and rattan furniture circa the 1930s and 1940s.

Across the street, the owner of the Alii shop runs the second part of the shop. This one offers jewelry, clothing, linens and collectibles filling the place from floor to ceiling.

Sightseeing

Popoia (Flat Island)

Wedge-tailed shearwater

Popoia (Flat Island) is one of a bunch of islands that comprise a designated seabird sanctuary (home to wedge-tailed shearwaters and Bulwer's petrels) where you will often see endangered green sea turtles. The island is about a quarter-mile offshore (across from the boat ramp by Alala Point in Kailua Bay) and is popular with surfers who paddle out on their longboards. The island, which is 3.7 acres in size, is also popular with kiteboarding and windsurfing.

Flat Island is open to the public during daylight hours and is accessible by kayak, surfboard or, when the tide is low and the water is calm, by foot.

Beaches

Kailua Beach

This picture-perfect beach, with its powdery white sand, is popular with swimmers and kayakers. The beach, officially called Kailua Beach Park and located at 450 Kawailoa Road, encompasses several small islets, some of which are considered bird sanctuaries, so be careful where you venture.

The beach is partly a state park but continues for several miles along Kailua Bay. Kitesurfers and windsurfers will find the strong tradewinds enticing. You can rent sailboards and kayaks at the beach.

There are three ways to get to Kailua Beach Park – the H3 Freeway, the Likelike Highway (Route 63) and the Pali Highway (Route 61).

Visitors to the beach will be happy to find lifeguards, picnic areas, phones, showers and restrooms.

Lanikai Beach

Lanikai Beach is a beautiful spot once you find it. The beach is on Kailua Road past Kailua Beach and access is available through footpaths between houses. These are private residences (many owned by celebrities) so be respectful when you walk by. The water is usually a spectacular blue and the scenery is highlighted by two islands (the Mokuluas) in the background. There are no lifeguards or facilities but Lanikai is worth the effort if you're looking for a nice swimming and snorkeling beach or a fantastic spot for a romantic walk.

Adventures in Water

Windsurfing

Kailua Sailboards & Kayaks, Inc., 130 Kailua Road, ☎ 808-262-2555, www.kailuasailboards.com, offers windsurfing lessons and rentals as well as equipment for kayaking, surfing and kitesurfing. The steady tradewinds and protective reef make Kailua Beach a premier spot for all of these sports. Kailua Sailboards & Kayaks has all the goodies you'll need for a good time – eco-tours, double kayaks, boogie boards and surfboard rentals, windsurfing gear, as well as lessons in all of the above and kayaking journeys.

Tours

Mokulua Kayak Guides, ☎ 808-206-8508, www.mokuluaguides.com, offers eco-tours where you can snorkel, kayak and explore small islands while learning about the Hawaiian culture and sea life from an expert. The company is dedicated to environmental awareness and limits the size of their groups, so call early. The tour includes all kayaking equipment, snorkeling gear, lunch and a free pickup from your Waikiki hotel.

Twogood Kayaks Hawaii, 345 Hahani Street, ☎ 808-262-5656, www.twogoodkayaks.com, runs guided kayak tours on regular or clear-bottom kayaks. This all-day tour is led by a naturalist and will take you to a seabird sanctuary, for a picnic on a secluded island, snorkeling with turtles and then enjoying Kailua Beach. This is the only company that offers clear-bottom kayaks that allow you to see tropical fish, turtles and other marine life as you paddle along. The company can also set you on your way with all the equipment for a self-guided tour. This package includes instruction, gear, a picnic lunch and hotel pick-up. Tours generally run from 8:15 am to 3:30 pm.

Surfing

Popoia (Flat Island) is about a quarter-mile offshore (across from the boat ramp by Alala Point in Kailua Bay) and is popular with surfers who paddle out on their longboards. The island (which is 3.7 acres in size) is great for beginning surfers, especially early in the morning when water is calm.

Where to Eat

Lanikai Juice, 600 Kailua Road (in the Kailua Shopping Center), ☎ 808-262-2383, www.lanikaijuice.com, offers smoothies, juice and bowls of fresh fruit. You can add spirulina, bee pollen, ginseng, protein powder and more to your smoothie! Lanikai Juice is open Monday through Friday from 6 am to 8 pm and Saturday and Sunday from 8 am to 7 pm. $.

Baci Bistro, 30 Aulike Street, ☎ 808-262-7555, www.bacibistro.com. Chef Reza Azeri described the bistro's cuisine as "European cuisine with an Italian flair." Veal, pork, chicken and fish highlight the menu. They make their own pasta, with ravioli being the house special. Baci Bistro has been open since 1997 and is a favorite among Kailua residents. Lunch is served from 11:30 am to 2 pm Monday through Friday and nightly from 5:30 to 10 pm for dinner. Reservations are recommended. Lunch $$. Dinner $$$.

Cinnamon's, ☎ 808-261-8724, 315 Uluniu St, www.cinnamonsrestaurant.com. Open for breakfast daily from 7 am to 2 pm. This is THE place for breakfast! The signature dish is eggs Benedict and the variety is amazing – traditional, veggie, mahi mahi, crab cake, kalua pork, lox or a combo. They also have a great selection of pancakes, including guava chiffon, banana and fresh carrot. Local favorite, loco moco, is also popular and if you're really hungry, there is a broiled prime rib breakfast or a skilled breakfast which is homefries topped with and egg and your choice of three extras (chicken, beef, ham, mushroom, etc.). $.

Morning Brew, ☎ 808-262-7770, www.morningbrewhawaii.com, is at 600 Kailua Road in the Kailua Shopping Center. The cute coffee house offers a large selection of coffee along with healthy sandwiches and salads. Morning Brew has free wi-fi and is open from daily from 6 am to 8 pm. $.

Pinky's Pupu Bar & Grill, ☎ 808-254-6255, 970 N. Kalaheo Ave. Seafood and local favorites are the specialties of the house. For something different, try an appetizer of fish tacos, boiled peanuts or crab cakes. Big appetites will be satisfied with "ohana style" family combination platters, including a local sampler with kalua pig, beer can chicken and fried mahi mahi. Pinky's is spacious with a large bar in the middle and a lively atmosphere.

This is a great place for kids and families and Tuesday is kids' night, with fun activities for the little ones. Pinky's is open from 3 to 10 pm Monday through Friday with happy hour from 3 to 6:30 pm; from 4 to 10 pm Saturday and Sunday with happy hour from 4 to 6:30 pm. $$.

Kalapawai Market, 306 S. Kalaheo Avenue, ☎ 808-262-4359, www.kalapawaimarket.com, has been around since 1932. This is a great place to grab a quick breakfast or a sandwich to go. They also offer 10-inch pizzas, salads and hot sandwiches. The deli has gourmet sandwiches that you can grab and go. The historic market is open from 6:30 am to 9 pm and the store from 6 am to 9 pm. The tapas menu is offered daily after 5:30 pm. $$.

Kalapawai Market recently opened a second branch in Kailua Town at 750 Kailua Road, ☎ 808-262-3354.

Boston's North End Pizza Bakery, 29 Hoolai Street, ☎ 808-263-7757. This is one of about a dozen restaurants in this popular pizza chain. The slices of pizza are huge so be cautious when ordering! This location is open from 11 am to 8 pm Sunday through Thursday and from 11 am to 9 pm (sometimes earlier, though) on Friday and Saturday. $.

Buzz's Original Steak House, 413 Kawailoa Road, ☎ 808-261-4661. Buzz's is considered a classic throughout the island and you will not be disappointed. This site was established in 1962 and sits across from Kailua Bay. They specialize in kiawe-broiled steaks and fancy fish dinner. All dinners include a trip to the salad bar. Lunch is served from 11 am to 3 pm and dinner from 5 to 10 pm. They don't accept credit cards – only debit cards. Lunch $$. Dinner $$$.

Where to Stay

Bed & Breakfasts

Beach Lane B&B and Studios, 111 Hekili St, ☎ 808-262-8286, www.beachlane.com. Just a few steps from Kailua Beach, this lovely B&B has been around for 17 years. Rates are $125 per night plus tax, based on two-person occupancy. The studios have private entrances and range from $95 to $135 per night plus tax. There is also a $40 cleaning fee (a charge I don't believe in!) Check out the website for pictures of the accommodations. $$.

Nightlife

Boardriders Bar and Grill, 201-A Hamakua Drive, ☎ 808-261-4600, is known for having 12 beers on tap, live entertainment and mediocre food. It has pool tables, dart machines and about eight TVs spread through the room. Local bands frequently play in this tucked-away spot. Open daily from 11 am to 2 am. $$.

Kane`ohe

At a Glance

Kane`ohe is a small town north of Kailua, marking the beginning of the beautiful Kane`ohe Bay. The eight-mile-long bay is the largest sheltered body of water in the main Hawaiian Islands and offers lots of recreational opportunities. At the southern end is the Mokapu Peninsula, better known as home to the Marine Corps Base Hawaii (www.mcbh.usmc.mil).

Sightseeing

Olomana Gardens

Olomana Gardens, 47-285 Pulama Road, ☎ 808-239-6775. This 725-acre garden was owned by former US Senator Hiram Fong and is full of banana and papaya groves, along with gardenias and ginger plants. There are narrated tram tours through five scenic valley and plateaus with palms, fruit and nut trees, ferns and fragrant tropical flowers.

Ginger plant

He`eia State Park

He`eia State Park, 46-465 Kamehameha Hwy, ☎ 808-247-3156, www.friendsofheeia.com. This small park is on an elevated peninsula called Ka Lae O KeAlohi, which means "the point of shimmering light." It has impressive views of Kane`ohe Bay and is a nice picnic and hiking spot. Beyond the visitor's center is a path that leads down to the 90-acre, 600-year-old He`eia fishpond.

To get to He`eia State Park take H-1 West to the Likelike Highway and stay on the Likelike for eight miles. Make a left on Kamehameha Highway and continue for 2½ miles until you see the park.

Where's Ginger & Mary Ann? Look across Kane`ohe Bay and see Coconut Island where the opening credits of Gilligan's Island were shot.

Valley of the Temples

Byodo-In Temple

Valley of The Temples is home to the Byodo-In Temple, 47-200 Kahekili Hwy, ☎ 808-293-9844, a re-creation of a 900-year-old Buddhist temple in Kyoto, Japan. Shaped like a phoenix landing, the temple was built in 1968 to commemorate the arrival of the island's first Japanese immigrants 100 years before. The temple, which features a giant Buddha, sits up against the amazing vertical cliffs of the Ko`olau Mountain Range. Don't forget to ring the three-ton sacred bell, an action believed to cleanse the mind of evil temptation. The Valley of the Temples Memorial Park is a great place to stop for a peaceful and uplifting break. The park has beautiful grounds and ponds filled with koi fish.

Mokoli`i Island (Chinaman's Hat)

Mokoli`i Island (Chinaman's Hat) is a well-known islet in Kane`ohe Bay named for its resemblance to a, well, Chinese hat. You can view this site from the northern edge of Kane`ohe Bay.

KUALOA RANCH

This 4,000-acre working cattle ranch stretches from the ocean to the mountains. Here, you can go for a horseback ride, take a trek on an ATV or hop onboard the Jungle Expedition Tour or the Ranch & Movie Set Tour. Hollywood has visited Kualoa Ranch for several movies and shows like *Jurassic Park*, *Mighty Joe Young*, and *Windtalkers*. You may even stumble upon the secret set of *LOST*. The ranch also has a Hawaiian Fishpond & Garden Tour. Kualoa is one of the most historically significant destinations on the island.

The ranch is only 45 minutes from Waikiki – take the H-1 Freeway west to the Likelike Highway, route #63. Proceed through the Wilson Tunnel and descend toward Kane`ohe and exit onto the Kahekili Highway (Route #83), heading north. Kahekili Highway turns into Kamehameha Highway as you pass the historic "Hygienic Store" in the village of Kahalu`u. In about 10 minutes, you'll see the entrance to Kualoa Ranch on your left.

Activities can be booked online at www.kualoa.com (the website is very informative!), activityinfo@kualoaranch.com, or ☎ 808-237-7321.

Have you heard about the Haiku Stairs?

This attraction has a fascinating history but, as of press time, these stairs, which stretch from a gulch bottom to a mountain top and scaling a nearly vertical cliff, are closed to the public due to safety concerns. The Haiku Stairs is a 3,922-step steel structure that begins at the bottom of the Haiku Valley, near Kaneohe, and takes you to an overlook 2,800 feet above the valley.

The stairs were created in 1942 as part of the war effort – they supported the US Navy's top-secret high-powered transmitter station in Haiku Valley. In 1955-56, the wooden steps were replaced with steel since the ladder still provided access for maintenance of radio equipment. Between 1975 and 1987, tens of thousands hikers climbed the stairs without any report of injury. In 1981, the TV show *Magnum P.I.* filmed a chase scene at the stairs, thereby increasing their popularity. In 1987, the stairs were closed to the public due to concerns about vandalism and liability.

A group called the "Friends of Haiku Stairs" was created to organize public support for the re-opening of the stairs. In 2000-2003, the City of Honolulu acquired much of Haiku Stairs and initiated repair work. The repairs were completed in June 2002 but the city had problems finding an appropriate access to the stairs. Illegal hikers were also creating problems and in spring of 2003, the illegal hiking increased to more than a hundred people per day on weekends. Security was beefed up to prevent the illegal access and, as of press time, the city and the Friends of Haiku Stairs were still trying to work out a solution to the problem of how to access the stairs and parking considerations.

Adventures on Land

Golf

**Ko`olau Golf Club**, 45-550 Kinoaole Road, ☎ 808-236-4653, www.ko-olaugolfclub.com. Located under the Nu`uanu Pali Lookout, which is carved out of the breathtaking rainforest of the Ko`olau Range, this 18-hole championship golf course is one of the most challenging in the nation.

Pali Golf Course, 45-050 Kamehameha Hwy, ☎ 808-266-7612, www.co.honolulu.hi.us/des/golf/pali.htm. This is a public 18-hole course run by the City and County of Honolulu. It offers picturesque views of the Ko`olau mountain range and Kane`ohe Bay.

Bayview Golf Park, 45-285 Kaneohe Bay Dr, ☎ 808-247-0451. This 18-hole course features 3,269 yards of golf from the longest tees for a par of 59. The course opened in 1997.

Hiking

Ho`omaluhia Botanical Garden, 45-680 Luluku Road, ☎ 808-233-7323, www.honolulu.gov/parks/hbg/hmbg.htm. This 400-acre nature conservancy specializes in fruits, flowers and trees native to Hawaii. The garden is geographically laid out and represents tropical regions from around the world – the Philippines, Hawaii, Africa, Sri Lanka, India, Polynesia, Melanesia, Malaysia and tropical America. There is a network of trails that introduce visitors to over 10,000 specimens.

From the gardens, you can get spectacular views of the Ko`olau Range and the Pacific Ocean. Ho`omaluhia (which means "to make a place of peace and tranquility") Botanical Garden has a Visitor Center with a lecture room, exhibition hall, workshop and botanical library.

Erythrina flowering tree

The garden was designed and built by the US Army Corps of engineers to provide flood protection for Kane`ohe. The gate is open daily from 9 am to 4 pm and later on the weekends. Call for more information about camping, permits and guided hikes.

Where to Eat

There's not a lot of fancy eateries in Kane`ohe but you won't starve – there's Jack in the Box, McDonald's, Taco Bell, Zippys, Arby's, Pizza Hut and a Panda Express.

Where to Stay

Ali`i Bluffs Windward B&B, 46-251 Ikiiki Street, ☎ 808-235-1124 or 800-234-1151 (toll free), offers two rental units that overlook Kaneohe Bay. The two rooms on the property are filled with Old World furnishings, oil paintings, antique toys and other collectibles. The Victorian Room has one double bed and the Circus Room has two twin beds. A continental breakfast is included and an afternoon tea is offered in the afternoon. Owners De and Donald ran an art gallery in New York before coming to Hawaii. There are also two Maltese dogs, Hector and Hamish, on the property. The Circus room is $70 a night and the Victorian room will cost you $80 per night.

Kahana

At a Glance

The Kahana area is home to several quiet beaches, secluded hiking trails and spectacular scenery. The beaches are smaller and more low-key than other beaches on the island.

Adventures on Land

Hiking

Experienced hikers will enjoy this trail that leads into Kahana Valley and provides breathtaking view of the valley. Over 140 native Hawaiians live throughout the community of Kahana Valley so act accordingly. To get to Kahana Valley, take H1 West and get off on the Likelike Highway and go through the mountain. Take Kahekili Highway west and Kahana Valley Park will be on the right side.

Beaches

Kahana Bay

Kahana Bay, 52-222 Kamehameha Highway, is a quiet beach cove surrounded by tall beach pines. This quiet, secluded beach has no lifeguards or facilities so use caution while swimming.

From Kahana Bay to La`ie (the beginning of the North Shore), there are a number of small beaches to check out. As you drive north you'll see Kaluanui Beach, Makao Beach, Aukai Beach Park, Hau`ula Beach Park and Kokololio Beach Park.

Where to Stay

Camping

Kahana Valley State Park, ☎ 808-587-0300. Located off Kamehameha Highway in Kahana, this park offers camping, a scenic, wild valley, beach activities, picnicking, hiking and even pig hunting. Call ☎ 808-587-0300 for more information about camping permits. $.

Central O`ahu

At A Glance

Central O`ahu lies between the Ko`olau and Wai`anae Mountain Ranges and include the small less-touristy towns of Mililani, Wahiawa, Waipahu and Poamoho. The area is also home to the Wheeler Army Air Field and Schofield Barracks.

IN THIS CHAPTER

Mililani

Shopping

The Farmers' Market at Mililani High School, ☎ 808-848-2074, is held every Sunday from 8 to 11 am. Check out the website, www.hfbf.org/FarmersMarket-Mililani.html, to see the day's specials as well as a list of vendors and their goods. A local-style breakfast and/or lunch is usually offered by one of the vendors for a small price.

Sightseeing

Dole Pineapple Plantation and Maze, 64-1550 Kamehameha Highway, ☎ 808-621-8408, www.dole-plantation.com. Memorialized in the 2001 *Guinness Book of World Records* as the world's largest maze, the plantation's huge natural puzzle encompasses nearly two miles of paths lined by 11,400 colorful Hawaiian plants. The maze is open daily from 9 am to 5 pm and costs $6 for adults or $4 for children.

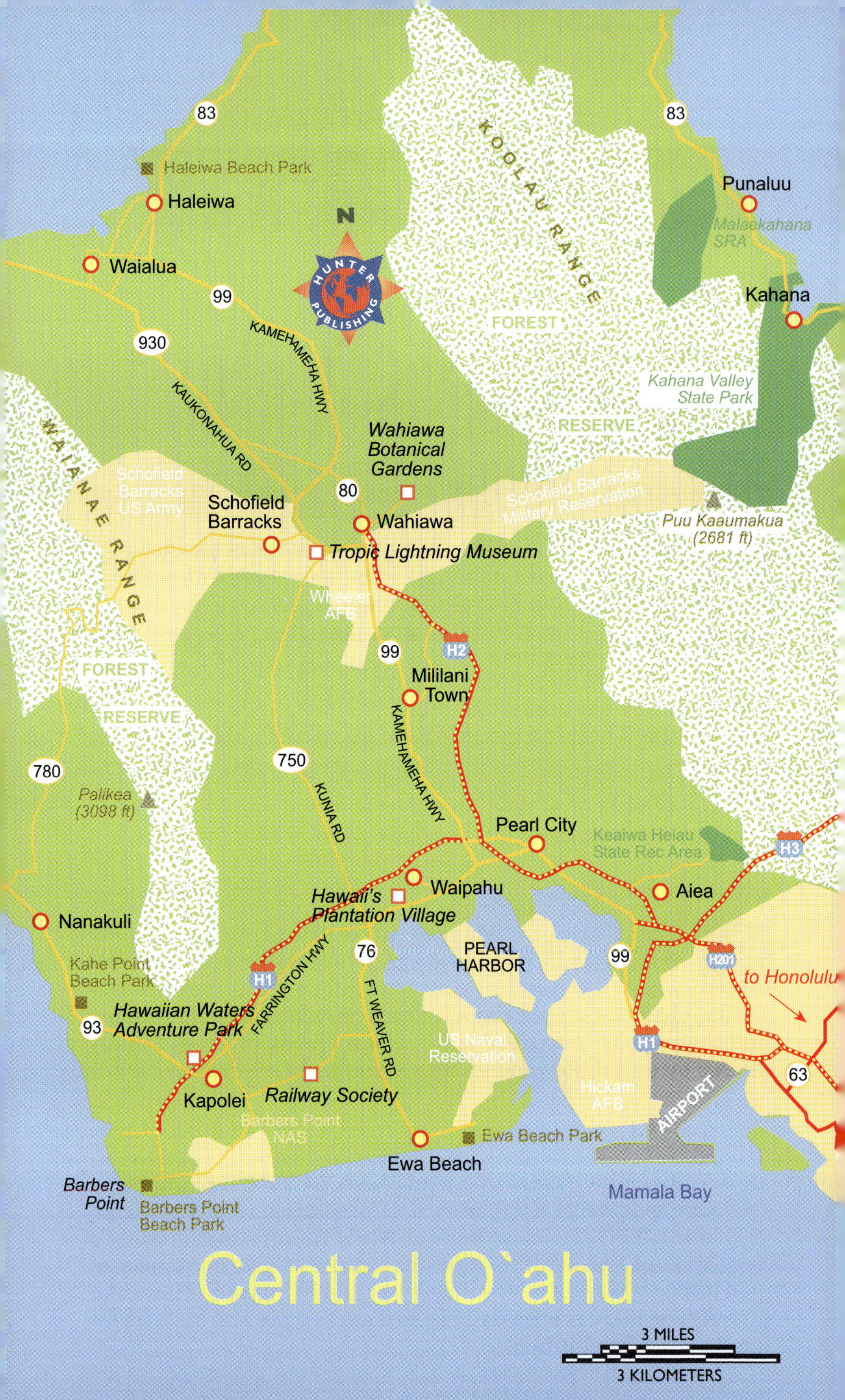
Central O`ahu
Haleiwa Beach Park
Haleiwa
Waialua
Punaluu
Malaekahana SRA
Kahana
Kahana Valley State Park
KOOLAU RANGE
FOREST
RESERVE
N
HUNTER PUBLISHING
KAMEHAMEHA HWY
KAUKONAHUA RD
WAIANAE RANGE
Wahiawa Botanical Gardens
Schofield Barracks US Army
Schofield Barracks
Wahiawa
Tropic Lightning Museum
Schofield Barracks Military Reservation
Puu Kaaumakua (2681 ft)
Wheeler AFB
Mililani Town
FOREST
RESERVE
Palikea (3098 ft)
KUNIA RD
Pearl City
Keaiwa Heiau State Rec Area
Aiea
Waipahu
Hawaii's Plantation Village
Nanakuli
PEARL HARBOR
to Honolulu
Kahe Point Beach Park
Hawaiian Waters Adventure Park
FARRINGTON HWY
FT WEAVER RD
US Naval Reservation
Hickam AFB
AIRPORT
Kapolei
Railway Society
Barbers Point NAS
Ewa Beach Park
Ewa Beach
Barbers Point
Barbers Point Beach Park
Mamala Bay
83
99
930
80
H2
750
780
H3
H1
76
H201
93
63
3 MILES
3 KILOMETERS

Afterwards, go for a ride on the Pineapple Express Train, which takes visitors on a two-mile tour in which you'll learn about the history of the pineapple and hear the story of James Dole, who pioneered the pineapple industry in Hawaii. The train departs every 30 minutes between 9 am and 5 pm, weather permitting. The cost is $7.75 for adults and $5.75 for children ages four-12.

The plantation also offers a self-guided garden tour of eight mini-gardens where you can get an up-close view of a large variety of native plants grown on O`ahu's North Shore. The tour also includes information about the plantation villages and contract laborers who came from all over the world to work in Hawaii's sugarcane and pineapple fields. Tickets cost $4 for adults or $3.25 for children ages four-12.

HISTORY LESSON

James Drummond Dole, fondly known as "The Pineapple King," arrived in Hawaii in 1899. The following year he bought a 61-acre tract of land in Wahiawa where he started his first pineapple plantation. In 1901, Dole figured out that the best way to transport the pineapple out of Hawaii would be in cans, so he built a cannery, which marked the start of the Hawaiian Pineapple Company. In 1907, the cannery was relocated to Honolulu Harbor, where it was closer to the labor pool, shipping ports and supplies. The Honolulu cannery was at one time the world's largest cannery and remained in operation until 1991.

In 1922, as demand for pineapples grew, Dole bought the island of Lana`i and converted it from a cactus-covered island with 150 residents into the largest pineapple plantation in the world, with 20,000 pineapple-producing acres and over 1,000 employees and their families. For nearly 70 years, Lana`i operated as a pineapple plantation and became widely known as the "Pineapple Island," providing nearly 75% of the world's pineapples.

By the 1930s, Hawaii was known as the pineapple capital of the world. Dole's Hawaiian Pineapple Company was now processing over 200,000 tons of pineapple a year and was responsible for 90% of all the canned pineapple produced in the world.

Dole passed away in 1958 at the age of 80. The enterprise he founded is known worldwide as Dole Foods Company.

The plantation also has a country store which offers many pineapple goodies as well as great gift options such as clothing, pineapple-based treats and made-in-Hawaii products. The plantation is open daily from 9 am to 5:30 pm and in the summer months of June through August, the plantation is open from 9 am to 6 pm.

The plantation is just three miles north of Wahiawa and 10 miles from Haleiwa and the North Shore. From Haleiwa, take the Kamehameha Highway (Highway 99) until you get to 64-1550 Kamehameha Highway. Follow the signs to the Dole Plantation. From Waikiki, take Highway 1 (H1) West to Highway 2 (H2) North and continue to Kamehameha Highway (99).

Hawaiian Railway Society. The Hawaiian Railway is the only active railroad on O`ahu. The Railway Society was formed in 1970 to save what remained of Hawaii's railroad history. Now an educational, non-profit organization, the Railway Society has been placed on the State and National Registers of Historic Sites.

Railway fans can ride the railway every Sunday, except the fourth Sunday in December. Departure times are 1 and 3 pm and the ride lasts 90 minutes. Seating is on a first-come, first-serve basis and costs $10 for adults or $7 for seniors and children ages two to 12. Remember, they only accept cash and checks.

The second Sunday of the month is a special day at the Railway, reserved for the Parlor Car 64, which was built in 1900. Tickets are $20 and seating is limited to 14 passengers.

For more information about the Hawaiian Railway Society call ☎ 808-681-5461 or visit www.hawaiianrailway.com.

Adventures on Land

Golf

Mililani Golf Club, 95-176 Kuahelani Avenue, ☎ 808-623-2222, www.mililanigolf.com, opened in 1966. It is set on a plateau, with the Wai`anae and Ko`olau Mountain Ranges on each side. The par 72, 6,455-yard golf club carves its way through a maze of Norfolk pines, eucalyptus trees, African tulip trees and tropical Hawaiian foliage.

Waipahu

Waipahu is a former sugar mill town in the `Ewa district of O`ahu. There's not much to see here and the eateries consist mainly of fast food restaurants.

Sightseeing

Hawaii's Plantation Village, 94-695 Waipahu Street, ☎ 808-577-0110, www.hawaiiplantationvillage.org. This outdoor museum showcases the lifestyles and experiences of Hawaii's plantation workers who came to Hawaii between the late 1800s and the 1940s. The site, which is part of the Waipahu Cultural Garden Park, opened in September 1992 and has a collection of 32 original structures as well as replica homes of these hard-working groups. Guided tours are conducted hourly Monday through Saturday from 10 am, with the last tour held at 2 pm. Admission is $13 for adults, $10 for seniors, $7 for military and $5 for children ages four to 11.

Traffic Alert: Kolekole Pass, a four-mile short cut through the Wai`anae Mountains that runs from Leeward O`ahu to Central, has been closed to the public since 9/11 due to security concerns and its proximity to military headquarters.

Adventures on Land

Golf

Royal Kunia Country Club, ☎ 808-688-9222, www.royalkuniacc.com. Only 20 miles from Waikiki, this club offers a great golfing experience for beginners or low handicappers.

Wahiawa

Sightseeing

The **Kukaniloko Birthstones State Monument** is one of the most significant cultural sites on O`ahu and is listed on the National and Hawaii Registers of Historic Places.

The monument itself is a site marked by 180 stones over an area of about half and acre. It is surrounded by a grove of eucalyptus and coconut trees surrounded by pineapple fields. The site is hundreds of years old and was used as a birthsite for royal births.

HAWAIIAN HISTORY

Beginning with the birth of Kapawa, Kukaniloko became recognized as the royal birthsite on O`ahu. Based on genealogical records, the dates of Kapawa's birth range from 1100 to 1400 AD, but historians believe the date could be even earlier. The site remained a significant spot for royal births into the late 1700s, as seen by the efforts of Kamehameha I to make sure his successor, Liholiho, was born at Kukaniloko in 1797.

The birth of a child at Kukaniloko was witnessed by 36 chiefs. Immediately after the birth, the child was taken to the nearby *waihau heiau* of Ho`olonopahu, where purification rites and the cutting of the umbilical cord were overseen by 48 chiefs.

At Ho`olonopahu, the beating of the sacred drums (Hawaea and `Opuku) announced the royal birth. There were seven days of purification for the chiefess after giving birth and great care was taken for the disposal of the navel cord of the child.

The Kukaniloko Birthstones State Monument is on the north side of Wahiawa at the intersection of Kamehameha Highway (Highway 99) and Whitmore Avenue).

Tropic Lightning Museum, Building #361, Wai`anae Avenue, Schofield Barracks, ☎ 808-655-0438. This museum's goal is to collect, preserve, and exhibit artifacts reflecting the history of the 25th Infantry Division from 1941 to today, as well as Wheeler Army Airfield. The museum supports education and training for military and civilian personnel.

The 25th Infantry began to gather the Division's history in August 1956 and held their first museum committee meeting in October of 1957. The new museum moved to more spacious quarters in November of 1958. The museum contains uniforms, displays of artillery guns and military vehicles, among other exhibits. From Honolulu, take H1 West and then merge onto HI-78 West via Exit 19B on the left toward Fort Shafter/Aiea. Then take I-H1 West exit toward Pearl City and merge onto Interstate HI West. Next take the I-H2 North exit (Exit 8A) toward Mililani/Wahiawa and merge onto Interstate H2 North, which becomes Wilikina Drive/HI-99 West. Turn left onto Kunia Road, then right onto Lyman Road, where gate access is required. Turn right onto Flagler Road and left on Waianae Avenue. The museum is in Building 361.

Wahiawa Botanical Gardens, 1396 California Avenue, ☎ 808-621-5463. Likened to a tropical rain forest, the Wahiawa Botanical Gardens are right in the center of O`ahu. They contain 27 acres of ferns, trees and flowers.

The idea of the gardens was conceived in the 1920s when the Hawaii Sugar Planters Association leased land from the State of Hawaii as a site for experimental tree planting. Most of the large tress you'll see were planted at that time under the direction of Dr. Harold Lyon. It was opened as a botanical garden in 1957.

The Wahiawa Botanical Gardens are open daily from 9 am to 4 pm, except for Christmas and New Year's Day.

Adventures on Land

Golf

Hawaii Country Club Golf Course, 94-1211 Kunia Road, ☎ 808-622-1744, www.hawaiicc.com. This 18-hole course features 5,916 yards of golf for a par of 72. The course opened in 1957 and was designed by John Uldrick.

Leilehua Golf Course, Bldg. 6505, Leilehua Road, ☎ 808-655-4653, is a premier Army golf course just outside of Wheeler Army Airfield. Locals, tourists and military members alike can enjoy this 18-hole course.

Central

Pearl City

Where to Eat:

Buzz's Original Steak House, 98-751 Kuahao Place, ☎ 808-487-6465. This is the ultimate steak and seafood dinner house – they have top sirloin, teriyaki steak, BBQ beef ribs, prime rib, Alaskan king crab, lobster tail and scampi. The lunch menu is on a smaller scale – more salads (including smoked salmon salad) and sandwiches (the teriyaki steak burger or a fresh fish burger). Warning: Buzz's does not take credit cards – only debit cards.

Open Monday through Friday from 11 am to 2 pm and 5 to 9 pm, Saturday and Sunday from 5 to 9 pm. Lunch $$, dinner $$$.

Index

Index